# To be a European Muslim

## Other titles by the same author

*Les musulmans dans la laïcité, responsabilités et droits des musulmans dans les sociétés occidentales*, Tawhid, Lyon, 1994, 2nd edition 1998

*Islam, le face à face des civilisations, Quel projet pour quelle modernité?*, Les deux Rives, Lyon, 1995, 2nd edition 1998

*Aux sources du renouveau musulman, Un siècle de réformisme islamique*, Bayard-Centurion, Paris, September 1998

*Peut-on vivre avec l'Islam?*, talks with Jacques Neirynck, Favre, Lausanne, March 1999

*Muslims in France: The way towards coexistence*, Islamic Foundation, Leicester, UK, 1999

## In collaboration:

*Péril islamiste?*, directed by Alain Gresh, Complexe, Brussels, 1995

*La tolérance ou la liberté? Les leçons de Voltaire et de Condorcet*, directed by Claude-Jean Lenoir, Complexe, Brussels, 1997

*Islam, Modernism and the West*, edited by Gema Martin Munoz, I.B.Tauris, London, January 1999

# *To be a European Muslim*

## A Study of Islamic Sources in the European Context

TARIQ RAMADAN

The Islamic Foundation

*Published by*
THE ISLAMIC FOUNDATION,
Markfield Conference Centre,
Ratby Lane, Markfield, Leicester LE67 9SY, UK
Tel: (01530) 244944, Fax: (01530) 244946
E-mail: i.foundation@islamic-foundation.org.uk
Web site: http://www.islamic-foundation.org.uk

Quran House, PO Box 30611, Nairobi, Kenya

PMB 3193, Kano, Nigeria



ISBN 0 86037 300 2 (PB)
ISBN 0 86037 315 0 (HB)

Cover design: Imtiaz Ahmad Manjra
Typeset by: N.A. Qaddoura

---

Cover Illustration: Map of North Africa and Europe drawn by al-Idrisi. Africa is on the top part of the globe, Europe is on bottom part of the globe.
Printed and bound in Great Britain by Antony Rowe Ltd, Chippenham, Wiltshire

***For Maryam,***
(*and Rum*)
for your infinite sensitivity.
Hoping you *never* let anyone
turn your qualities into faults

***For Sami,***
"Saʿīd"
for your outlandish imagination.
May you be ready to help everybody,
attentive to all, *ever*

***For Moussa,***
for your playful sweetness.
A rebel, if you can be,
in the name of justice,
in the name of *all* men

*God love and protect you*

بسم الله الرحمن الرحيم

# Contents

# Along the Road – Acknowledgements

The present book was written two years ago as I was carrying out a year's research in Leicester, in the "Islam in Europe" unit of the Islamic Foundation. I must first of all acknowledge the excellent research facilities offered me at the Islamic Foundation. I particularly want to thank the Foundation's Chairman, Professor Khurshid Ahmad, and its Director, Dr. Manazir Ahsan, for their warm welcome. Numerous discussions with Dr. Ataullah Siddiqui, Dilwar Hussain, Sohail Nakhooda, Mokrane Guezzou, Anwar Cara and Batool al-Toma enabled me, thanks to their help and advice, to develop the present research in the desired direction. To them all, I am fraternally grateful. I do not forget Khurram Murad (God have mercy on him) who more than once deeply touched me with his kindness. A word, also, for all those who have been following my work for years and who help make it accessible. This book could not have been completed without the questioning and suggestions of Yamine Makri.

This book also owes a lot to the memory of my father (God have mercy on him) and to his very specific approach to legal issues – slowly elaborated and fashioned all along my theoretical studies on Islamic law and jurisprudence. It is also greatly indebted to all those who, in one way or another, accompanied me along the road and who, through their own studies and reflections and/or through their own field experience, have enriched me with their opinions and remarks: I am thinking in particular of Tarek Oubrou, Fouad Imarraine, Mamadou Daffe, Abd al-Halim Herbert, Larbi Kechat, Abdelaziz Chambi, Didier Bourg, Tayyeb Shah, Malika Dif, 'Ubaid Allah Gloton, Yusuf Islam, Ahmad Jaballah, Ahmad Bouziane, Farid Abdelkarim, Yacoub Mahi, Ibrahim Hewitt, 'Abd as-Samad, and many others, who have also directly or indirectly helped fashion the contents of the present work and who have encouraged me to present its substance in a new manner. They are my attentive and friendly brothers and sisters: I pray God to protect and love them. My thoughts, my invocations, my fraternity and my love accompany you, all.

The friends, companions or partners in the long, intense and sometimes repeated debates over the issues of coexistence, pluralism and secularism are also present in my memory: Jørgen Nielsen, Peter Clark, Jocelyn Cesari, Philippe Lewis, François Burgat, Pierre Dufresne, Isabelle Ducret, Albert Jacquard, Michel Morineau, Pierre Tournemire, Patrice Mugny, Guy Coq, Juan Martinez, Nathalie Dolle, Claude Torracinta, Alain Gresh, Robert Bistolfi, Jean Boussinesq, Henri Tincq, Jacques Neirynck, Jacqueline Costa-Lascoux, Christian Delorme, Richard Friedli, Jean-Claude Basset, Patrick de Laubier, Jean Offredo, Gilles Couvreur, Edmond Blattchen, Olivier Roy, Gema Martin Muñoz, Dominique Roulin, among so many other interlocutors. Their friendly or critical, direct or indirect contributions were of the most helpful, along with those of other interlocutors. Though it would be impossible to mention them all here, I extend to every one of them my heartfelt gratitude.

My wife Iman does more than accompany me. Along the road, she challenges, argues, questions, criticises. For so many years, she has been the mirror in whose reflections an important part of my thought has found its source and orientation. I have been able to understand a dimension of God's love by pondering over the priceless value of His gifts: my wife, her heart, her intelligence, and our children. Thanks for her presence, thanks for her patience.

Geneva,
March 1999

**Tariq Ramadan**

# Foreword

It is now a generation since western Europeans began to notice that there were Muslim communities settling in our cities. The days of the temporary migrant worker had been replaced by the establishment of families in a process which was clearly going to be permanent. The first mosques started appearing, and we began to pay attention. As we looked behind the superficial developments we discovered that there had been Muslims in Western Europe for a long time, in some cases for centuries, although in smaller numbers. The new presence in Western Europe served also to remind us that there were already well-established Muslim communities in parts of Eastern Europe – even if we thought we could safely ignore them hidden away behind the Iron Curtain. The new presence reminded us of our own presence in the Muslim world, in the form of empire.

But, of course, while we were paying attention to the changes we had to deal with – and the reluctance to do so in some quarters – assumptions were also being made about the impact of this new situation on Muslims themselves. The early simplistic conclusions were that with the passage of time, perhaps over one generation, the new immigrant communities would have become assimilated, at least in the sense that their attitude to religion and its requirements would have been "Europeanised". Some observers suggested that intermarriage in particular would be a major factor in this expected process of assimilation. Now, one generation later, the picture looks radically different from what those earlier – we might now call them naïve – observers thought.

So what has happened? The fact that we Europeans were reluctant to accept people who were different, except on our own terms, has certainly contributed to Muslims' assertion of their own distinctiveness in response. But, as I have argued on a number of occasions, it is really the Muslims' own attachment to their traditions which has forced local communities, politicians and academics to take them seriously and forget about the original naïve, assimilationist scenarios.

At the same time, it cannot be denied that Muslims themselves have been obliged to think increasingly deeply about the implications of their situation for their faith and its practice, and the ways in which that faith might continue to form an appropriate and functional foundation for their daily lives. It was beginning to become clear that, in so doing, they were having to reopen many of the questions which had faced Muslim scholars and thinkers at the height of Islamic civilisation a thousand years ago. The irony of the situation has become that living on the margins of the Muslim world has taken European Muslims back into the theological centre. In so doing they are being watched also from the geographical centre.

In the summer of 1995 I was speaking to a seminar of young Islamists in Jordan about the situation of Muslims in Western Europe. One perceptive young man posed the question: Is it possible that the experience of Muslims in Western Europe, as they struggle with this issue, is one from which we in the Arab world can benefit? After all, they are faced much more directly and intensely than are we with having to deal with the encounter of Islam with modern technological and secular society.

What is happening here is that the first generation of European Muslims, those who have grown up in western Europe, are asking fundamental questions about Islam. They have discovered that the cultural traditions of their parents, firstly, have difficulty functioning in a modern urban and bureaucratic society and, secondly, that much of that cultural tradition is not essentially Islamic in any case. In some instances some would even regard particular aspects as unacceptable in Islamic terms.

For a long time much of this debate has taken place in the language of the legal tradition, of *fiqh*, and in some minority circles this has been conceived of in inflexible conservative terms and the debate has been conducted almost in isolation from the larger society. Some observers of this process have therefore suggested that, if Muslims are going to be able to "cope" successfully with modernity, they have to drop the *fiqh* discourse and engage in a root-and-branch theological reformation. This reformation would have to start with a rethinking of the nature of revelation and thence the understanding of the revealed text. We know that there are also Muslim thinkers who take this line. Other observers have suggested that the Muslim response should be to abandon *fiqh* as something which cannot work any longer and instead emphasise issues of faith and theology. Again there are also Muslims who think along this line.

What has not been done systematically before in the contemporary European context has been to explore the resources of the mainstream tradition and their usefulness in this new environment. This is something which is being done extensively in the Muslim world, especially in the Arab Muslim world. Now Dr. Ramadan has provided us with the first major attempt to apply this process to the situation of Muslims in Europe.

His method is that used also by significant contemporary Muslim scholars, his debt to whom he explicitly acknowledges. He thus places himself squarely within a mainstream modern (as distinct from modernist) Islamic tradition. Starting from a systematic restatement of theological foundations, Dr. Ramadan then discusses in some detail the techniques developed traditionally for translating principles into the practice of a particular time and place: keywords *māṣāliḥ* and *maqāṣid*. This is the field which has suffered most in the popularisation of Islamic thought which has been such a strong phenomenon over the last century or so, as a consequence of the spread of Western structures of education and intellectual reasoning. It is a field which has enormous resources for relating the universal and eternal principles of Islam with the contingencies of human time and place, which is precisely the task which the Muslims of Europe are faced with.

Part Two of this fascinating study is then an analysis of particular practical issues and suggestions for how to proceed to solutions. This is where many readers – Muslims and others – will find the most interest. But in the longer term I would suggest that it is actually the first, more theoretical part which needs the closest scrutiny, because it is here that we find the foundations and the methodologies which will help Europe's Muslims to develop practical solutions to being European Muslims. While they may come up with different answers than those particularly suggested by Dr. Ramadan, they will have arrived at them in ways which both reassert their belonging within the mainstream Islamic tradition and assert their cultural and social belonging in Europe. On these foundations difference of opinion, *ikhtilāf*, is a blessing not a threat of conflict.

May 1999

**Professor Jørgen S. Nielsen**
Director, Centre for the Study of Islam
and Christian-Muslim Relations
University of Birmingham, UK

# Introduction

There is strong pressure today on Muslims living in European countries. The wave of immigration, which started after the Second World War, brought into Europe first Muslim men, then their wives and their whole families. Fifty years later, the number of Muslims living in West European countries borders on 15 million, if not more. The mere mention of this figure should satisfy us: the Muslim presence in Europe is important and we can find in each country a community which is more or less structured. This is a fact, a new one, of which Muslims are not always aware. They naturally turn their eyes towards another reality, one closer to their day-to-day life, whereby they face the difficulty of regular practice, genuine respect for Islamic rules, the weight of being part of a minority often labelled as foreign, different, if not barbarian, fundamentalist or fanatic. Even if they try to carry on despite this permanent pressure, the situation nevertheless influences their thoughts and actions: a reactive posture creeps into their conciousness and, in order to protect themselves from a non-Islamic environment, they finally determine their own identity in contrast with what it is not. Alternatively, they sometimes either forget their origin and religion or they try to erase their specificity in order to dilute themselves in society and, thus, become as invisible as possible, become *one of theirs*, an *authentic* European.

Nevertheless, in both cases one notices that Muslims do not define their Islamic identity by and of itself, from the inside, for what it is *per se*. This is true not only for those with extremist attitudes, but also for the great majority of Muslims who experience difficulties in merely saying *who and what they are*. Why should this be so? Is there an inherent difficulty in defining what a Muslim is *vis-à-vis* Western civilisation? Is this the result of the new European context? Has the experience of being a minority, and living as such, developed a kind of syndrome within the Muslim-European mind which prevents Muslims from considering themselves except through the mirror of a rejected world? Each of these assumptions carries a part of the truth. Notwithstanding this, it would appear, however, that we can find a more global cause for this type of attitude.

We should not forget that, in Islamic history, the nature of our current presence in the West is of a new kind. We have certainly experienced the fact of being a minority throughout our history, but this has nothing to do with the presence we are witnessing now. Essentially, it is our contemporary European context which confounds the data. Nowadays, the Western way of living is not only a specific attitude which we observe or detect in a man or a woman as a particular feature within his or her behaviour. It is obviously much more complicated and subtle: Western civilisation, with its machinery of values, is armed with such powerful means that it makes it difficult for anyone living in Europe[1] to define what he or she is or is not. The media, popular culture, music, the cinema and advertising serve as a vehicle to diffuse the concepts of individual and society, freedom and morality, entertainment and duty. Without warning, these concepts take root in the hearts and minds of the individual, if they do not subjugate him completely, and make it difficult for him to determine what is really from him, of his own volition, and what is due to external contributions or influences. Muslims are not spared these tensions. Moreover, it is made more evident by the presence of two contradictory tendencies: an initial and intimate culture of duty and community in contrast to an environment promoting freedom and autonomy but which, in fact, exerts a natural attraction over people. Who are we then? For those who have been brought up in Europe the question becomes even more complex. This is the lot of all teenagers of the second, third, and fourth generations. Who will answer? Who will restore to them the elements and the sense of their identity? Who will reconstruct it or, at least, give them some milestones which should permit them to find, consciously and freely, their own way?

One could present Islam, and this often happens inside European Muslim families, by means of a whole series of rules, interdictions or prohibitions, rulings which explain Islam within the framework of a specific relation of protection from an environment which is perceived as too permissive and even hostile. This was, mainly, the attitude of the first generation whose members, with a weak knowledge of Islam, sought first to protect themselves from the loss of their traditions. This latter concept represented, in fact, a vague idea, an indistinct mix of different kinds of elements such as familial or local tradition imported from the country of origin, with its own peculiar rules and principles (and sometimes superstitions), without necessarily being linked to Islam, but often confused with it, or to a clear idea of what is the content of their identity.

Before being a means of protection, however, Islam is an affirmative Faith which carries within itself a global understanding of creation, life, death, and humanity. This understanding is, or should be, the source of Islamic rules of thinking and behaviour and, at the same time, it should be shaped by a specific type of worship which encompasses the sphere of worship (*ʿibādāt*) and, more widely, the whole domain of social affairs (*muʿāmalāt*). One finds, expressed throughout the Qur'ān, a perpetual movement, back and forth, between a global vision of the universe and humanity – which is given birth to by the very essence of Faith – and, consequently, its implications in practice with the five daily Prayers, the annual payment of *zakāt*, the fast of Ramaḍān and the duty of permanent social involvement. The latter are all acts of worship and, in turn, they reinforce, strengthen and mould Faith itself.

In order for people to understand the Islamic identity we must explain this global vision of what the Islamic faith *is* – with its specific horizon – and what its immediate consequences on the diverse fields of human life are. Moreover, we should explain to people the essential principles as they are, but above all make them understandable in the light of our new context within European society. This is the way, we believe, that will allow us to remain faithful to both the Qur'ānic way of presenting the link between

Faith and the rules of action, and to the problem of being Muslim in Europe. To try to solve this problem implies then that we present our religion through our belief in its universality but in a manner relevant to our context: this should be the way that permits Muslims to understand their presence in Europe positively.

Lack of Islamic knowledge, added to specific circumstances such as an often difficult exile, the feeling of being foreign, economic problems and so forth, lead to the reactive posture we are witnessing today. This attitude was naturally widespread within the first generation, but one still finds its evident scars among younger generations: self-assertion, very often linked with a total oblivion of one's origin, and attempts to remain faithful to Islamic references is translated, both in thinking and acting, by reaction, rejection, refusal and sometimes aggression.[2]

We shall try in Part One of this work to draw the global framework of the Islamic concept of God, creation, worship, morality and social affairs. This should help us to understand the Islamic sources from which, downstream, are taken the general principles of the foundations of Islamic jurisprudence (*uṣūl al-fiqh*). The second section of the first part will treat some essential aspects of Islamic jurisprudencial rules in order to clarify some concepts – often misunderstood – and to offer a framework which should support Muslims in their attempts to treat and solve the sensitive questions they are facing today, especially in Western countries. In Part Two, we shall study some important questions regarding our situation in Europe: where are we? and who are we? This will provide elements of response to certain thorny problems such as defining notions like *dār al-Islām*, *dār al-ḥarb* or *dār al-ʿahd*, and give a clear definition of what the Muslim identity is. Such a study is necessary in order to lay down the first milestones for a genuine coexistence.

For us to face our problems in Europe it is essential that we bear in mind the very nature of the Islamic sources also understand their practical implications. We need to accept that our religion holds all the global principles by means of which we can face contemporary problems and find appropriate solutions to them. Basically, we have to carry on our research armed with at least three tools: first, a clear understanding of the Islamic references; second, a deep consciousness that they have to be considered as universal by the Believer and, finally, that any failure today to provide appropriate answers is due to the negligence of the Muslims themselves and has absolutely nothing to do with Islam whose teachings, on the contrary, incessantly encourage both scientific and juridical researches and discoveries.

## Notes

1 Except for some very traditional tribes and ethnic groups, this is also the case in the Third World because of the diffusion of Western culture throughout the world. See the analysis of this process in *The Westernisation of the World* (Serge Latouche, La Découverte, Paris, 1990).

2 Aggression towards the West is sometimes the scale by which Muslims measure both their own and their fellow Muslims' genuine belonging to Islam. As if it is sufficient to define Islam by what it is not and, above all, through a conflicting attitude. See our discussion below.

# Part One

# At the Heart of the Sources

## Faith and Religious Practice

### Introduction

As we have indicated in our general Introduction, the question of the Muslim presence in Europe necessarily requires that one has a clear idea about the fundamental teachings of Islam and also about the juridical tools which are at the Muslims' disposal. This so as to address the challenges we encounter nowadays.

The way in which Islam is, very often, presented in Europe is not without consequence. Perceived as a problem in secularised societies, Muslim men and women are expected to find solutions in order to adapt their religion and practices. Muslims are forced, almost automatically, to adopt a reactive attitude, just as they are quickly tempted to justify their beliefs and practices. In such an atmosphere, it is impossible, as much for Muslims as for their interlocutors, to present the essential Islamic teachings, those that take their sources in acknowledgement of a unique God, and which are nourished by a daily spirituality that radiates the totality of life and gives it value and meaning.

Muslims themselves, unfortunately, lose their sense of priority, not only in the manner in which they present their Faith but also in the way they end up conceiving of the same. Compelled to explain themselves in a society in which, as a minority, they are perceived as the source of malaise and conflict, the form this account takes, ends up gaining the upper hand over Faith and spirituality. We see Muslims reducing their religion to prescriptions and rules, to the lawful (*ḥalāl*) and unlawful (*ḥarām*), and idealising the Islamic sciences. Indeed, the latter are reduced to the apparatus of rules of jurisprudence (*fiqh*) whose knowledge and mastery is taken as sufficient guarantee for suitable responses to all problems. Priorities are, thus, reversed and we enter a vicious, vertiginous circle. This because by observing Islam from the reduced side of an opera-glass, it becomes impossible to give birth to an affirmative, confident and constructive perception of Muslim identity which develops real abilities to inscribe itself in the European landscape. In other words, the manner in which Muslims in Europe are perceived and questioned puts them in a reactive and defensive posture and this prevents them from producing an original and serene attitude.

It is, therefore, most urgent that we come out of this incriminating and, as such, infernal circle in order to accede to the profound dimensions of Islamic teachings. Such an approach is of the utmost usefulness and necessity both for Muslims as also for Western societies. Before there can be any consideration of adaptability, evolution or modernisation of the law, it is imperative that we take the time to approach Islam's essential teachings, its spiritual entrenchment and its universal dimension. Likewise, it is appropriate to better situate the role, place and typology of the Islamic sciences. Such a study of itself would give access to the juridical notions and tools we need nowadays so as to think our presence in the West. The savants of the science of jurisprudence (*uṣūl al-fiqh*) have elaborated, throughout the centuries, a methodology based on fundamental rules that are even more precious today because they allow, as Islam teaches, for us to remain faithful to the Revealed Message without preventing us from addressing changes in our environment or the evolution of history. We must, therefore, go back to these principles – this is done in the second section of Part One – just as it is also necessary to study the notions of *maṣlaḥa*, *ijtihād* and *fatwā*. Armed with such an understanding of the sources, it will then be possible to launch a constructive, dynamic reflection which is far removed from accusations and justifications. By means of this reflection, it will be possible to draw the horizon of living in Europe and, more profoundly, of the European Muslim, with all the priorities and stages that such an horizon entails.

Such is what we propose to undertake in Part One, starting, intentionally, from the fundamental teachings of Islam that have come to clarify the diverse sciences. These give us access to a thoughtful mastery of our sources by means of juridical tools that encourage a dynamic interpretation which is untiringly new and yet in perpetual search, because such is the exactness imposed by faithfulness to Revelation.

# I

# Islamic Teaching and Sciences

## A. The Essential Teachings

Paradoxically, one of the most important teachings regarding the organisation and typology of the Islamic sciences appears when we return to the time in which they did not exist, that is to the epoch of Qur'ānic Revelation during the Prophet's lifetime. The Prophet Muḥammad received Revelations while he was living among his people, some of whom were to become his nearest Companions. Considering the 23 years during which he received these Revelations, one can easily discern the steps of a very penetrating spiritual and religious teaching. The Prophet and his Companions had the benefit of neither sciences nor specialisations, they were educated by God, swept along by a Message which deepened their perception and their understanding of the universe and so moulded the nature of their individual and community bond with God, the One. From the consciousness of God to the clear and profound comprehension by which they behaved and acted in accordance with His teachings, there were 23 years of education, coupled with silence and explanation, peace and struggle, victory and defeat and, sometimes, death. The Prophet, chosen by God, to remind, guide and warn his people as well as the whole of mankind, was nothing but a man, with noble qualities certainly, but a man, just as we are,[1] and a mortal. We find in the Qur'ān – among the earliest Revelations – the three essential aspects of the nature of this prophethood. These are respectively (a) his quality of being a Messenger sent for the whole of humanity who has to remind people of the Presence of God, (b) of being a human and a guide and, finally, (c) of being a model, fashioned in the best manner with the best moral qualities.

*Now (as for thee, O Muḥammad), We have not sent thee otherwise than to mankind at large, to be a herald of Glad Tidings and a warner; but most people do not understand (this).*[2]

*Hallowed is He who from on high, step by step, has bestowed upon His servant the standard by which to discern the true from the false, so that to all the worlds it might be a warning.*[3]

*Say (O Prophet): "If you love God, follow me, (and) God will love you and forgive you your sins; for God is much-forgiving, a dispenser of grace."*[4]

*Say (O Prophet): "I am but a mortal like all of you. It has been revealed unto me that your God is the One and Only God(...)"*[5]

*Verily, in the Apostle of God you have a good example for everyone who looks forward (with hope and awe) to God and the Last Day, and remembers God unceasingly.*[6]

*For, behold, thou keepest indeed to a sublime way of life.*[7]

Man among men, chosen to be the paragon of virtue, his main duty, as a Prophet and a Messenger – with the call of worshipping the One God – was to permit and go along with a new way of considering the elements, the universe, indeed the whole of creation. The first verses and *sūrahs* revealed, for hearts newly filled with the light of Faith, were to totally modify and perturb the shallow glance people had hitherto given the world and, above all, themselves:

*Read in the name of thy Sustainer, who has created – created man out of a germ-cell! Read – for thy Sustainer is the Most Bountiful One who has taught man the use of the pen – taught man what he did not know!*[8]

Initial access to the understanding of *Tawḥīd* – Oneness of God – was to be deepened by a new and profound comprehension of His Signs within and through His creation without. Believers were encouraged to observe the world and to meditate on its purposes:

*In time We shall make them fully understand Our Messages (through what they perceive) in the utmost horizons (of the universe) and within themselves, so that it will become clear unto them that this (Revelation) is indeed the Truth.*[9]

The universe (*al-kitāb al-manshūr,* the displayed book) was to become, by the Will of God, the first support and confirmation of the Truth of Revelation (*al-kitāb al-masṭūr,* the written book) and, of course, of the presence of the Creator. This is confirmed by many verses throughout the Qur'ān which enable human beings to have access to a new sight fed by recognition of God:

*The seven heavens extol His limitless glory, and the earth, and all that they contain; and there is not a single thing but extols His limitless glory and praise: but you (O men) fail to grasp the manner of their glorifying Him!*[10]

This is in fact, with Faith in the Oneness of God, the expression of a profound spirituality which was henceforth opened to men and women who attained to Faith. To see with a new seeing:

*(At His behest) the sun and the moon run their appointed courses; (before Him) prostrate the stars and the trees.*[11]

To calculate the course of planets or stars is intellectually feasible as they are concrete and visible elements: hence, the first part of the verse clearly addresses our minds. The second part appeals to our inward vision, to our hearts, such that we see the ceaseless prostration of the trees and the stars. Clearly, Faith is a specific path to a new reality by which one reaches – or has to reach – the vicinity of what is apparently non-existent, unreal. *Apparently*, because the Message of the Qur'ān is quite the opposite regarding what *is* and what *can be perceived*:[12]

*Have they, then, never journeyed about the earth, letting their hearts gain wisdom, and causing their ears to hear? Yet, verily, it is not their eyes that have become blind – but blind have become the hearts that are in their breasts!*[13]

To observe the world and oneself, to ponder the purpose of creation is the first step towards a deep understanding of Faith and, then, to the proximity of the Creator. This was the meaning of the Prophet's tears after a wakeful night. The Companion, Bilāl, came at *fajr* time to call the Believers to Prayer and he found the Prophet sitting in the dark crying. Asking the reason for his tears, he was answered with: "Would I not cry while this verse has been bestowed on me from above the seven heavens?!" and the Prophet went on to recite:

> *Verily, in the creation of the heavens and the earth, and in the succession of night and day, there are indeed Signs (Messages) for all who are endowed with insight.*[14]

He added: "Woe betide him who hears this verse and who does not muse over it." What made the Prophet cry was not the announcement of a calamity or the fear of chastisement but clearly the pure and genuine revelation of the meaning of the whole of creation nourished by visible Signs and Messages of the latter's total submission to God. This, for he who could *see* and feel, hear and listen; for he who could *understand*. By contrast, those who are bent on denying the Truth are depicted as severed from those qualities:

> *They have hearts with which they fail to grasp the Truth, and eyes with which they fail to see, and ears with which they fail to hear.*[15]

This is the first stage of a penetrating teaching: everything in space bears testimony to God's presence. Hence, by means of this one reaches a deep God-consciousness (*taqwā*) and this, in turn, confirms the truth of the Qur'ān in the Believer's heart:

> *This Divine writ – let there be no doubt about it – is (meant to be) a guidance for all the God-conscious.*[16]

This Divine writ, confirmed by the heart and addressing the mind, reports episodes of the long human history from Adam to the Prophet Muḥammad and his Companions and even speaks about events to come.[17] Thus, Revelation sheds a new light on *history* once Faith and God-consciousness have transformed our way of considering the *space* around us and that far beyond. Here, with our immersion in the past, a new dimension, a new category of the invisible world arises, for "we were not present, we did not see", and God did not make us witnesses of His creation of the heavens and the earth, nor the creation of our own selves.[18] Divine Revelation, thus, sweeps us along to a time which just precedes man's creation:

> *And lo! Thy Sustainer said unto the angels: ... "Behold, I am about to establish upon earth one who shall inherit it."*[19]

And then we are in the first morning of His creation:

> *And He imparted unto Adam the names of all things, then He brought them within the ken of the angels and said: "Declare unto Me the names of these (things), if what you say is true." They replied: "Limitless art Thou in Thy glory! No knowledge have we save that which Thou hast imparted unto us. Verily, Thou alone art all-knowing, truly wise."*[20]

With the story of Adam, the first Prophet, Divine Revelation gives Believers intellectual access both to a past that no human witnessed and to a universe, beyond our capacities of perception – "outside the realm of previously realised experiences"[21] – to an *invisible* world in which the angels live who, at every hour, at every minute, at every second, everlastingly extol the limitless glory of Almighty God. This is the realm of *ghayb*, of a reality beyond that with which the sciences or rationalist and analytical philosophies deal: here one has access to a profound feeling, an intimate conviction, of the existence of spiritual beings and forces, of life after death, of purpose underlying the universe, along with faith in God. Faith is both at the origin and at the end of this initiatory process during which, in fact, it strengthens itself and increases.

Human history is read, henceforth, in this new light. A light that irradiates all the domains of thought, all events: it grants meaning to and reveals a global project of history beyond the reported stories and history itself. The Qur'ān teaches us that all the Prophets, after Adam, who followed each other over the course of centuries were first sent to remind people of the One Truth:

> *Not an apostle did We send before thee without this inspiration sent by Us to him that there is no god but I; therefore worship and serve Me.*[22]

From Adam, Noah, Abraham, Moses, Jesus to Muḥammad, it was the same essential Truth – God's Oneness – with its immediate consequences: God, the One, is the Sustainer of all the worlds, both physical and spiritual. He created us and to Him everyone will return after his/her death, in the Hereafter, and He, alone, is the Lord of the Day of Judgement.[23] The Revealed Books, punctuating the time of our human history, answer the needs of our nature which, kept occupied and preoccupied with the present life, can easily forget God, the Signs, the angels, the Life to Come and the Day of Judgement. It was said to Adam, during the first morning after the first forgetfulness:

> *There shall, nonetheless, most certainly come unto you guidance from Me; and those who follow My guidance need have no fear, and neither shall they grieve.*[24]

This guidance, mentioned in the above verse in its generic meaning, actualised itself within history by specific Revelations for one people (*qawm*) among peoples and for one limited era till the Qur'ānic Revelation which is considered by Muslims as the last one for the whole of mankind. To every Messenger, God taught the guidance, the direction and the way by which He wanted to be worshipped:

> *And unto thee (O Prophet) have We vouchsafed this Divine writ, setting forth the Truth, confirming the Truth of whatever there still remains of earlier Revelations, and determining what is true therein (...) Unto every one of you (as a community) have We appointed a (different) law and way of life.*[25]

The Qur'ānic Revelation confirmed the truth of earlier Messages but, at the same time, the Qur'ān teaches us that every previous community was appointed "a different law and way of life". Thus, during history the message was the same – there is only one God – but the ways of worshipping Him were and are diverse. There is, moreover, another essential teaching revealed in this verse: our relation to God is not only a matter of heart, pure faith or oral testimony that *we believe in God and in His Prophets.* To believe, on the contrary, is to behave in a certain manner, by trying to apply all that is laid down by Revelation and the Prophets.

This was utterly plain to the Prophet and his Companions from the very outset of his 23-year mission. To believe requires that we worship through a codified form revealed to the Prophet. This was the case for the first Muslims during the early years: they immediately understood that they had to pray by following certain rules. The third *sūrah* revealed, according to aṣ-Ṣuyūṭī's classification *al-Muzzammil* (The Enwrapped One), mentions the night Prayer – which was compulsory – in its initial form:

> *Behold, (O Prophet) thy Sustainer knows that thou keepest awake (in Prayer) nearly two-thirds of the night, or one-half of it, or a third of it, together with some of those who follow thee. And God, who determines the measure of night and day, is aware that you would never grudge it: and therefore He turns towards you in His grace. Recite, then, as much of the Qur'ān as you may do with ease.*[26]

Afterwards, some Revelations were bestowed upon the Prophet from on high in order to teach him, as all the Muslims, gradually, what was to be the definitive form and number of their daily Prayers.[27] Finally, the Prophet said to his Companions: "Pray as you have seen me pray."[28] Little by little, step by step, the first community was directed, through the educational method of the interspersed revelation of the Qur'ān, towards a definite way of worshipping God, based on precise rules and complete worship. After 23 years of this directed teaching, the Muslims were to hear:

> *Today have I perfected your concept and way of life for you, and have bestowed upon you the measure of My blessings, and willed that self-surrender unto Me shall be your religion.*[29]

Every element of the four pillars (Prayer, *zakāt*, fasting, and Pilgrimage) was now determined and definitively set either by the Qur'ān or by the witnessed practices of the Prophet. This worship was taught, and understood, as the practical way by which the Believer responds to God and, thus, testifies to his/her deep comprehension of the *shahāda*'s meaning: "There is no god but God and Muḥammad is His Messenger." These four *practical pillars* are in fact nothing but the means of remembrance, a reminder in one's human life, just as is the Qur'ān within human history.[30] They enable the human being, who by nature is forgetful and neglectful, to nourish the genuine life of Faith, *īmān*, a Faith which needs to be constantly strengthened if the person is to reach the world beyond sense perception, the world of *ghayb*. These pillars are only means, yet they are the indispensable and essential arbiter for mastering our inward and outward life so as to be totally and perpetually imbibed by Faith and its light.

This specific meaning of Divine teaching was plain and evident in the minds and hearts of the Prophet and his first Companions: the profound link between the mystery of *īmān* and the visible testimony of fixed worship (*ʿibādāt*) left no doubt as to the intrinsic meaning of Revelation. In fact, the first and essential principle of a life of Faith is that it is tied to a daily performed worship which requires, of itself, that intimate efforts be made to deepen and strengthen it.

This principle is the first, it is cardinal, yet Revelation and the Prophet were to teach Believers that it is not sufficient. Relations with God cannot be confined to Faith and worship, to *īmān* and *ʿibādāt*. These two domains are by no means the end, an aim *per se*, but, rather, the beginning. *Īmān* and *ʿibādāt* lie within the process and scope of Divine Revelation which glows in all spheres of life. They are both reminders and lights by which the Believer is able to *see*, find his way and make conscious choices. The Qur'ānic teaching is clear: to believe is to act and hence Islam, more than a simple and codified link between the Believer and God (a *Religion* in its strict and etymological meaning is "*to link*"), is a concept and a way of life. The Muslim Believer is lightened by Faith, guided and reminded by his/her daily worship in order to bear witness, in his general behaviour as well as in every personal action, to the authenticity and profoundness of his Faith. The genuine Muslim, as it is often said in the Qur'ān, is one who "*attains to Faith and does good works*".[31]

Before God, every human lives among other people, with whom he has to speak, share goods, entertain many kinds of social relations, from love and marriage to opposition and even adversity. One finds, both in the Qur'ān and the *aḥādīth* of the Prophet, many recommendations and instructions regarding the Believer's day-to-day life with oneself, one's parents, relatives, Muslims, non-Muslims, and foes, etc. The paragon, says the Qur'ān, is the Prophet:

> *For, behold, thou keepest indeed to a sublime way of life.*[32]

The Prophet showed the way, by his day-to-day behaviour, to love, bounty, generosity and justice. He tirelessly repeated to his Companions that they be good to one another, that they respect life, other human beings, animals, nature and, above all, that they be fair with all Muslims or non-Muslims, men or women, young or old. "Righteousness is a good way of life (*khuluq*, morality)"[33] said he, and "The most perfect in Faith among the Believers are those who possess the best way of life (morals), and the best among you are those who are kindest to their wives."[34] In another *ḥadīth*, one reads: "The best of you is he who is best to his family, and I am the best among you towards my family",[35] and "No one among you attains true Faith, until he likes for his brother what he likes for himself",[36] and "He is not a true Believer who eats his fill while his neighbour is hungry."[37] Many other traditions of this kind of moral teaching could have been quoted here and all direct the Believer to the same course: one has to behave in a good way in order to perfect one's Faith.

The presence of the Muslim on this earth, during his limited life-span, must be an active presence, involved in the affairs of the community. This is the essential way by which one bears witness to one's God-consciousness. This is, as a whole, the role of the Muslim community, which, says the Revelation, has not been chosen according to a supposedly inherent quality, but rather because of the good deeds that should distinguish its members:

> *You are indeed the best community that has ever been brought forth for (the good of) mankind: you enjoin the doing of what is right and forbid the doing of what is wrong, and you believe in God.*[38]

The Prophet urged Muslims to go forth in this way in every circumstance, imbued with a vivid consciousness of their duty: "Whosoever of you sees an evil action, let him change it with his hand; and if he is not able to do so, then with his tongue; and if he is not able to do so, then with his heart – and this is the weakest of Faith."[39] The commitment of the Muslim must be permanent inasmuch as it is the immediate consequence, and yet the best testimony, of the reality of his Faith. In fact, there is no true Faith without a deep requirement of justice and the Muslim, at the very moment he decides to live in and by his Faith, has to be a strict defender of justice, *with* the oppressed and wronged – whether Muslim or not – and *against* the oppressor – whether Muslim or not. The Prophet amazed his Companions by making a seemingly paradoxical statement: "Help your brother, whether he is doing wrong to others or is being wronged." One of the Companions asked: "O Messenger of God, I can understand helping one who is being wronged, but how can I help him when he is doing wrong?" The Prophet replied: "Stop him from doing wrong, this is your help to him."[40] To defend justice cannot be to defend Muslims only: the best witness of the excellence (*iḥsān*) of the Islamic way of life lies in respecting the ideal of justice over and above the failings and weaknesses of Muslim Believers. The Prophet Muḥammad, himself, was directed by God towards a deep comprehension of what is justice (*ʿadl*) and equity (*qisṭ*) and that both are an essential part of Faith. Eight verses of *Sūrah* an-Nisā' (The Women) were revealed to Muḥammad in order to acquit a Jewish citizen of a false charge and to condemn a Muslim instead. The latter, Ibn Ubayriq, had stolen a coat of mail and, afterwards, accused the Jew. The Revelation, bestowed upon the Prophet, illustrated the truth at a time when certain Jewish tribes were plotting with the Quraysh, the enemy of the still fragile Muslim community of Madina:

> *Behold, We have bestowed upon thee from on high this Divine writ, setting forth the Truth, so that thou mayest judge between people in accordance with what God has taught thee. Hence do not contend with those who are false to their trust.*[41]

Notwithstanding the precarious position of the Muslim community, the application of justice had priority over any other consideration and this was what the Prophet immediately understood and implemented. The same idea is conveyed by two other verses whose meaning leaves no doubt as to the requirement of justice and the deep link between God-consciousness and equity:

> *O you who have attained to Faith! Be ever steadfast in upholding equity, bearing witness to the Truth for the sake of God, even though it be against your own selves or your parents and kinsfolk. Whether the person concerned be rich or poor, God's claim takes precedence over (the claims of) either of them. Do not, then, follow your own desires, lest you swerve from justice: for if you distort (the Truth), behold, God is indeed aware of all that you do.*[42]

The other verse follows the same direction:

> *O you who have attained to Faith! Be ever steadfast in your devotion to God, bearing witness to the Truth in all equity; and never let hatred of anyone lead you into the sin of deviating from justice. Be just: this is closest to being God-conscious. And remain conscious of God: verily, God is aware of all that you do.*[43]

Thus, along with Faith (*īmān*), God-consciousness (*taqwā*) and regular worship (*ʿibādāt*), the way of life and personal morality (*khuluq*), bounty, generosity, love of mankind, efforts to spread righteousness and to do good deeds are, altogether, perpetual testimony to a true understanding of the Islamic teachings and of their authentic implementation. These three spheres are intimately linked and each one draws vigour and energy from the presence and intensity of the other two within a process which permits the Believer to reach, a little more every day, a deeper proximity with God. To apply absolute justice to our own self, within our inward and outward life, alone or in society, with our friends or with our foes, all this seems to be the greatest level a Believer can achieve. This is a very high level indeed, but the Qur'ān teaches us that there is even more than this:

*Behold, God enjoins justice, and excellence (sincerity).*[44]

More than the mere implementation of a visible justice – which has to be fulfilled – the Muslim must go beyond this stage and reach a state within whereby he is in permanent remembrance and, thus, has a continuous link with God so as to nourish the notion of justice (and its accomplishment) with the intense light of a wakeful Faith. In this way, the requirement of justice, before God and deep inside the Believer, becomes a demand of the heart. This is much more profound and intense than any intellectual propensity which can be disturbed by material, social or political interests. Within the heart, moulded by deep Faith, *justice* and *equity* are no longer notions or categories of the mind, but are rather the required stations of a genuine access to bounty, generosity, mercy and love which permit the Believer to be in God's vicinity. This is the path of *individual* Islamic spirituality which, by virtue of the effort required of everyone, should lighten the hope of the whole *community*.

In a well-known *ḥadīth*, the Prophet, answering the angel Gabriel's questions, first describes what *Islām* is, then what *īmān* and finally *iḥsān* are. The latter is presented in such a manner that it is clear that it represents the highest level of Faith a man can reach. Moreover this *ḥadīth* gives definition for the three domains we have just been speaking about.

"O Muḥammad, tell me about *Islām.* The Messenger of God (blessings and peace of God be upon him) said: *Islām* is to testify that there is no god but God and Muḥammad is the Messenger of God, to perform Prayers, to pay the *zakāt*, to fast Ramaḍān, and to make the pilgrimage to the House if you are able to do so.

He said: You have spoken rightly, and we were amazed at him (said ʿUmar) asking him and saying that he had spoken rightly. He said: Tell me about *īmān*. He said: It is to believe in God, His angels, His books, His Messengers, and the Last Day, and to believe in Divine destiny, both the good and the evil thereof. He said: You have spoken rightly. He said: Then tell me about *iḥsān*. He said: It is to worship God as though you are seeing Him, and while you see Him not, yet truly He sees you."[45]

Performing worship – *Islām* (*ʿibādāt*) – and feeling and understanding the specific world of *īmān* (*ghayb*) are like elements, or milestones, on the path of "excellence" (*iḥsān*), namely a complete and permanent submission of the heart and the mind to God's Will. Prayer, the payment of *zakāt*, remembrance of angels, Prophets, the Day of Judgement, all partake of a progression by which the Believer, the servant, tries to come closer to God and feel His presence, His love, His mercy. Forgetfulness though is part of our nature and hence why this process requires constant effort in order to overcome our negligence, our laziness. To put the memory and service of God at the heart of our life, at the heart of our hearts, demands constant awareness. A determination to master our natural tendency to go astray, far from the Divine reminder. This is not easy and God – through *Islām* and *īmān* – has provided us with the means – which are both rules, intimate recall and spiritual protection – to master our human nature and purify it. Prayers, fasting, and *zakāt* are *means* – required means of course, but they remain nothing but means – which fit our human condition. Nevertheless, they are not the ultimate aim of our worship. The latter is, once more, through any kind of good deed and action, to love God, to serve Him and to please Him. It is good, sometimes, to remind Muslims of this essential Truth. Too often, they confuse means and ends and waste their time engaging in sterile disputes concerning some detail of jurisprudence (*fiqh*) and so neglect the essential aspect of their worship, namely to purify their hearts through sincere love of God.

The Prophet taught this sense of priority to his Companions from the very beginning and he was helped by the Divine Revelations whose order followed a course which was to become clear over the 23 years of his mission: it was a question of educating individuals – men and women – of diffusing the Divine Message, of building a community of Believers who love the Creator and His Prophet and who are deeply conscious of their duties before God and the whole of humanity. The first Companions understood, through the impulsion and life of their Faith, that to adore God, to perform worship and to behave in a good way were all aspects of the same thing, partaking of the essence of their fundamental testimony (*shahāda*) among humankind: "*There is no god but God and Muḥammad is His Prophet and Messenger.*"

## B. The Birth of Islamic Sciences

### 1. *During the Prophet's lifetime*

The first Muslim community lived around the Prophet who was both the Messenger and the reference. He directed Believers, answered their questions and, thus, calmed and soothed their hearts and minds. His was the path of wisdom, knowledge and science. Initially, in his presence, there was no need to determine different domains of knowledge or to think of any kind of specialisation within the strict *religious* field. The teaching was unique, global, and affected all areas of human life but the Prophet made it clear that he was only a man and that as regards world affairs he could be wrong or wronged. For instance, when the Prophet arrived in Madina, he found the people grafting their date-palm trees. He said: "Perhaps it would be better if you did not do that." The *Anṣār* subsequently abandoned this practice but the yield from the date-palms became less: they informed the Prophet of this and he answered: "I am a human being. So when I tell you to do something pertaining to Religion, accept it, but when I tell you something from my personal opinion, bear in mind that I am a human being. You have better knowledge in the affairs of this world."[46]

Many other situations like this latter one were reported, all of which confirm the Prophet's status as a depository of Divine norm (*furqān*) and, as such, a reference for everything religious, yet a fallible human being in all other matters.[47] This distinction was clear for the Companions and the Prophet variously consulted them in order to take a decision according to the majority opinion.[48] This first distinction is very important not only because it clarifies the role of the Messenger as such, but also because it sheds new light on the Prophet's encouragement to his Companions to make legal rulings. Just as he did his best concerning world affairs, so they had to do their utmost with both matters religious and legal rulings all the while remaining true to their Faith, the Islamic practice and the right path. Two main factors were to bring about considerable changes within and for the Muslim community once it had settled in Madina. First, it was a question then not only of a living intimate Faith in one's heart, but of organising a whole society in the name of this Faith, bearing witness that the community was now able to be faithful to the meaning and prescriptions of the Qur'ānic Message. Second, the very rapid increase in the numbers of the Muslim community and its steady geographical expansion proportionately increased the difficulties. At the outset the Muslims had to understand Islam in order to apply it to a very well-known environment, i.e. the Arab society of the Hijāz, but, henceforth, they had to think of how best to implement Islam in a totally different context, with new populations, new habits and customs.

During the second part of his mission – and because of these substantial disruptions – the Prophet increasingly relied on the competence of some Companions, delegating his responsibilities to them in certain areas or merely taking maximum advantage of the qualities present in his community. He was already accustomed to employing Companions according to their knowledge or competence: for example, Zayd ibn Thābit for writing down the Qur'ān and Mus'ab ibn 'Umayr for the first predication in Yathrib, before the *Hijra*. However, the needs of the community went deeper than this: not only people who could write and speak were needed, but moreover those Companions who could understand the Islamic principles enough to give *religious* judgements. Circumstances dictated this internal development and, at the same time, it represented the first efficient step towards preparing the Companions to carry on the Islamic way of life, the *Sharīʿa*, after the Prophet's death.

Applying this practical methodology, the Prophet sent ʿAlī ibn Abī Ṭalib to Yemen. The latter was surprised for he thought he was too young and had "no knowledge of giving judgements". The Prophet replied: "God will guide your heart and keep your tongue firmly (attached to the Truth). When two litigants sit before you, do not decide until you have heard what the other has to say the way you heard the first, for that is more suitable for the correct judgement to become clear to you."[49]

Along with his continuous teaching of the meaning, both of recent Revelations and new obligations, the Prophet always took into account the competence of each Companion, encouraging some of them to give judgements or formulate religious rulings (*fatāwā*). He said plainly: "Whoever makes a reasoned decision (*ijtihād*) and is correct will receive two rewards, while he who does so and is incorrect will receive one reward."[50] Before sending Muʿādh ibn Jabal to Yemen, he asked him: "According to what shall you judge?" He replied: "According to the Book of God." "And if you find nought therein?" "Then I will exert myself to form my own judgement." Thereupon the Prophet said: "Praise be to God Who has guided the messenger of His Prophet to that which pleases His Prophet."[51]

Both the new challenges faced by the Islamic society of Madina and the original environment were to spur the Muslim community into developing the various skills of its members. Thus, the general orientation was already drawn: Qur'ānic Revelation had taught the Muslims what *īmān*, *Islām* and *iḥsān* are, it had taught them the essence of life, the priorities and global rulings to enable the community to remain faithful. All the means were in their hands to facilitate the most accurate implementation of Islamic teaching, taking into account cultural and geographical diversities.[52] Their intelligence, coupled with their skills, had, thereby, to be at the permanent service of their Faith.

The process of specialisation within the still global and unified Islamic teaching was to start during the last years of the Prophet's life. This was perceptible, albeit in embryonic form, in the way the Prophet organised and delegated his responsibilities during the Madinan period when the Muslims were fighting the Quraysh tribes and their allies. The Qur'ān plainly directed the Prophet towards a rethinking and a reorganising of people's various roles within the community. At the time of the northern expedition to Tabūk, the verse below was revealed:

> *With all this, it is not desirable that all of the Believers take the field (in time of war). From within every group in their midst, some shall refrain from going forth to war, and shall devote themselves (instead) to acquiring a deeper knowledge of the Faith, and (thus to be able to) teach their home-coming brethren, so that these (too) might guard themselves against evil.*[53]

The majority of commentators on the Qur'ān (*mufassirūn*)[54] explain that this verse relates to the Tabūk expedition, when the Revelation commanding the Prophet to keep some Companions close to him while others were sent on campaign, was given. This to ensure the continuity of Islamic knowledge spread through the Revelations and the Prophet's sayings. From this verse, scholars (*ʿulamāʾ*) have extracted some important teachings including the idea of a possible, and sometimes a necessary, distribution of functions within the Muslim community in light of personal or collective obligations (*farḍ ʿayn* or *kifāya*).[55] In his commentary (*tafsīr*), Qurṭubī highlights that we have to understand the notion of "acquiring a deeper knowledge of Faith" (*li yatafaqqahū fid-dīn*) in its widest meaning: in other words, it refers to all kinds of knowledge, not only the religious.[56] At the same time, it is clear that the early stages of specialisation are contained within this verse, even if one reads it in a very literal and contextualised way. The Prophet's attitude clearly confirms this interpretation since he distributed functions among the Companions according to needs and competencies.

With time this process would be accentuated with more specific domains of Islamic knowledge appearing. For example, in the field of recitation and understanding the Qur'ān, knowing and quoting the Prophet's sayings and behaviour, judging among people according to Islamic references, giving juridical rulings (*fatāwā*) and so forth. The Prophet's death was to intensify the need of the community to gather together all the surviving Companions so as to take up the challenge of pursuing his mission. The more proficient Companions contributed in preserving the content, meaning, intensity and the social, political and economic implications of God and His Messenger's teachings. In the absence of the Prophet though the questions remained the same: How to protect the Faith, how to apply Religion, how to reach excellence? In other words, *how to remain faithful*?

## 2. *The formation and typology of the Islamic sciences*

As we have stated above, the expansion of the Islamic community and the transformations in the social, cultural and historical context were, taken as a whole, one of the two main factors which led to the necessary formation of the distinct Islamic sciences. The other factor relied on the essence of the two fundamental Islamic domains and the way they presented themselves to the Believer's mind. We have already quoted *ḥadīth al-iḥsān* and a sole reading shows three (later four) separate fields which were to correspond to specific Islamic sciences: *īmān* and its elements would become *ʿilm al ʿaqīda*, *Islām* would become *fiqh al-ʿibādāt* (the first part of which is called *al-fiqh al-islāmī*, Islamic jurisprudence) and *iḥsān* according to its two-fold meaning linked with human action would become in its individual and intimate aspect *ʿilm al-akhlāq* (*taṣawwuf*, sufism, is linked with this field), and, regarding its social, commercial or juridical implications, *fiqh al-muʿāmalāt* (the second part of *al-fiqh al-islāmī*). All these studies were of course thought out, considered and elaborated upon in light of the Qur'ān and the Prophet's *Sunna*, which, as such, were to constitute two new domains of knowledge: *ʿulūm al-Qur'ān* and *ʿulūm al-ḥadīth*, respectively.

Before presenting a detailed typology of the Islamic sciences, it is necessary to remind ourselves that the formation process of these sciences occurred over a long period of time; it was slow and sporadic and spanned more than two centuries (roughly between the 7th and 9th centuries CE). As we have said, during the Prophet's lifetime, things were clear and the teaching was one and global. During the era of the *Khulafā' ar-Rāshidūn* (the Righteous Caliphs, between 632 and 661 CE),[57] the close Companions and the community preserved in their hearts and minds the meaning of the Revelations and the teachings of the Prophet. One of the first needs that appeared, after the battle against the southern Arab tribes which refused to pay *zakāt*, and the death of more than 70 *ḥuffāẓ* (Companions who knew the Qur'ān by heart – sing. *ḥāfiẓ*), was the writing down – as a possible reference source – of one copy of the whole Revelation according to its definitive order. Up until then, the proximity of these Companions to the Prophetic mission, both in their hearts and in time, made any such kind of codification unnecessary. Decisions were taken in common, in light of their deep comprehension of their Religion and its implications for individual and communal life. The reference was well known and Abū Bakr stated: "I have been appointed as your ruler, but I am not the best among you. If I am right, then help me. If I am wrong, you should set me right."[58] It was clear that the only two parameters of right and wrong were, in Abū Bakr's mind as well as in the mind of the whole community, the Qur'ān and the *Sunna* for all understood and applied the Prophet's statement: "There is no obedience to a creature in disobedience to the Creator."[59]

During this period, the consultative meetings were frequent and the majority of juridical or political decisions were taken in common and very often based on a consensus between the Companions. These Companions were reluctant to make individual legal rulings (*fatāwā*) and tried, when so tested, to direct the questioner to another Companion they considered more qualified. Essentially, they stuck very close to the literal meaning of the Revelation in question[60] and avoided excessive quotation of *aḥādīth* lest they misquoted the Prophet[61] and, above all, they concentrated their efforts on the study of the Qur'ān. This had in any case been 'Umar's recommendation both before and during his reign.

The way of ruling and dealing with problems was of a very practical nature during this period: the community and leaders were far from any kind of conceptualisation, of determining spheres of distinct science, of prescribing a set of procedures to be followed or of recording the laws resulting from their legal rulings. It was only during the last years of the period of the Righteous Caliphs that the first signs of turbulence appeared and made necessary a rethinking of the way to deal with the Qur'ān and the *Sunna*.

At the end of ʿAlī's reign, the Muslim community was facing one of its most difficult times since the Prophet's death. The first open power conflicts occurred which led to great social unrest and the birth of divisions within the community. After ʿAlī's death and the accession of Muʿāwiya ibn Abī Sufyān, the problems were to increase and, then, to effect a genuine implementation of the Islamic teachings. During the Umayyad era (661–750 CE), initiated by Muʿāwiya, at least four symptoms of deviation were to bring about the first compilations of *aḥādīth* along with the birth of specific studies on Islamic references by the *ʿulamā'*. The first symptom was the introduction of new practices in the Islamic State's affairs influenced as such by the Persian, Byzantine and Indian cultures: in 679 CE, for example, the office of Caliph was converted into that of an hereditary kingship and the State Treasury, *Bayt al-Māl,* was turned into the personal property of the Caliphs and their families. Thus, the principle of consultation (*shūrā*) and social participation had been lost and the first reaction of the *ʿulamā'* who refused to submit themselves blindly and cowardly to the desires and personal ambitions of the new kings, was to collect and compile the legal rulings – these were to become the elements of Islamic jurisprudence (*fiqh*).

The second sign was the dispersion of the *ʿulamā'*: some had fled the corruption of the capital or other political centres, others had merely migrated to remote cities and, therefore, it was impossible to gather them together to obtain juridical decisions based on consensus (*ijmāʿ*). Scattered, facing geographical, cultural and social diversities and, moreover, alone in their search for appropriate decisions (*ijtihād*), the *ʿulamā'* initiated and founded, often unwillingly, a multiplicity of schools of thought by virtue of the students around them. This was the case, to mention just a few examples with Abū Ḥanīfa and ath-Thawrī in Kufa, Mālik in Madina, al-Awzāʿī in Syria and al-Layth in Egypt.

The third symptom was the new phenomenon of fabrication of *aḥādīth* due both to an increasing need for information and various political interests. These periods witnessed not only deeper researches and studies in the religious field but also the development, for the first time, of false sayings and actions attributed to the Prophet. This was a period of trouble and turmoil and different parties tried to justify their respective positions by basing them on alleged *aḥādīth*. The scholars' reaction was to compile *aḥādīth* they knew to be true and so they initiated the science of *ḥadīth* criticism. The last phenomenon – which was both a cause and an effect of the three others – was the numerous conflicts between different tendencies and parties within the community. The two best known splits are the Battle of Ṣiffīn (657 CE) which would lead to the creation of the *Khawārij* (secessionists) group and the Battle of Karbalā (680 CE, in which Ḥusayn, ʿAlī's son, died) that brought about the reaction of ʿAlī's partisans and the strengthening of the *Shīʿa* (partisans) branch. Other minor conflicts took place over this hundred-year period increasing the turbulence and, in turn, bringing to the fore the need for some codification and rules in matters relating to Islam, especially in the juridical field.

The two main elements mentioned above – the dispersion of the *ʿulamāʾ* and the fabrication of *aḥādīth* – engendered serious upheaval in the nature of the transmission of Islamic knowledge. For the first time Muslims witnessed a multiplication of qualified and authorised opinions; not only were these diverse but, sometimes, on some secondary issues, they were totally at odds. Even the way of dealing with situations and problems was completely different: at Madina, the *ʿulamāʾ*, following the example of Ibn ʿUmar, confined themselves to a strict reading of the Qur'ān and the *Sunna* by avoiding personal interpretations (they were called *Ahl al-ḥadīth*);[62] while in Iraq, at Kufa, the scholars – called *Ahl ar-ra'y* – followed in Ibn Masʿūd's footsteps by using reasoning, analogical considerations and did not hesitate in imagining and speculating original problems and situations. Both history and the differences in socio-political context could explain these disruptions but, henceforth, it became clear that this diversity – which was still considered as *inside* the lawful sphere – had to be regulated so that opinions could be defined as being within the legal authorised field or not. The Umayyad era was the first milestone, one which directed scholars' studies and from which the diverse branches of the Islamic sciences were brought to bear.

In the course of the first two centuries of the ʿAbbāsid Dynasty (approximately 750–1258 CE) things went quicker and one could say that it was during this era that the specific fields of Islamic sciences were determined and shaped: social and political troubles gave birth to the worry and danger that the Muslim community would become forgetful in its requirements of Faith, that it would betray its sources and, finally, that all this would lead to its destruction. The first hundred years is known as that of the *great imāms* (750–850 CE): this period saw the flourishing of the Islamic sciences, especially within the field of jurisprudence (*fiqh*) and that of the *ḥadīth* criticism. The early ʿAbbāsid Caliphs made a great show of respect for Islamic Law and its scholars. Many of them, such as Harūn ar-Rashīd (ruled 786–809 CE) or al-Manṣūr (ruled 754–75) were either scholars themselves or commissioned others to compile authoritative books of *Sunna*. There was considerable freedom of opinion and, throughout the realm, the numerous centres of thought, learning and debate were lively and stimulating in their approaches. Additionally, this time witnessed an impressive number of great scholars who not only taught but also engaged in deep discussions among themselves, and so we have all the ingredients which explain the intellectual vitality of this era.

Many schools of thought were to appear around prominent *ʿulamā'* such as Abū Ḥanīfa (703–67 CE) in Kufa, al-Awzāʿī (708–74 CE) in Syria, Mālik (717–801 CE) in Madina, Zayd (700–40 CE) in Kufa and Wasit, al-Layth (716–91 CE) in Egypt, ath-Thawrī (719–77 CE) in Kufa, ash-Shāfiʿī (769–820 CE) in Baghdad and Cairo, Ibn Ḥanbal (778–855 CE) in Baghdad, Abū Dāwūd (815–83 CE) in Kufa or aṭ-Ṭabarī (839–923 CE) in Egypt and Ṭabaristān. All these *ʿulamā'* were the means by which important progress was made within Islamic studies. Everyone made a specific contribution during his lifetime and helped develop a positive evolution in the comprehension of Islamic sources. Each was considered as a founder – willingly or not – of a *madhhab* (school of thought): some disappeared during history and others are still known today throughout the Muslim world (particularly the Ḥanafī, Mālikī, Zaydī, Shāfiʿī and Ḥanbalī *madhāhib*). For the first scholars, such as Abū Ḥanīfa, al-Awzāʿī and Mālik, the distinction between the different sciences was not very clear. The well-known compilation of the latter's *Al-Muwwaṭṭa'* (The Beaten Path), is still a mixture of personal legal rulings, *aḥādīth* and the opinions of the Companions or their successors.

Historical circumstances coupled with the influence of the great civilisations the Muslims encountered – Greek, Roman, Persian or Indian – were to modify widely the way of reasoning and presenting the outcome of scholars' researches. Little by little, the phenomenon of distinction and specialisation in Islamic thought and study appeared and even within the field of *Fiqh* as such. Henceforth, the *ʿulamā'* distinguished – in *Fiqh* – between *al-uṣūl* (fundamental principles) and *al-furū'* (secondary principles). More generally, ash-Shāfiʿī, in his *ar-Risāla,* was the first scholar to systematise global principles and determine the frame within which and by which specific juridical rulings had to be stipulated. Due to distances in time and space from an immediate understanding of the sources, he felt that scholars were in need of rules and methods which should avoid – or put a stop to – unfounded and unqualified interpretations. Ash-Shāfiʿī's decision to fix a framework and formulate global rules was to see the creation of a new Islamic science of the utmost importance and whose objective was "to determine and define the global rules used to extract and deduce the specific juridical rulings – of *fiqh* – from the sources of reference".[63] This kind of research, necessitating a close, deep and technical study of the Qur'ān and the *Sunna,* not only encouraged evolution and improvements within other fields but also directed them towards a new way of dealing with the sources, one which required memory, precision and authentication along with a complete mastery of the Arabic language.

It was approximately during the same era that the *science of ḥadīth* saw a rapid development. Ibn Ḥanbal and Mālik, following the Companions, had already compiled numerous *aḥādīth* (there are more than 30,000 in Ibn Ḥanbal's *al-Musnad*), but the specific work of systematic authentification was to start with al-Bukhārī (810–70 CE) and his student Muslim (817–75 CE) who looked for *aḥādīth*, collected and authentified them and, then, classified them according to the themes and format pertaining to *Fiqh* studies. They, consequently, established a respective frame of rules concerning authentification through which they were able to decide whether or not a *ḥadīth* could be accepted as *ṣaḥīḥ* (authentic).

Through contact with other civilisations and due to the need for in-depth studies on the Arabic language, its structures and grammatical rules (so as to understand the linguistic structures of the Qur'ān and the *Sunna*), the first linguistic studies concentrated on Arabic morphology (*ṣarf*) and grammar (*naḥw*). To complement this, but through independent works, commentaries and exegetical studies on the Qur'ān (*tafsīr*) also appeared and the first important contribution in this context was by at-Ṭabarī (839–923 CE) with his *Jāmi' al-Bayān*. (He also wrote a well-known history of humanity from Adam onwards, *Tārīkh ar-Rusul wal-Mulūk*.)

Much has been said about the origins of Sufism (*taṣawwuf*) as a path to proximity with God, as a form of mysticism. Was it a strictly Islamic science, or was it the manifestation of outright borrowing from neighbouring Christian traditions? Different opinions have been stated on the subject, whether by Muslim scholars or by Christian Orientalists, some going so far as to argue that sufism, as opposed to the different legal sciences the evolution of which we have just described, is "another Islam". Some Muslims, often little conversant with Islamic sciences, even went so far as to "exclude" Sufis and their initiatic schools (*ṭuruq*, sing. *ṭarīqa*) from "authentic Islam". Such statements, which in fact express ideological, religious or scholastic standpoints, do not resist factual analysis.

The Prophet of Islam was the first to show the way of meditation, of *dhikr* (reminder) and of asceticism, also identified through the concept of *zuhd*. The Companions, during their nocturnal Prayers, experienced the dimension of proximity, knowledge and love of God. The concept of *rabbānī*, found in the Qur'ān in the plural, already bore the mystical intensity which the great scholars of *taṣawwuf* were to give to initiation. Ḥasan al-Baṣrī (died 728), both globally and specifically, then the famous mystic Rābi'a al-'Adawiyya (died 801), paved the way to what was to become an authentic Islamic science, with its scholars, its vocabulary and its norms. In Kufa first of all, with 'Abd al-Wāḥid ibn Zayd (died 793), then more specifically from the 9th century in Baghdad, Sufism was to flourish and gradually clarify the specificity of its approach. In the course of centuries, a few authorities stood out by fixing the norms of the exacting mystical approach: Abū 'Abd Allah Hārith ibn Asad al-'Anazī, better known as al-Muḥāsibī (died 857), his disciple al-Junayd (died 910), Dhu'l-Nūn al-Miṣrī (died 859), Abū Ṭālib al-Makkī (died 996), al-Qurayshī (died 1074) and 'Abd al-Qādir al-Jilānī (died 11660, the founder of the first recorded *ṭarīqa*, al-Qādiriyya, were all Sufi scholars (most of them also highly qualified in the canonical sciences of faith and Islamic law) who, along with many others whom it would take too long to mention here, were to define and direct the mystical path by considering it as one of the spheres, one of the paths of Islam. It never occurred to them to distinguish 'one Islam' from 'another Islam' nor to stress the excellence of "another Islam" as opposed to the formalism of jurists. It is clear that they considered themselves as Muslims, in complete accordance with the fundamental teachings of 'Islam' which they did not conceive as anything but a single entity. Most of them clearly stated that no esoteric approach could develop without being deeply rooted and firmly grounded within the so-called esoteric sciences; the two approaches are indissociable, they both follow the same path, lead to the same destination, express the same disposition of the heart submitted (Muslim) in the name of the single message of the one Islam.[64]

Finally, translations of the great philosophers of antiquity opened another field and initiated the Greek tradition of philosophical debates in some Islamic centres of learning. This process forced the *'ulamā'* to determine more clearly what the exact elements and contents of the Islamic Faith (*īmān*) were in order to

## Chart I: The Developmental Stages of *Fiqh*

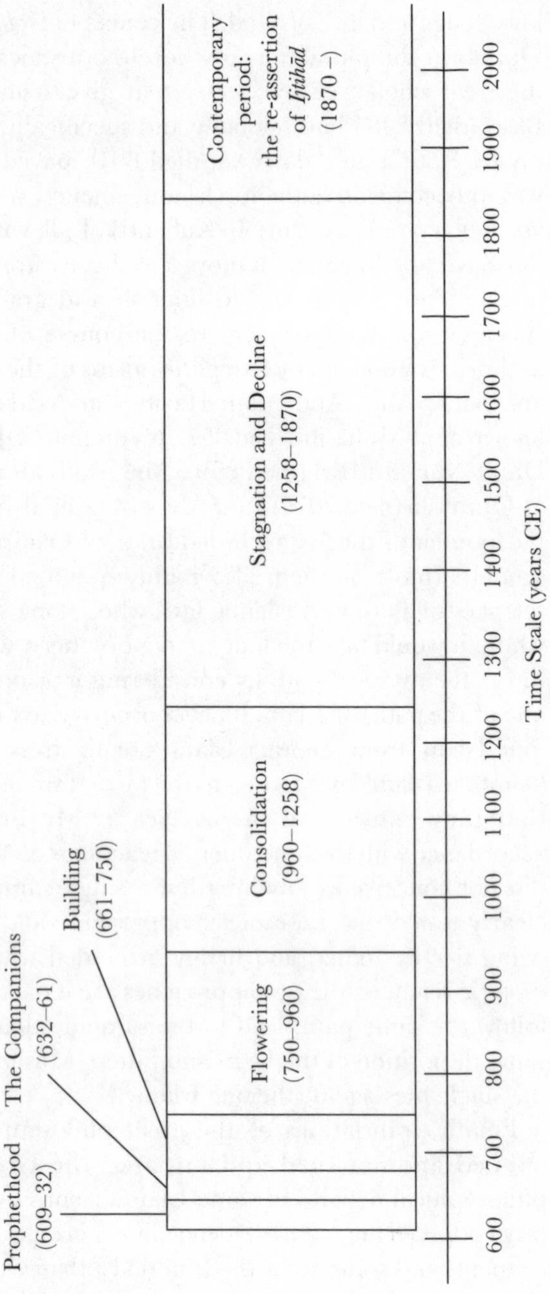

## Chart II: **The Era of the Early *Fuqahā'***

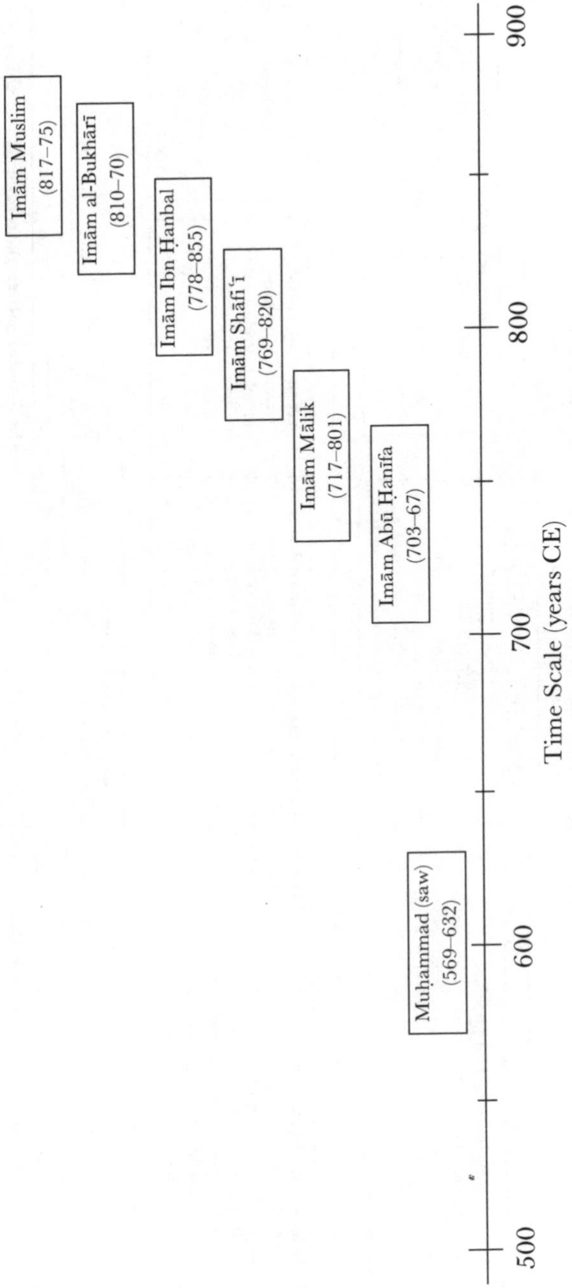

## Chart III: **Typology and Classification of the Islamic Sciences**

**Qur'ān** ***Sunna***

***Sharīʿa***

General concept of the Creation, of existence, of death, and of way of life, derived from normative reading and understanding of the scriptural sources.

***Sciences of the Qur'ān***

Makkan and Madinan revelations; occasions of revelation; abrogation; etc. One may include among these sciences exegesis (*tafsīr*), as well as styles and rules of recitation (*tajwīd*).

***Sciences of the Ḥadīth***

Compilation about the transmitters and authentication of the routes of transmission (*isnād*), together with study and analysis of the content (*matn*). Degrees of authenticity (*ṣaḥīḥ*, *daʿīf*, etc.) Necessarily dependent on study of the life of the Prophet (*sīra*).

***Science of ʿaqīda*** **(the creed)**

Study of *Tawḥīd* (oneness of God), the names and attributes of God, the Angels, the Prophets, the Books, Destiny, the Day of Judgement. ***ʿIlm al-kalām***, Islamic philosophy (theology), grew by extension out of the debates carried on in the domain of *ʿaqīda*.

***Uṣūl al-fiqh*** **(principles of jurisprudence)**

Foundations of Islamic Law. It expounds the principles and methodology by means of which the rules of law and jurisprudence are deduced and extracted from their sources. Study and formulation of the rules of interpretation, of prescription and prohibition, of general principles (*ijtihād*, *ijmāʿ*, *qiyās*), etc.

***Science of akhlāq*** **(morals, ethics)**

Study of individual behaviour in relationship with God, one's self, the family, neighbours, and society in general.

***Taṣawwuf*** **(Sufism)**

Study of the mystic's path, the respective stages and states of the inward journeying towards God.

***Fiqh*** **(jurisprudence)**

Study of Islamic Law and jurisprudence presented in two fields.

***ʿibādāt*** **(rites/modes of worship)**

Study of the rules related to ritual purification, Prayer, *zakāt* (alms-tax), fasting, Pilgrimage.

***Muʿāmalāt*** **(other than formal worship)**

Study of the rules in respect of collective affairs: legislation, commerce, marriage, inheritance, etc.

***Fiqh al-wāqiʿ*** **(events, cases) and *Fiqh al-awlawiyyāt* (priorities)**

Study of the determination of priorities in the application of the Islamic laws and regulations in the light of period and context.

***Fiqh al-daʿwa*** **(communicating Islam to others)**

Study of the methods of explaining and transmitting the Message of Islam according to period and context.

prevent the community from deviating and going too far towards sophist or rationalist disputes, sometimes only for the pleasure of arguing, without really understanding or even referring to the sources. Such a context pushed them into defining exactly what was and what was not part of the Islamic Faith and so enabled them to establish the contents, principles and rules of *ʿilm al-ʿaqīda* (the science of faith, which is sometimes called theology, by analogy with Christian studies).[65]

Thus, before the middle of the 10th century, all the Islamic sciences had appeared and had had, more or less, their specific field of study already circumscribed. This due to the double influence of history and the consequent need for a more meticulous application of the Qur'ān and the *Sunna* in order to identify solutions and solve individual or social problems in a new context. One could say, in the light of our study, that the sciences in Islam – through their initial formation, evolution and improvement over the course of history since the 7th century – have had only one purpose, one objective, and that is to answer one fundamental question: How to maintain a vivid Faith and yet remain faithful to the Qur'ānic and Prophetic teachings in new historical, social and political situations? The sciences, enlightened and directed by the Faith and its requirements, are the *means* of the Believer's faithfulness and these means have to be more and more sophisticated in order to fit a world which is much more complex and becoming still more so. Faith requires a mind and a reason in constant awareness and activity.

This is what the *ʿulamā'* of the first generations clearly understood and during three centuries, in spite of problems, corruption and persecution,[66] they did their utmost to serve God, Islam and the Muslim community. They offered to their descendants a rich legacy constituted by an original *geography of the Islamic sciences* with clearly marked fields and a set of great subjects to explore and think about. It was also clear to them that their contemporary Muslims as well as future generations should not confine themselves to the opinions they themselves held and formulated in a specific time for a very specific context. In the sight of history their studies and opinions *were no more than useful means rather than everlasting solutions.*

Since the 10th century, the Muslims have had a framework which should have permitted them to progress in their researches and to develop their skills to provide their community with appropriate answers to their questions. These sciences and their typology should have been a foundation, a vivid source for further studies. Unfortunately, it has, however, very often been like the walls of an intellectual prison preventing the *'ulamā'* from providing or imagining original, but still faithful, Islamic solutions to contemporary problems. For more than seven centuries, despite the ceaseless efforts of prominent scholars (such as ash-Shāṭibī or Ibn Taymiyya during the 13th and 14th centuries respectively), Muslims have followed the path of blind imitation (*taqlīd*) without being able to find again the genuine and dynamic Message contained in the Qur'ān and the *Sunna*. Moreover, they have often taken means for ends by making Islamic knowledge an objective *per se*, dressed in and covered with complicated fields, issues and useless details.

Notwithstanding this negative evolution, it is necessary to come back to these first attempts to establish a geography for the Islamic sciences. For Muslims living in Europe, it is of the greatest importance not only to know what these sciences actually are – and how they are inter-connected – but, more deeply, to be able to re-read the Islamic Message with its original life force and acquire a global vision of the fields, studies and means at their disposal so that they can face their current situation. So that they do not confuse one moment of their history with the essence of their Religion since, by means of the latter, the means are numerous and Islam's global rulings offer a wide field of exploration and investigation. It is necessary to master these juridical instruments and, at the same time, know and understand the European context so that it is possible to answer *the* question, ever the same question: How to maintain a vivid Faith and be faithful to the Qur'ānic and Prophetic teachings in Europe, in our new historical, social and political situation? In other words, how to be a European Muslim? How to develop, despite our materialistic environment, accurate Islamic sciences at the service of our Faith and our faithfulness. It is a question, in fact, of refinding the dynamism of our ancient scholars in order to formulate answers for questions that have never been asked, of doing so without confusing means and ends, but remaining exclusively in the service of science and the humble service of God.

The diverse Islamic sciences taken together serve an aim which is beyond their respective existence. That is, they allow everyone to come nearer to God, to be in His proximity, to love and serve Him, with heart, mind, and action. This is how, it seems, one has to understand the utility of every Islamic science which is part of the typology presented below.

## C. Comments (Typology and Classification)

By the end of the 10th century CE (3rd AH), each Islamic science already had its own specific field with its specialists and renowned scholars. Many of them were of course qualified in several areas but their names were, however, associated with one particular discipline.

As we can see, the Qur'ān and the *Sunna* are the two sources on which the whole building of the Islamic sciences is based. Together they constitute *Sharīʿa*, the exclusive references which direct the way Muslims must go to be faithful to the Revealed Message. The science of *uṣūl al-fiqh*, relying on studies of *ʿulūm al-Qur'ān* and *ʿulūm as-Sunna*, expound the rules and the methodology by which it becomes possible to extract (*istinbāṭ*) the global principles of Islamic law. With a clear comprehension of these roots and this framework, one should be able to apply a qualified and faithful *ijtihād* (through the community as with *ijmāʿ* or through the individual as with *qiyās*). This fundamental work permits the codification of Islamic law (*fiqh*) and its two sections: the *ʿibādāt* (worship) which is fixed and permanent, and the *muʿāmalāt* (social affairs) which deals with matters subject to change (because of context or time) like trade, marriage, customs, and the penal code and which need constant reflection and adaptation in order to permit their faithful enforcement in light of the global principles of *Sharīʿa*.

The sciences (*ʿilm al-ʿaqīda*) relating to *tawḥīd* (Oneness of God), God's names and attributes consider the essential aspect of Islam and are based on the study of the Qur'ān and the *Sunna* through this very specific angle. The fields relating to the intimate and spiritual link with God (*taṣawwuf*) as well as individual and social morality (*ʿilm al-khuluq*) are yet other ways of considering and extracting particular teachings from the sources (about *ghayb*, spirituality, intimacy and mysticism). All these different fields benefit from the inference and methodology used in *uṣūl al-fiqh.*

The three domains of *Fiqh* (considered here in its etymological meaning of understanding) have been developed and more or less codified since the end of the 19th century, whereas before then Muslim scholars had to face totally original social, political and economic situations. With the end of the implementation of Islamic laws within the Ottoman Empire (approximately during the mid 19th century) and their replacement by secular rulings imported from France, Britain and other Western countries, it became impossible to think about a genuine implementation of Islamic teachings without taking into account the new state of affairs (*wāqiʿ*) throughout the Islamic world and reconsidering ways through which it should be possible to formulate and apply Islamic jurisprudence. This leads, consequently, to a consideration and study of the order (*awlawiyyāt*) the Muslim community has to follow – the global strategy – to refind a deep and dynamic understanding of *Sharīʿa* in light of the international political and economic order.[67] With the progressive diffusion of Western culture, it has become necessary to re-think the way of presenting Islam among the Muslims themselves. The concept of *Fiqh ad-daʿwa* was first formulated in Egypt during the 1930s and has become a very productive field of thought because of the important challenges Muslims are facing to their Religion, values and cultures.[68]

## The notions of *Shahāda* and *Sharīʿa*

It has often seemed difficult to define the concepts which, in Arabic, determine and outline either a state of "being Muslim", or an action, or, more broadly, a frame of reference or a science.

The problem is twofold: it is first of all the 'mere' difficulty of translating from one language to another, but to this is added the fact that scholars themselves, according to their field of specialisation, or because of the particular perspective arising from the debates which occupied them at the time, have given different definitions, which were sometimes voluntarily precise and sometimes purposefully broad and vague.

In the classical presentation of Islamic sciences, the two basic sciences, *'ilm al-'aqīda*, the science of faith and all that cannot be perceived by the senses on the one hand, and *Sharī'a*, here understood as the Law including all the prescriptions drawn from the Qur'ān and the *Sunna* concerning worship in the broader sense and behaviour (the exoteric dimension) on the other hand, are presented as complementary. A third dimension is often added: that of *ḥaqīqa*, the Truth in the sense of spiritual Reality, which is the path towards the knowledge of God particular to Islamic mysticism (the esoteric dimension).

Disagreements over definitions, over the delimitation of fields of attribution, or even over the priority of one science or one approach over another, have been numerous and sharp. *Fiqh* specialists often tried to reduce the notion of *Sharī'a* to their field of specialisation alone, that is to law only. Other scholars, and in particular those who were conversant both with law and with mysticism, recalled that the meaning of *Sharī'a* is far broader than that and that the word literally refers to the notion of the *path leading to the source*, that it expresses the idea of *the Way* including and embracing all aspects of Islam, from the essential and primary axis of *'aqīda* (the science of faith) to *fiqh* (law and jurisprudence) and to *taṣawwuf* (mysticism). They thus wished to return to the unique and all-embracing vision which reigned at the time of the Prophet of Islam, when faith, spirituality and practice were all moved by the same inspiration. They above all strove to oppose the extremely shallow vision of those for whom Islam had come to be reduced to the primacy of the law and its implementation: for these scholars, specialised in *fiqh* and in the disputes related to it, law was no longer *a means* of being faithful to the message but *an end*, and Islam, which had originally included faith, spirituality and law, was now reduced to legal prescriptions and to their codification and commentary.[69]

Such discussions have led us far away from Islam's original simplicity. We must return to essentials and present things clearly, synthetically, and above all in a way that will again enable us to find the source of this single inspiration in whose glow Islam is all at once a faith, a law and a mysticism. Islam is one and it is based on two essential axes: "being a Muslim" and "how to be a Muslim". *Being a Muslim* means testifying that one believes in God in one's heart and mind and that one recognises the truthfulness of the Qur'ānic revelation and of its Messenger; it is the testimony of the *shahāda* that makes a man or a woman enter Islam (There is no god but God and Muḥammad is His Messenger). *How to be a Muslim* covers all the dimensions of action which enable us to remain faithful to the testimony of faith, as well in the intimate sphere of spiritual and mystical approach and in that of law and jurisprudence at the individual and collective levels; it is the *Sharīʿa*, the way, the path to how to remain faithful to the source.

To make things even clearer, we may present this as a graph (chart IVa). The horizontal axis represents "being a Muslim" (*shahāda*) while the vertical axis is the projection of "how to be a Muslim" (*Sharīʿa*).

In the first chart below, the curves represent the implementation of law and jurisprudence elaborated in the light of the sources and taking into account the historical and geographical context (the general situation, the type of society, the state of legislation, etc.). Each of these curves is an implementation, both individual and collective, actualized in a given time and place while being faithful to the framework of being a Muslim (*shahāda*) and of how to be a Muslim (*Sharīʿa*). The plurality of curves represents the necessary plurality of implementations of *fiqh* during different periods or in different environments (possibly during the same period).

Chart IV a: *Diversity of fiqh (in time and space)*

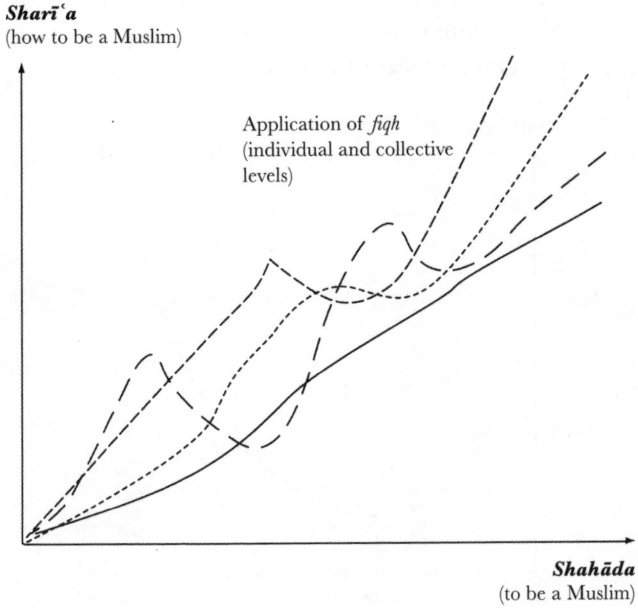


## Comments:

1. *Whenever an individual breathes, drinks, eats or prays while being conscious of faith, he or she is already in the living experience of Islamic Sharīʿa.*

2. *The implementation of law and jurisprudence (fiqh), necessarily takes into account the sources and the social, cultural, political and economic context. This implementation is flexible and open to change (it progresses or regresses) and it represents "how to be a Muslim", the Sharīʿa, at a given time in history, in a given society, and sometimes for a particular individual (in the case of a specific fatwā).*

Chart IV b: *Spiritual accomplishment*

In the chart below, the axes are the same but the curve represents the individual's inner spiritual and mystical progress through the three dimensions, which are also stages, of Islamic teaching as presented in our first section:

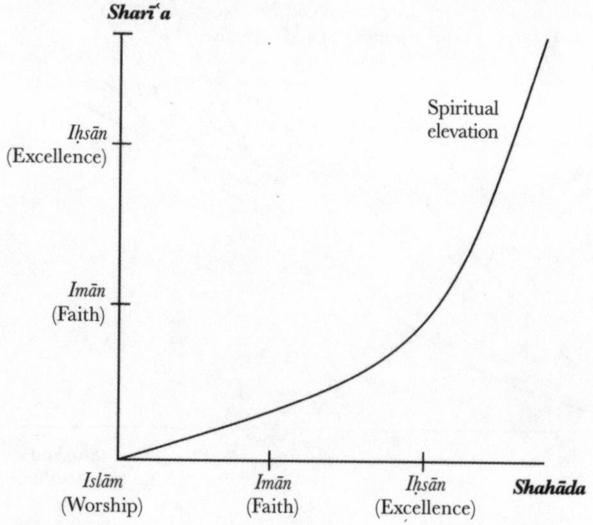


## Comments:

1. *On the two axes of shahāda and Sharīʿa, we can find the three dimensions of being and how to be a Muslim. Islām (the practice of worship) which, with the essential condition of shahāda, covers the field of the four practical pillars (Prayer, zakāt, fasting and Pilgrimage). Īmān (faith and its pillars) implants, deepens and develops the meaning and scope of the bond with God and with the universe beyond what the senses can perceive. Iḥsān, excellence (the permanence and depth of God-consciousness), which marks the initiation of those who are engaged in the knowledge of God (maʿrifa), His proximity and His love.*
2. *The ascending curve marks the stages in the purification of the heart and being (tazkiyat an-nafs) and represents the path of progressive, and sometimes slowed or halted, elevation followed by the believer who seeks proximity.*
3. *This spiritual progression and this mystical initiation clearly pertain to "how to be a Muslim" on the level of inner life and of the heart: they are clearly within the sphere of the Sharīʿa.*

Chart IV c: *Global application of fiqh in history*

If we now present the *Sharīʿa* on the vertical axis and if we project ourselves into history in order to know "how" Muslims were actually faithful to the implementation of their message, here in the field of law (*fiqh*), the resulting graph might be as follows:

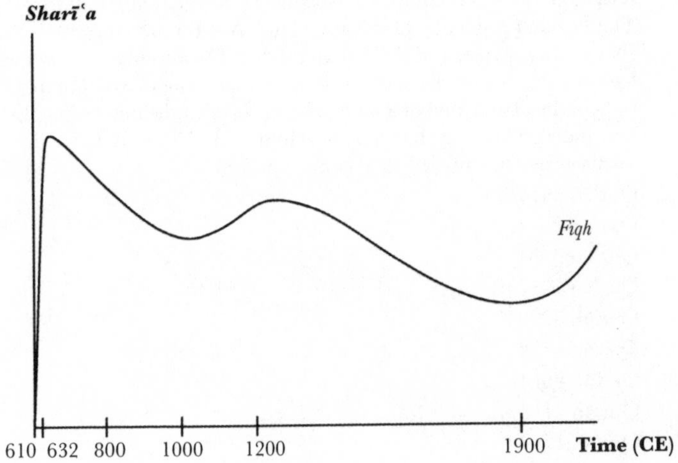


**Comments:**

1. *The projection into time makes it possible to visualise the evolution of the implementation of Islamic Law and jurisprudence on a level which remains very schematic because it is very global.*
2. *The dates on the time scale approximately correspond to those in Chart I. The periods of progress, stagnation and decline can be noticed.*
3. *The curve could also represent the evolution of dynamism in Muslim intellectual production in the fields of law and jurisprudence. The rising part, at the end of the curve, represents the renewal of Islamic thought thanks to the contribution of contemporary Muslim reformists. It also expresses a hope.*

## Notes

1 In matters of Revelation, the Prophet is considered infallible (*ma'ṣūm*) but there is a clear distinction to make between the Prophet receiving Revelation and his human state organising his – and that of his community's – day-to-day life. His Companions understood this distinction and many stories are quoted specifying this fact. For instance, in the Battle of Badr, al-Ḥubāb ibn al-Mundhir, asked the Prophet: "This place where we have been stationed, is it God's ordained selection (by Revelation), or is it your plan?" The Prophet replied, "This is my plan." Al-Mundhir suggested that they change their place, and the Prophet did so. On another occasion when he had to judge a case, he said: "It may be that some of you fail to prove his right in the case. I am but a human being. If my judgement wrongly favours one undeserving, this shall only take him to Hell." See Ibn Hishām, *As-Sīra an-Nabawiyya* (Cairo, 1955), Volume 3, p. 150.

2 Qur'ān 34: 28.

3 Qur'ān 25: 1.

4 Qur'ān 3: 31.

5 Qur'ān 18: 110.

6 Qur'ān 33: 21.

7 Qur'ān 68: 4.

8 Qur'ān 96: 1–5.

9 Qur'ān 41: 53.

10 Qur'ān 17: 44.

11 Qur'ān 55: 5–6.

12 Contrary to Latin or Indo-European languages, the notion of being does not exist in the Arabic: to convey the idea of being, one has to refer to the reality of the perception "to be seen or perceived" through the passive construction of the verbal root: *wa-ja-da, mawjūd*. The mere use of the language disturbs the common categories of the *philosophy of being* known since its first development with the classical philosophers (Socrates, Plato and Aristotle) until its very recent contribution through the school of phenomenology (Husserl, Heidegger).

13 Qur'ān 22: 46.

14 Qur'ān 3: 190.

15 Qur'ān 7: 179.

16 Qur'ān 2: 2.

17 For example, in *Sūra* ar-Rūm (The Byzantines) one verse predicts a Byzantine victory "*within a few years*" (the Arabic word *biḍ'* means a certain number, between three and nine: this happened about seven years after the initial prediction). We also find in the Qur'ān announcements relating to a long historical sequence such as the end of time, the Day of Judgement, and the life in the Hereafter.

18 See this expression in Qur'ān 18: 51.

19 Qur'ān 2: 30.

20 Qur'ān 2: 31–2.

21 Muḥammad Asad, *The Message of The Qur'ān* (Dar al-Andalus, Gibraltar, 1980), p. 989.

22 Qur'ān 21: 25.

23 These fundamental elements constitute the framework of *Sūrah* al-Fātiḥa (The Opening) which is repeated at least twice in each daily Prayer and which embodies the essential Islamic teachings.

24 Qur'ān 2: 38.

25 Qur'ān 5: 48.

26 Qur'ān 73: 20.

27 During the Makkan period (609–22 CE), the formal Prayers consisted of two of two *raka'āt* (cycles), respectively at the beginning and end of the day. The second stage took place at Madina, where the number of daily Prayers increased to five of four *raka'āt* each, except for *Maghrib* (three) and *Ṣubḥ* (two).

28 *Ḥadīth* (Bukhārī).

29 Qur'ān 5: 3.

30 One of the names of the Qur'ān is *adh-Dhikr*, the Reminder, according to the verse: "*Behold, it is We Ourselves who have bestowed from on high, step by step, the Reminder: and, behold, it is We who shall truly guard it (from all corruption)*" (15: 9).

31 Qur'ān 95: 6.

32 Qur'ān 68: 4. Muḥammad Asad has aptly translated *khuluq* as way of life according to the explanation of this verse by Ibn 'Abbās. He quotes the words of 'Ā'isha, who speaking of the Prophet many years after his death, repeatedly stressed that "his way of life (*khuluq*) was the Qur'ān" (Muslim, Ṭabarī, Ḥākim).

33 *Ḥadīth* (Muslim).

34 *Ḥadīth* (Tirmidhī).

35 *Ḥadīth* (Bukhārī and Muslim).

36 Ibid.

37 *Ḥadīth* (Bayhaqī)

38 Qur'ān 3: 110.

39 *Ḥadīth* (Muslim).

40 *Ḥadīth* (Bukhārī and Muslim).

41 Qur'ān 4: 105. The following verses as far as 113 refer to this story. Nevertheless, Muḥammad Asad aptly pointed out that "The '*thou*' in this and the following two verses – as well as in verse 113 – refer, on the face of it, to the Prophet; by implication, however, it is addressed to everyone who has accepted the guidance of the Qur'ān." Nevertheless, we do not see, for our part, a contradiction between reporting the context in which these verses were revealed (*sabab an-nuzūl*) and the comprehension of the general ethical teaching of the latter. See Muḥammad Asad, *The Message of the Qur'ān*, op. cit. p. 126.

42 Qur'ān 4: 135.

43 Qur'ān 5: 8.

44 Qur'ān 16: 90. *Iḥsān* here could mean excellence or sincerity (according to several interpretations of this verse by *mufassirīn*), the doing of good (Yūsuf 'Alī, Muḥammad Asad), right action or charity.

45 *Ḥadīth* (Muslim).

46 *Ḥadīth* (Bukhārī and Muslim); the two versions were reported by Rāfi' ibn Khadīj and Anas respectively.

47 Regarding legal judgements where he had to rule between two persons or parties, the Prophet said: "I am only a human being, and you bring your disputes to me. Perhaps some of you are more eloquent in your plea than others, and I judge in your favour according to what I hear from you. So, whatever I rule in anyone's favour which belongs to his brother, he should not take any of it, because I have only granted him a piece of Hell" (Abū Dāwūd).

48 For example, before the Battle of Uḥud. He put aside his own opinion and followed the majority which wanted to fight the Quraysh outside the city of Madina. The Muslim community was defeated at the hill of Uḥud but the Qur'ān confirmed, after this defeat, that the Prophet had to maintain the principle of consultation (*shūrā*): "*Pardon them, then, and pray that they be forgiven. And take counsel with them in all matters of public concern: then, when you have decided upon a course of action, place thy trust in God: for verily, God loves those who place their trust in Him*" (3: 159).

49 *Ḥadīth* (Abū Dāwūd in *Sunan*).

50 *Ḥadīth* (Bukhārī and Abū Dāwūd).

51 *Ḥadīth* (Muslim).

52 Later, they would have to consider the changes brought about by history.

53 Qur'ān 9: 122.

54 See, for example, Ṭabarī, Qurṭubī and Ibn Kathīr.

55 The ruling, here, is that both the duty to fight during a war and to acquire knowledge are collective obligations (*farḍ kifāya*) in the sense that if a group or a part of the community is fighting or studying, the obligation is not compulsory for the rest of the community.

56 Abū 'Abd Allah Qurṭubī, *Jāmi' al-Aḥkām al-Qur'ān*, 8th Vol., pp. 293–7. Muḥammad Asad, in his comments, follows the same direction and quotes some important *aḥādīth*. See op. cit. p. 285.

57 The four closest Companions of the Prophet and his successors as head of the Islamic State of Madina were Abū Bakr (632–34), 'Umar (634–44), Uthmān (644–56) and 'Alī (656–61).

58 See Al-Khudarī, *Tārīkh al-Umma al-Islāmiyya*, 1st Vol., p. 170.

59 *Ḥadīth* (Bukhārī).

60 Very early on two tendencies appeared among the Companions as a result of the influence of two eminent figures of this era: 'Abdullāh ibn 'Umar, who generally avoided giving personal interpretations, and 'Abdullāh ibn Mas'ūd, who made wide use of personal opinion if no answer or plain ruling could be found either in the Qur'ān or in the *Sunna*. We find these two postures among scholars (*'ulamā'*) and schools of thought (*madhāhib*):

respectively, they are known as *ahl al-ḥadīth* (based at Madina) and *ahl ar-ra'y* (based at Kufa in Iraq).

61 The Prophet said: "Whoever tells a lie in my name will find his seat in the Fire" (Bukhārī and Abū Dāwūd).

62 They treated only practical and real problems. They avoided applying analogical deductions (*qiyās*) if the Qur'ān or the Prophet had not clearly defined the purpose of an obligation or an interdiction.

63 See the interesting and clear introduction of ʿAlī Ḥassab-Allāh, *Uṣūl al-Tashrīʿ al-Islāmī* (Roots of Islamic Jurisprudence), (Dār al-Maʿārif, le Caire, 1985) in Arabic or, in English, *Principles of Islamic Jurisprudence*, by Mohammad Hashim Kamali (Cambridge, UK, 1991), pp. 2–15. Kamali gives another clear definition: "*Uṣūl al-fiqh*, or the roots of Islamic law, expound the indications and methods by which the rules of *fiqh* are deduced from their sources. These indications are found mainly in the Qur'ān and *Sunna*, which are the principal sources of the *Sharīʿa*" (p. 1).

64 There were indeed very violent disputes and struggles, as early as the 9th century, between traditionists (*muḥaddithūn*) and Sufis, the former fearing the doctrinal deviations of the latter or more simply their verbal excesses. Some Sufis did actually go very far in their claims, in particular when they experienced a kind of mystical intoxication (*shaṭaḥāt*). Understanding and evaluating such claims requires a lot of caution and especially the mastery of their coded language, which some law scholars were not always careful to do, hurriedly judging the said claims on their apparent meaning alone. Abū Hāmid al-Ghazālī was one scholar who advocated balanced judgements, as indeed Ibn Taymiyya also did on a number of conflictual issues. They themselves had followed Sufi paths, and we must recall that the great Muslim jurists of the flourishing period, such as Abū Ḥanīfa, Mālik, as-Shāfiʿī, Ibn Ḥanbal and so many others, were mystics themselves. It is also important to stress that great later reformers belonging to the Sufi tradition were to confirm their total adherence to Islam and faithfulness to the *Sharīʿa*: the famous Egyptian Sufi ʿAbd al-Wahhāb ash-Shaʿrānī (1493–1565), like the Indian Aḥmad al-Fārūqī as-Sirhindī (died 1625), firmly stated that the path of Sufism, of spiritual Reality, of *Ḥaqīqa*, was not outside the Islamic Way and Law (*Sharīʿa*), but that it was its heart, its essence and its light. Thus, the distinctions between the dry and formalist Islam of the "orthodox" on the one hand, and on the other hand the mystical outpourings of those who were supposed to have got beyond a mean preoccupation with rules and norms, must be totally reconsidered. *Taṣawwuf* is a science which lies at the heart of Islam, and it requires in-depth study before any judgement or evaluation. It pertains to the realisation of the *Sharīʿa* in the same way as all the other Islamic sciences, which it directs, deepens, completes and enlightens. Too many Muslims today, keeping their eyes fixed on the rules of Islam only, forget priorities and, with but little knowledge, bring "Sufism" into disrepute in the name of the opinions stated by some scholars, while they often have not read them entirely nor taken into account their moderation nor the context in which they wrote. Yet this is indispensable, for such questions are indeed delicate and require knowledge, precision and balance.

65 Some Muslim scholars also called this field *ʿilm al-kalām* (science of speech), an appellation which plainly expresses the influence of the more ancient philosophical traditions. It is both interesting and important to note here that the first Islamic science was related to the juridical domain with concrete and practical questions to solve. The first generations of Muslims were not involved in theoretical debates concerning God, His names and attributes or the nature of Faith; they confined themselves to the plain and simple Qur'ānic and Prophetic teachings. The Muslims' new proximity with other civilisations (particularly with Greek books, and the proximity of some Christian scholars), slowly modified this disposition and led several *ʿulamā'* to initiate theological and theoretical debates within the Islamic tradition and, furthermore, the art of dispute. As we have just explained above, this process provoked a reaction from those Muslim scholars who were aware of the risks which would be incurred if the field was left open to every kind of philosophical or rationalist consideration which would detract from the framework of Divine Revelation.

66 The list of great Muslim scholars who were persecuted by political authorities – from Abū Ḥanīfa (who died in prison) to recent times – is almost interminable.

67 See Yūsuf al-Qarḍāwī, *Al-Marjiʿiyya al-ʿUliyā fil-Islam lil-Qur'ān was-Sunna* (Maktabat al-Wahbat, Cairo, 1990), *Awlawiyyāt al-Ḥaraka al-Islāmiyya fil-Marḥala al-Qādima* (Maktabat al-Wahbat, Cairo, 1992), *Fī Fiqh al-Awlawiyyāt wa Dirāsa Jadīda fī Ḍaw'i al-Qur'ān was-Sunna* (Maktabat al-Wahbat, Cairo, 1996).

68 See ʿAlī ʿAbd al-Ḥalīm Maḥmūd, *Fiqh ad-Daʿwa* (Dār al-Wafāʿ, 1990), 2 Volumes in Arabic, and *Manhaj at-Tarbiya ʿind al-Ikhwān al-Muslimīn* (Dār al-Wafāʿ, 1991), 2 Volumes, *Wasā'il at-Tarbiya ʿind al-Ikhwān al-Muslimīn* (Dār al-Wafāʿ, Cairo, 1989), *Maʿa al-ʿAqīda wal-Ḥaraka wal-Manhaj fi-Khayri Ummatin Ukhrijat lin-Nās* (Dār al-Wafāʿ, Cairo, 1992). Shaykh Al-Bahī al-Khūlī, *Tadhkirat ad-Duʿāt* (Maktabat al-Falāh, Kuwait, 1984).

69 This latter, highly fragmentary, vision of Islam was indeed useful and legitimate, but when analysing the evolution of Islamic sciences and the debates which accompanied it, one cannot but admit that it has been, and remains, the upstream cause of sterile and endless disputes between the advocates of one field of specialisation or another, of law, philosophy or mysticism. Each one relativised the other's approach, or even simply ceased to consider him as a "good Muslim" or did not hesitate to exclude him from the acknowledged sphere of "real Islam", that is to say his own. The history of Islamic sciences, from yesterday to the present, is strewn with debates of this kind and it is because of such divergences that some Orientalists have found it possible to speak of "Islams", because it seemed clear to them that the law defended by the "orthodox" could not be confused with the sufism of "mystics" nor with the speculations of *kalām* "philosophers".

# II

## Some General Rulings of *Uṣūl al-Fiqh*

The science of *uṣūl al-fiqh* is elaborate and complex for it is both a methodology of linguistic, religious and juridical interpretations of the sources and, at the same time, a large frame constituted by a synthetic collection of global rulings whose function is to direct the application of *ijtihād* both theoretically and practically. It requires an excellent knowledge and a deep understanding of the Qur'ān, the *Sunna* and the Arabic language if only to grasp the meaning and scope of the concepts used in its elaboration. This is what one must master in order to be considered a *mujtahid*, a person able to apply an absolute (*muṭlaq*) or restricted (*muqayyad*) *ijtihād* and give juridical advice or rulings (*fatāwā*).[1] It is not possible, within the limits of our current study, to delve very far into the analysis of the different domains of *uṣūl al-fiqh* but, at least, we should present – and reflect on – some of the fixed general rulings of this fundamental science so as to provide a backdrop against which it is possible to consider our situation in Europe. It is especially important to remember these rulings and all the more so in a Western society as they determine the frame within which Muslims can formulate juridical decisions to take account of the new context: in other words, who chooses or decides? What is immutable and absolute and what is subject to change or related to a specific context? In the Islamic juridical landscape, what is the meaning of *ijtihād* and *fatwā*?

Some Muslims, acting – or rather *reacting* – out of fear of Western permissive culture rather than in the light of a deep comprehension of Islamic science, present the Islamic juridical frame as if it was in itself, or everything in it, *entirely immutable*, fixed once and for all, because it is from God or because our previous *'ulamā'* have already formulated all that it has to be known and followed. Such a position reveals a profound lack of knowledge and, above all, tends to define what Islam is not, in and by itself, in light of its own principles, but in contrast with what it is not, namely Western civilisation. If the latter accepts change, evolution, freedom and progress then, *logically*, *reasonably* and *as opposed to it*, Islam does not. Moreover, in their minds, the more one – whether an individual, group or society – refuses change, freedom and progress, the more he or they are genuinely Islamic. One can easily see where this state of mind leads the Muslim community but, what is more, this kind of reflection, even if understandable in a time of social and political weakness, crisis and acute pressure, has no justification within the fundamental Islamic frame of reference.

On the other hand, we find some Muslims who, because they have heard about *ijtihād*, hastily define this as "the freedom to stipulate rational rulings when the sources do not give clear and adapted answers". Far from considering the basic frame and methodology of Islamic jurisprudence, they declare that *ijtihād* permits Muslims to live in accordance with their time, but they apply it chaotically without any reference to rules, knowledge or science, and they are often deeply influenced by their desire to please their modern and progressive compatriots or to prove that they are not fanatics or fundamentalists. The concept of *ijtihād* and its practical application tends then to justify everything. The phenomenon, however, is the exact opposite of the one described above: because Western civilisation is nowadays in a position of strength, we must take it as a model and follow its evolution, for better and for worse. One should not worry if the essence of the Islamic teaching is betrayed, one has to be, by any means available, open-minded, progressive, and *modern*!

These are the two opposite aspects of the same fundamental mistake: that is, to consider Islamic Religion and civilisation from outside, through the prism of another civilisation and in this way either reject or follow it. In fact, both postures are equally wrong and can be explained by the Islamic community's current situation throughout the world and particularly, of course, within Western societies. Apart from a few exceptions, the great majority of Muslims are living in deprivation and poverty. Islamic civilisation, moreover, is going through a deep crisis due in part to the Islamic countries' fragile situation but also due to the forgetfulness and negligence, by many Muslims, of their own identity and values. To avoid both reactive and submissive postures, it is necessary to return to the sources and study the global rulings in order to identify the parameters against which we have to measure the accuracy of our positions, interpretations and solutions. Such a close examination should allow us to think differently about our attitudes and to formulate some original rules which, even if they seem – and are effectively – new, nonetheless remain faithful to the teachings of the Qur'ān and the *Sunna.* We shall soon see that this room for manoeuvre is important and that the scope of Islamic jurisprudence is both precise and wide and that it requires the permanent involvement of human reason.

## A. Who Decides?

For Muslims, the Qur'ān, revealed over a period of 23 years, between 610 and 632 CE, is the Word of God bestowed from on High through the intermediary of the Angel Gabriel. In this sense, of course, the Qur'ān represents a world of absolutes since it was Revealed by the Creator of the heavens and the earth, of space and time. In the Qur'ān, Believers will find, beyond the events and contingencies of history, the profound and essential message of *tawḥīd*: there is only One God and human beings must answer His call.

This was the quintessential Message revealed to all previous Messengers: Adam, Noah, Abraham, Moses, Jesus and all other Prophets in the course of history. The Qur'ān, then, is *a Reminder*, the last one, which is preserved by God Himself:

> *Behold, it is We Ourselves who have bestowed from on high, step by step, this reminder: and, behold, it is We who shall truly guard it (from all corruption).*[2]

The heart of this Divine teaching, constituting the foundation of all Revelations, is present in the Qur'ān with all its implications for us humans: there is One God, He has created everything, from

Him we come and belong and to Him we shall return, everyone will be judged according to his Faith, his intentions, his sincerity and his behaviour: this life is not the Life but a passage, of a very short time. Basically, this life is a test:

> *He (God) who has created death as well as life, so that He might put you to a test (and thus show) which of you is best in conduct.*[3]

All revealed religions are based on this understanding of what life means. According to Islamic teaching, God, along with this fundamental teaching, provided diverse peoples with a specific way of worshipping Him, adapted to a certain era and in a certain context and that this consequently explains the diversity and coexistence of the various creeds, *wanted* by the Creator:

> *And unto thee (O Prophet) have We vouchsafed this Divine writ, setting forth the Truth, confirming the Truth of whatever there still remains of earlier Revelations and determining what is true therein.*

And further:

> *Unto every one of you have We appointed a different law and way of life (shirʿa, sharīʿa). And if God had so willed, He could surely have made you all one single community: but (He willed it otherwise) in order to test you by means of what He has vouchsafed unto you. Vie, then, with one another in doing good works!*[4]

Thus, religious diversity is wanted by God and He gave a specific Message to each people. However, these Divine Messages, in the course of history, were, in one way or another, modified and altered by human hands. So much so, that every successive Revelation had to rectify what was wrong and falsified in its predecessor.

For the Muslim, the Qur'ān confirms what was sent previously and, at the same time, it corrects and rectifies the errors and alterations which – according to the Qur'ān itself – had been introduced within earlier Messages. As it is the last Revelation, the Qur'ān represents the last guidance, the last frame of reference whose teachings are suitable, henceforth, for all places and times to come, until the end of human history. Thus the Qur'ān, the very Word of God, conveyed by the Angel Gabriel, is the first and essential source for Muslims in both religious and juridical fields. Nine-tenths of it deal with spirituality in the widest sense of the term: the presence of God, creation, Faith, worship, morality, the Hereafter, etc.[5] We also find general rulings concerning social affairs: in its last Revelation, God fixed a global frame within which Believers have to exert themselves in order to find the most appropriate law which is both faithful to the Qur'ān and which also fits their context.

According to some *'ulamā'*, there are only about 250 verses (out of 6,632)[6] which deal with legal issues and they were, for the majority, a response to specific problems encountered by the community during the time of Revelation. From these verses, the *fuqahā' al-uṣūl* have extracted global rulings which should direct both *'ulamā'* and Believers' comprehension and behaviour. This is what the Prophet's Companions first, and then Muslim jurists (*fuqahā'*), soon understood and they tried (the latter basing their works on Qur'ānic studies), to expound the general rulings behind the revealed responses given to Muslims during the 7th century CE.

To assist them in this work they also referred to the Prophet's teachings, his *Sunna*. The latter contains all that is narrated from the Prophet, his actions, sayings and whatever he tacitly approved. The *Sunna*, the second source of Islamic jurisprudence, confirms, specifies and, more rarely, adds some elements to what is already present in the Qur'ān. The *aḥādīth*, whose process of authentication has over time become an independent study, permit the *'ulamā'* to understand the Divine teachings more completely and deeply and they further assist Muslims along the path they should follow. Together with the Qur'ān, the *aḥādīth* provide a complete and global frame of principles which express the *Sharī'a's* teaching regarding the juridical domain.[7] In fact, this global frame, these general principles and rules are what, in the Muslim's belief, has to be considered as *absolute* and *immutable*: revealed by God in His last Revelation and through his last Messenger, they are suitable whenever and anywhere. This partakes of the Islamic belief and it is one of the most important principles and teachings of *Tawḥīd:*

that is for Muslims to remain faithful to the revealed path, the *Sharīʿa*.

Nevertheless it must be clear that faithfulness to such absolute principles is an important and permanent work of the *ʿulamāʾ* from whom it is expected that they formulate specific and precise rules and laws tuned to the historical and geographical context. This is exactly the function of *ijtihād*: we will come back to this concept in a specific section but suffice to say here that, just as the *fuqahāʾ* of the Muslim community have to provide their fellow Believers with appropriate answers fitting their environment, so they must also exert themselves in forming individual or community judgements so as to preserve the essential link between the absoluteness of the sources and the relativity of history and geography. They must set about a two-fold work: a deep and precise interpretation of the Qur'ān and the *Sunna* along with an appropriate analysis of the social, political and economic situation they are facing. They have to determine the *Fiqh* (Islamic Law) which is the product of rational human elaboration based on the unchangeable rulings of the *Sharīʿa* but with responses, adaptations and formulations which are in constant evolution.[8]

These remarks allow us to clarify at least two confusions concerning the *Sharīʿa*, its contents and scope. First, the *Sharīʿa* is not restricted to the penal code; in our typology and classification, it is an element, a part of a global path, methodology and philosophy of life. To consider one element out of the context which gives it meaning is not only unfair but methodologically incorrect. The teachings of the Qur'ān and the *Sunna* give shape to a complete way of life and this is, in fact, the *Sharīʿa* we are commanded to follow: from performing daily Prayers to defending social justice, from studying to smiling, from respecting nature to helping an animal. The second confusion has to do with the *Sharīʿa* and *Fiqh* being taken as one and the same thing when, in fact, there is an essential difference between them. *Fiqh* represents the product of human thought and elaboration; more precisely, it is the state of juridical reflection reached by Muslim scholars at a certain time and in a certain context in light of their study of the *Sharīʿa*. Thus, if the *Sharīʿa* is the revealed and immutable path, it is quite different from *Fiqh* which, to be faithful to its function, has to be dynamic, in constant elaboration since evolution is the characteristic of our world. To be faithful to the Message of the Qur'ān in no way means to confine oneself to a very restrictive and lazy reading of the two main sources and their commentaries made by great *'ulamā'* in the past, but, on the contrary, to exert one's intelligence to provide solutions which, by fitting the social and political reality, will express our individual and community intention to be genuine Muslims.

By knowing the function of Islamic sources and understanding the scope of the *Sharī'a*, one can more easily understand the different spheres and stratum of Islamic thought. God alone decides the path, the direction and the ends, and within the general and global rulings He revealed to them, Muslims have to develop their knowledge and understanding of both sources as also the social reality so that they can implement these teachings in a faithful way. God has decided the way to worship Him, to pray and also what is lawful and what is not: human beings cannot modify this, yet at the same time they cannot merely rely on the general rulings of the *Sharī'a* to solve their problems in a world which becomes more complex every day. We have, for instance, to study, understand and consider the ten verses which deal with economy in the Qur'ān, but it is impossible to propose an alternative economy, a specific system, appropriate to our contemporary situation, without directing all our efforts and resources – intellectual and financial. Only then can we bring to the fore the priorities, the steps and prospects which could let us hope for a future free from the domination of capitalism.

The Prophet's Companions were afraid to give rulings which could have been in contradiction with the Qur'ān and the *Sunna*. For, to determine what is lawful (*ḥalāl*) and unlawful (*ḥarām*) is the exclusive prerogative of God:

> *Hence, do not utter falsehoods by letting your tongues determine (at your own discretion), "This is lawful and that is forbidden", thus attributing your own lying inventions to God: for, behold, they who attribute their own lying inventions to God will never attain to a happy state!*[9]

*O mankind! Partake of what is lawful and good on earth, and follow not Satan's footsteps: for, verily, he is your open foe, and bids you only to do evil, and to commit deeds of abomination, and to attribute unto God something of which you have no knowledge.*[10]

The Companions' fear of making such errors was, in fact, salutary and it shows the two aspects of their understanding which are the specific qualities of the Muslim scholar (*'ālim*): a deep and absolute respect of God's and the Prophet's teachings coupled with an intense fear of betraying them. At the same time, they never hesitated to formulate rulings where they did not find an appropriate answer in the sources. Linked with God, they knew that they were living in a world in perpetual evolution. They knew, and that is perhaps their greatest gift, that to be a genuine Believer does not mean to neglect our mind, that to seek God's proximity with our heart does not mean to forget intellectual elaboration. Through them we learn that an intensive Faith does not mean a deficit of intelligence. We need both, a heart and a mind, a Faith and an intellect in order to draw our path and to stipulate rulings in accordance with the direction He gave to mankind.

## B. Permissibility is the Base

*'Ulamā' al-uṣūl* (the scholars studying the principles of *Fiqh*) have extracted some important global rulings in the course of their researches on the Qur'ān and the *Sunna*. The first principle upon which depend many essential Islamic rulings is that of permissibility: the rule concerning things and natural utilities is that permission in accordance with the verse:

*He it is who has created for you all that is on earth.*[11]

The whole universe is the creation of God: in the absolute, this work is good *per se* and it is the manifestation of the good for mankind. The whole of nature welcomes the human being and his own natural origin directs him. Regarding our relations with the world and the priority of permission, it would appear clear that the first two states we have to recognise are those of *freedom* and *innocence vis-á-vis* a creation which has been placed at the service of mankind:

> *Are you not aware that God has made subservient to you all that is in the heavens and all that is on earth, and has lavished upon you His blessings, both outward and inward?*[12]

The human being has to consider the world, of which he is a part, as a gift and all the elements as kindness offered to him, a witnessing of his responsibility before his Creator. What is prohibited is very small when compared to the large latitude of what is permitted. This is confirmed by a mere reading of the Qur'ān and also by the Prophet's clear statement:

"God the Almighty has laid down religious duties, so do not neglect them; He has set boundaries, so do not overstep them; He has prohibited some things, so do not violate them; about some things He was silent – out of compassion for you, not forgetfulness – so seek not after them."[13]

Adam and Eve, both disobedient to the only prohibition expressed by God, were forgiven, and their life on earth was to be *a test which took its source in innocence and its meaning within responsibility*:

> *And We said: "O Adam, dwell thou and thy wife in this garden, and eat freely thereof, both of you, whatever you may wish; but do not approach this one tree, lest you become wrongdoers." But Satan caused them both to stumble therein, and thus brought about the loss of their erstwhile state. And so We said: "Down with you, (and be henceforth) enemies unto one another; and on earth you shall have your abode and your livelihood for a while!" Thereupon Adam received words (of guidance) from his Sustainer, and He accepted his repentance: for, verily, He alone is the Acceptor of Repentance, the Dispenser of Grace.*[14]

On earth, the human being has been born innocent and successive Revelations from God have been bestowed upon him as directions and pointers to the path (*Sharīʿa* in its original and literal meaning) and in order to specify limits. Everyone, according to his/her capacities, is responsible for respecting the Revelation and the recommendations it contains, and everyone will have to account to God for their deeds:

> *God does not burden any human being with more than he is well able to bear.*[15]

> *... no bearer of burdens shall be made to bear another's burden.*[16]

This is life, and this test is our common lot since the dawn of time:

> *He who has created death as well as life, so that He might put you to a test.*[17]

Within the juridical field, a plain rule could be stipulated from a reading of the Qur'ān and the *Sunna* to the effect that *whatever is not prohibited is in fact permissible.*[18] Prohibition acts both as limitation and direction: by imposing limits the Creator reveals to mankind the dimension of finality and directs us towards an horizon of values whose respect will shape our humanity and dignity. Yūsuf al-Qarḍāwī aptly notes that the original permission not only concerns nature, food and drink but, more widely, actions, habits, dress and culture; namely the whole gamut of social affairs (*muʿāmalāt*).[19] Everything is permissible except that which is at variance with a stipulated and known prescription. Human dignity relies on this capacity to think and undertake whatever is possible for the good of the human community while carefully and cautiously respecting the limits. The Prophet said:

"That which is lawful is plain and that which is unlawful is plain and between the two of them are doubtful matters about which not many people know. Thus, he who avoids doubtful matters clears himself with regard to his Religion and his honour, but he who falls into doubtful matters falls into that which is unlawful, like the shepherd who pastures around a sanctuary, all but grazing therein. Truly every king has a sanctuary, and truly God's sanctuary is His prohibitions. Truly in the body there is a morsel of flesh which, if it be whole, all the body is whole and which, if it be diseased, all of it is diseased. Truly it is the heart."[20]

An awareness that the universe is offered to us and that everything in it is a gift we can freely use, with confidence, is the original attitude we have to adopt towards life and nature. This would provide us with serenity and an intense feeling of love for He who gives us everything and creates us innocent.[21] Therein a deep sense of limitation materialises, one which places in the human conscience the conviction of being permanently responsible rather than being – in essence – guilty.

This essential principle of *uṣūl al-fiqh* is of the greatest importance when we reflect upon our situation in Europe. It makes clear that Islam allows us to consider its intrinsic possibilities for adaptation to space and time; that is to say, to accept and make ours what, within every civilisation or culture, does not contradict a clearly stipulated juridical prescription. This requires first that we overcome our tendency – quite natural in the early days of immigration and the formation of a communal minority within Western countries – to think of our identity by comparison, and often in contrast, with the majority pattern. We should be able to define ourselves in the exclusive light of our references by respecting what – according to them – is lawful and what is not. This is the way by which we shall not only gain in maturity but, furthermore, be drawn to rediscover the essence of our Religion. A Religion based on one major pillar (that is the Oneness of God, *Tawḥīd*), founded on a few global rulings and ready to accept and incorporate cultures, traditions and customs in their rich and immense diversity. We have to remember this at the same time as trying to define what a European Muslim is and showing the way by which the Islamic sources permit us to so determine it.

## C. Rulings Outlining Liability[22]

The human being is born innocent and, according to the Islamic concept, he *naturally* expresses his link with the Creator and follows His recommendations. This is, in fact, what is conveyed by the notion of *fiṭra* which means both the *natural* and immediate expression of human adoration of God as well as the *natural*, deep and intrinsic aspiration of humanity towards the transcendent dimension. The human, like all creation, bears in himself –

before any kind of codified worship – the expression of his submission to the order wanted by God which we used to call the *natural* order:

> *Art thou not aware that it is God whose limitless glory all (creatures) that are in the heavens and on earth extol, even the birds as they spread out their wings? Each of them knows indeed how to pray unto Him and to glorify Him; and God has full knowledge of all that they do: for, God's is the dominion over the heavens and the earth, and with God is all journeys' end. Art thou not aware that it is God who causes the clouds to move onward, then joins them together, then piles them up in masses, until thou canst see rain come forth from their midst? And He it is who sends down from the skies, by degrees, mountainous masses (of clouds) charged with hail, striking therewith whomever He wills, (the while) the flash of His lightning well-nigh deprives (men of their) sight! It is God who causes night and day to alternate: in this (too), behold, there is surely a lesson for all who have eyes to see!*[23]

> *The seven heavens extol His limitless glory, and the earth, and all that they contain; and there is not a single thing but extols His limitless glory and praise: but you (O men) fail to grasp the manner of their glorifying Him!*[24]

The human being, like all the other beings and elements in the universe, extols – *per se*, through his essence – the limitless glory of God by his immediate obedience to the created order; literally he is *Muslim*, naturally and instinctively *submitted*. The Islamic concept of human being adds the fact that there exists – inherent in human nature – an initial aspiration towards God whose source has to be found at the very origin of the creation of the first man:

> *And whenever thy Sustainer brings forth their offspring from the loins of the children of Adam, He thus calls upon them to bear witness about themselves: "Am I not your Sustainer?" – to which they answer: "Yea, indeed, we do bear witness thereto!" (Of this We remind you) lest you say on the Day of Resurrection, "Verily, we were unaware of this!"*[25]

Once again, this aspiration precedes all types of intellectual awareness of God's presence, it is inscribed in man's being as one of his constitutive elements. We find the same identified in the Qur'ān:

> *And so, set thy face steadfastly towards the (one ever-true) Faith, turning away from all that is false, in accordance with the natural disposition which God has instilled into man: (for,) do not allow any change to corrupt what God has thus created – this is the (purpose of the one) ever-true Faith; but most people know it not,*[26]

as also by the Prophet's saying: "Each child is born in a state of *fiṭra*, but his parents make him a Jew or a Christian. It is like the way an animal gives birth to a normal offspring. Have you noticed any (young animal) born mutilated before you mutilate them?"[27] Naturally submitted and imbued with this aspiration, the human being, is *Muslim* in the widest sense of the word.

There comes, however, the time of awareness and responsibility towards God. For He has drawn, through His Messengers, the way which fits the freedom partaking of the human condition, the path we have to follow to remain faithful to our original essence while perfecting our free beings' destiny. By following the path and respecting its rules, we find, rediscover, the way of the submission to the Creator: this use of freedom allows us to reach, both in our hearts and intelligences, the level animals immediately reach by living instinctively. In fact, we reach the harmony which is expressed by the link between God's will and nature's order: to follow the path prescribed by God is for our intelligence what the natural order is for all the other elements. Our awareness of limits is a harmony of God's rights and our responsibilities:

> *These are the bounds set by God: do not, then, offend against them – for it is thus that God makes clear His Messages unto mankind, so that they might remain conscious of Him.*[28]

This awareness of limits lies within the global Islamic concept of human responsibility before God. "*Unto God belongs all that is in the heavens, all that is on earth,*"[29] and, on the latter, the human being is but a trustee who will be asked about his behaviour, his management during his lifetime. This account will not only concern external things such as nature, social, political or economic issues but also the way he deals with his own self for, before God, *the human does not utterly belong to himself.* He has to respect his being, his soul, his body and its needs as they are God's gifts and the way he treats them is part and parcel of his test on earth. The Prophet made this very clear in a well-known statement directed to one of his Companions, ʿAmr ibn al-ʿĀṣ, who used to go to extremes in his performance of worship. He said: "Behold, your body has rights over you, your eyes have rights over you, your wife has rights over you, your guest has rights over you."[30]

In fact, this *ḥadīth* summarises the content of our discussion and sets us at the source of the Islamic concept of human responsibility and, consequently, of one's duties and rights. Initially innocent and submitted to God and to the order of the universe, the dawning of one's intelligence, and then of one's conscience, is in fact the awakening of mankind's sense of responsibility along with that of freedom. God has offered the earth to mankind but He has prescribed certain limits everyone has to respect as soon as one becomes able to understand, apprehend and act according to one's own will. The individual becomes *mukallaf* (has to respect the rules) at the very moment he/she reaches the age of puberty and is in full possession of his/her faculties. The Prophet said: "Responsibility has been removed from the child, the one who sleeps and he who is not in full possession of his faculties."[31] In fact all the topics with which *Fiqh* deals depend on this first condition: to apply and respect juridical rules, one has to be *mukallaf.* Here lies a second difference between *Sharīʿa* and *Fiqh*, the former being a global concept of life and death providing us with global rulings beyond the specific field of jurisprudence and individual responsibility (*taklīf*); the latter being the concern of *Fiqh.*

The *ʿulamāʾ* of *uṣūl al-fiqh*, through their studies of the Qur'ān and *aḥādīth*, have extracted five values, or more precisely five rulings (*ḥukm sharʿī*), relating to our behaviour when we have the choice. Their purpose was essentially to classify the different kinds of injunctions which are presented in a variety of forms within the sources: to establish distinctions between different types of prescriptions so as to know which were plainly and absolutely binding and which were subject to analysis and *ijtihād*, which were commands or prohibitions and which were mere recommendations. Therefrom, they applied a precise methodology of reading through which they were able to link the different types of formulation with their respective value relating to human behaviour.

A close study of their efforts is outside the purview of our current research, nonetheless it is necessary to present here, even succinctly, the outcomes of their classification. At the two extremes of *al-aḥkām at-taklīfiyya* (the law which defines rights and obligations), we find *wājib* (or *farḍ*) and *ḥarām*: the former relates to an act which has been evaluated as obligatory and the latter to one which is absolutely forbidden. If, for instance, the Qur'ānic prescription is formulated in the imperative (such as "*Perform the Prayer and pay the tax*")[32] or through an interdiction (such as "*And do not commit adultery*"),[33] then we are drawn to identify an obligation (*wājib*) and a prohibition (*ḥarām*) respectively.[34]

Between these latter, the *'ulamā'* have identified three other values relating to human actions: the recommendable or preferable (*mustaḥab, mandūb*), the reprehensible (*makrūh*) and the permissible (*mubāḥ*). The different actions linked with these three categories do not fall under the strict application of Islamic law (which is concerned only with *wājib* and *ḥarām*) and, as we have already mentioned, the permissible is the base for social affairs. Nevertheless, this classification of human actions permits the Believer to recognise his way and, by avoiding the reprehensible and following what is recommendable, to evolve positively, on secure ground, in order to please God and come nearer to Him.

### 1. *Lawful and unlawful (al-ḥalāl wal-ḥarām)*

This classification enables us to have a clearer understanding of the sources. As soon as we remember that God alone decides what is right and what is wrong, that permissibility is the base and, eventually, that we have been provided with milestones to direct us on the appropriate path, we are able to apprehend the two notions of *ḥalāl* (the permissible in its wide meaning, containing not only *mubāḥ* but also *wājib*, *mustaḥab* and *makrūh*) and *ḥarām* (what is absolutely prohibited).

According to Muslim belief, God knows what is good and what is evil for His creatures who, at the same time, were provided with freedom. Thus, He points out limits and rules, both global and precise, to encourage them to live in accordance with His Will. Through His different Revelations, and more particularly in the last one, He has transmitted the means to distinguish right from wrong, good from evil and this is one of the names of the Qur'ān: *al-Furqān*, that which establishes a distinction.

God, in His bounty, has shown us the path. By placing permissibility along with innocence as the two basic principles, He has made it easy and attainable:

> *God wills that you shall have ease, and does not will you to suffer hardship.*[35]

The human being is free and has the choice: he should know that what is forbidden by God is bad for him since it is a prescription bestowed from his Lord who knows better. The path of Islam is both easy and demanding. The responsibility of the true Believer is to follow it by making the appropriate choices to prevent himself from becoming a wrongdoer or allowing doubts to creep in. The *'ulamā'* have provided us with a precious contribution, that is of elaborating a classification of the five different Islamic moral values linked with every law and every behaviour or action related in the Qur'ān and the *Sunna*. Thus, not only the distinguished domains of *ḥalāl* and *ḥarām* appear more plainly but the *'ulamā'* of all times to come hold a frame, an instrument, enabling them to face new situations and contexts and, from these, formulate appropriate rulings (*fatāwā*).

This is also of much value to the average Believer who can discern and penetrate first the wide extent of permissibility in Islam and, then, the different levels regarding the values of human action (intrinsically, but also in light of a specific context).[36] Trying to steer away from wrong deeds and all that leads and attracts to them,[37] one could, and should, perceive and choose the successive steps one has to follow to protect one's heart, soul and body. Seeking a *ḥalāl* way of life, and apprehending the wide field of *mubāḥ* in Islam, the Believer has to make choices and first avoid – as far as possible – what is *makrūh* and then direct himself to the *mustaḥab* in all the different aspects of his life. Once again, the choice of *ḥalāl* and *mustaḥab* by no means signifies that we have to opt for the more strenuous and austere solution or ruling. Unfortunately, many Muslims, both *ʿulamāʾ* and common Believers, forgetting the Qur'ānic prescription and spirit, confuse the two options. A *fatwā* is not more Islamic if it is more rigid: rather, a *fatwā* is *Islamic* from the moment it respects the Qur'ān and the *Sunna*. No more, no less.

To respect the limits decided by God first requires a deep and permanent God-consciousness nourished by a vivid Faith and a continuous reminder (*dhikr*). A Muslim has to know, in order to keep alive this aspiration and to feel a steady improvement in coming nearer to the Creator, that within the field of actions there are priorities and steps and that he must make his choices according to the Islamic sources. Thereafter, he should take into account the environment in which he lives as well as his own personality. This is the path of wisdom that Revelation itself has taught us: during the 23 years of successive Revelations, many prohibitions and obligations were revealed step by step in order both to make the new ruling easily attainable and to uplift Muslims' hearts and intelligence towards a deeper respect and a more profound spirituality. In light of *ḥalāl* and *ḥarām*, this is the ascending path everyone of us has to take and stick to, in order to reform his own person.

The *ʿulamāʾ*, understanding the frame, aim and function of *ḥalāl* and *ḥarām* in Islamic jurisprudence, have to provide the Muslim community with legal Islamic guidance appropriate to its time and environment. The dual task of reading the sources and comprehending the context (we shall discuss this below when analysing the notion of *ijtihād*) is the essential contribution of the *fuqahāʾ* to the Muslim community of their time. That is, to have a deep knowledge of the sources, to understand the people of their era as well as their environment and, finally, to bring to the fore the successive stages the Muslim community (as a whole or in each country) has to follow to be able to reform itself, its members and institutions. *Ḥalāl*, *ḥarām* and the other three values or rulings are a frame as well as a direction, they are the source and the path of one exclusive and sole objective: to please God and to answer His call *today*, in Europe as anywhere on this earth, as the Prophet and his Companions, *yesterday*, tried to please Him and were so successful in responding to His Call.

## 2. *The meaning of silence in the sources*

To lay down what is lawful or not is the exclusive prerogative of God and neither the Prophets themselves nor the *ʿulamāʾ* could modify the revealed rulings or make new decisions out of the Revelation framework.[38] In fact, to make unlawful what is lawful or lawful what is unlawful is similar to *shirk*, assigning oneself or another as God's partner. This is the gravest sin in Islam and the Qur'ān reads:

> *Surely God will not forgive the association of partners (shirk) with Him, but He forgives (sins) less than that of whomever He wishes.*[39]

Man, by fixing or modifying what has been clearly revealed, takes rights which are absolutely not his, and, consciously or not, places himself beside the Creator. Be this through prophethood, an institution organised into a hierarchy (Church or Council) or an individual claiming authority, all is totally unacceptable in Islam. Many stories have been quoted in this regard regarding our great *ʿulamāʾ* from among the followers (*tābiʿīn*). Ash-Shāfiʿī, in his book *al-Um*, quoted Abū Yūsuf, Abū Ḥanīfa's student, as saying, "I have met numerous scholars (*mashāyikh min ahl al-ʿilm*) who detested formulating a ruling (*fatwā*), that is to say 'this is lawful and this unlawful' unless it was plainly stipulated in the Qur'ān and did not need interpretation."[40] Aḥmad ibn Ḥanbal, when asked about a ruling, used to answer "I detest it", "This does not please me" or "I do not like it", so avoiding determination of anything as unlawful and pronouncing it *ḥarām*.[41] Ibn Taymiyya also mentioned that the *ʿulamāʾ* of the first three generations (*salaf*) did not say that something was unlawful unless its unlawfulness was based on indisputable evidence, that is through a clear statement in the Qur'ān or the *Sunna*.

Thus, the Believer must understand the importance of sticking firmly to what God has revealed and not go beyond allowed rights. Neither in the sense of limitless liberality or inordinate excess in prohibiting things or activities: these attitutes were present among the Prophet's Companions and he strongly warned Muslims for all times: "Truly, lost are they who are extreme/excessive (*mutanaṭṭiʿūn*)! Lost are they who are of extreme!"[42] The Qur'ān is similarly clear on this:

> *O you who have attained to Faith! Do not deprive yourselves of the good things of life which God has made lawful to you, but do not transgress the bounds of what is right: verily, God does not love those who transgress the bounds of what is right. Thus, partake of the lawful, good things which God grants you as sustenance, and be conscious of God, in whom you believe.*[43]

As regards the unlawful itself:

> *He (God) has clearly spelled out to you what He has forbidden.*[44]

The Prophet confirmed the content of this verse on many occasions and we have already quoted the whole *ḥadīth* starting with: "That which is lawful is plain and that which is unlawful is plain." The two Islamic sources, the Qur'ān and Sunna effectively give Believers a clear frame of reference within which they have to consider their life and their affairs and from which they should apprehend new situations or problems. As a universal frame of reference, everything is covered in the Qur'ān, but we will not find in it every answer for every specific question. This is the meaning of the two verses below, which whilst apparently contradictory, should be read at different levels:

> *We have bestowed from on high upon thee, step by step this Divine writ, to make everything (that pertains to knowledge of good and evil) clear,*

> *and to provide guidance and grace and a Glad Tiding unto all who have surrendered themselves to God.*[45]

And:

> *O you who have attained to Faith! Do not ask about matters which, if they were to be made manifest to you (in terms of law), might cause you hardship; for, if you should ask about them while the Qur'ān is being revealed, they might (indeed) be made manifest to you (as laws). God has absolved you (from any obligation) in this respect: for God is much-forgiving, forbearing. People before your time have indeed asked such questions – and in result thereof have come to deny the Truth.*[46]

The first verse alludes to the last global rulings mankind needs – as a frame of reference: in this respect, everything is clear and *God has perfected (for us) our religious law.*[47] On more specific topics, which could concern either issues of worship or individual, social, political or economic contingencies, the prescriptions – even if plain – were not so detailed at the time of Revelation and God advised the Prophet's Companions to avoid asking for too much detail so that they would not restrict the field of the permissible and make heavy the burden for generations to come. In other words, the frame is absolute and perfect but it embodies some *silence* which lightens the Believers' burden, facilitates their worship and permits them, as opposed to people of earlier Revelations, to stay close to the Revealed Truth. This is the first meaning of silence and we have already quoted the *ḥadīth* which clarifies our current discussion:

> *God the Almighty has laid down religious duties, so do not neglect them; He has set boundaries, so do not overstep them; He has prohibited some things, so do not violate them; about some things He was silent – out of compassion for you, not forgetfulness – so seek not after them.*[48]

God, in His bounty, has decided to remain silent about some things "*out of compassion for (us)*" since the answers "*might cause (us) hardship*". This silence is a gift and it is, in fact, the juridical and practical translation of the basic principle of permissibility studied above (*ibāḥa*).

However, there is a second meaning to the notion of *silence* which we can extract from the two verses quoted. The Qur'ān conveys to the Muslim community a guidance and a Glad Tiding: all who surrender themselves to the Revealed teaching will be rewarded in the Hereafter. These teachings, nevertheless, are global and require from the Muslims, and especially the *'ulamā'* among them, to be, first, deeply and clearly understood and, second, apprehended in light of every specific era and environment. Armed with the general rulings, tied to them, the silence of the sources on very precise questions, obliges the *'ulamā'* to ponder on the revealed matter, to think about their era and to formulate adequate rulings for their contemporaries. The *silence* is, in fact, the specific part given to human analytic reason to stipulate inevitably diverse *Islamic rules*, through space and time, but ones which are still *Islamic*, i.e. in complete accordance with the global ordinances to be found in the sources.

This process has nothing to do with the excessive questioning we were just speaking about or the addition of unwarranted prohibitions; it is rather a question of adaptation, of *inner dynamics* in the words of Muḥammad Iqbāl,[49] of permitting Muslims to accept and face, in an appropriate way, geographical and historical changes. The universality of the Qur'ānic ordinances is made practical and tangible through an active process within which human reason has to stipulate *Islamic answers* – which are faithful to the sources – to original questions.[50] This is the origin of *ijtihād* and the function of *fatwā*. The *silence*, then, is the sphere which permits *Fiqh*, within social affairs (*mu'āmalāt*) to be in constant development, evolution and formulation. Furthermore, the sources themselves make it compulsory for Muslims to direct their thoughts and their legal works in this regard: this was confirmed by the *ḥadīth* already quoted where Mu'ādh was sent to Yemen. To remain attached to rulings stipulated by scholars of the 9th century – as great and respected as they were – or to refuse to consider the evolution of time is, indeed, a treachery against Islamic teachings.

## D. *Al-Maṣlaḥa* (Considerations of Public Interest)

The notion of *maṣlaḥa* as a juridical term has provoked many debates since its first use, mainly by the *ʿulamā'* of the Mālikī school of thought and the firm opposition manifested by the *Ẓāhirī* school and especially Ibn Ḥazm. These disputes were not always well-founded and it seems that, very often, it was, above all, a question of definition in relation to the *Sharīʿa*'s sources and framework.

In recent times, this notion has been used to justify any kind of new *fatāwā*, even if they are clearly in opposition with the plain evidences of the Qur'ān and the *Sunna* as for rules concerning interest (*ribā*) or inheritance. It is, thus, important to refer roughly to the first researches and works done in this field to be able to understand not only the scope of *maṣlaḥa* but also to assess the advantages we can take of its aim over time and within a diversity of contexts.

Imām Mālik referred to the notion of *istiṣlāḥ*,[51] which means to seek what is good. Within his juridical researches, he relied on the example of the Companions – who formulated numerous legal decisions in light of the public interest while respecting the framework of the sources – to justify the fact that to seek what is good (*istiṣlāḥ*) is one component of the *Sharīʿa*. After the codification work of ash-Shāfiʿī, the *ʿulamā'* began to establish distinctions about what exactly the sources were, their judicial domains of application, and their hierarchy of values among the rulings, etc.

Many *ʿulamā'*, such as al-Juwaynī in his *al-Burhān* or the *Muʿtazilī* Abū al-Husayn al-Baṣrī in *al-Muʿtamad fī Uṣūl al-Fiqh*, both during the 11th century, referred, in one way or another, to this notion. The polemics to define what this concept exactly meant and what its status was within the Islamic legal instrument had already begun. It is Abū Hāmid al-Ghazālī (d. 1111) who, through his strict codification, provided the clearest framework around which this question was to be discussed, and this is still the case today. In his *al-Mustaṣfā min ʿIlm al-Uṣūl*,[52] he states very precisely:

"In its essential meaning, (*al-maṣlaḥa*) is an expression for seeking something useful (*manfaʿa*) or removing something harmful (*madarra*). But this is not what we mean, because seeking utility and removing harm are the objectives (*maqāṣid*) at which creation aims and the goodness (*ṣalāḥ*) of mankind's creation consists in realising objectives (*maqāṣid*). What we mean by *maṣlaḥa* is the preservation of the objective (*maqṣad*) of the Law (*shar*ʿ) which consists of five things: the preservation of Religion, life, reason, descendants and property. What assures the preservation of these five principles (*uṣūl*) is *maṣlaḥa* and whatever fails to preserve them is *mafsada* and its removal is *maṣlaḥa*."[53]

This overall definition circumscribes a way, one which almost all ʿ*ulamā*' are agreed upon[54] for it implicitly refers to the sources without making a distinction between the aim of goodness lying in the Qur'ān and the *Sunna* and the human stipulation of it when there is nothing clearly stated in the sources. In fact, al-Ghazālī, with this clarifying definition, placed himself beyond the ʿ*ulamā*''s debate and his further codification was the sort that permitted a clear understanding of *maṣlaḥa* and the relevent issues: thus, his contribution was great.

Al-Ghazālī, still referring to the wide meaning of *maṣlaḥa*, mentions its three different types: *aḍ-ḍarūriyyāt* (essentials) which deals with the five elements of *maqāṣid ash-Sharīʿa* (objectives of the Law) as the preservation of religion, life, reason, descendants and property.[55] *Al-ḥājiyyāt* (complementary), which concerns the prevention of what could lead to hardship, but not to death or collapse, in the life of the community.[56] Finally, we have *taḥsīniyyāt* or *kamāliyyāt* (improvement, perfection) which relates to what permits the improvement of worship.[57] These three levels contain all that can be thought of relating to the human *maṣāliḥ* (public interests) for a human being as much as a worshipper, and this categorisation leads neither to debate nor to polemics.

What did lead to disagreement and conflict in the juridical field, however, was the question of knowing if there was an actual need for this notion within the Islamic framework,[58] or of recognising *maṣlaḥa* as an independent source – even though supplementary – of the *Sharīʿa* (and, thus, a part of it whose scope has to be delimited),[59] or of considering it as a part of another source such as *qiyās*.[60] These different positions rely on another classification which distinguishes three types of *maṣāliḥ* (differentiated with regard to their class and not their hierarchical value such as essential or complementary). The *'ulamā'* have established a typology according to the degree of proximity of *maṣlaḥa* with the sources. If the *maṣlaḥa* is based on textual evidence, extracted from the Qur'ān or the *Sunna*, the *maṣlaḥa* is called *mu'tabara* (accredited) and, thus, considered as definitive, not open to debate. If, on the contrary, the stipulated *maṣlaḥa* is contradicted by a plain text (*naṣṣ qaṭ'ī*), we call it *mulghā* (discredited) and it is considered null and void. The third type relates to a situation where there is no text: the Qur'ān and the *Sunna* neither upheld nor nullified the *maṣlaḥa* which appeared after the time of Revelation. This kind of *maṣlaḥa* is named *mursala* (meaning unrestricted) for it allows the *'ulamā'* to refer to their own analysis and reasoning in order to stipulate juridical decisions taking into account their historical and geographical context. This by trying at the same time to remain as faithful as possible to the commands and spirit of the Islamic legal framework since the text, the letter of the law, is missing.

It is the latter type which has provoked so many debates and polemics, whose analysis is beyond the limits of our current study. Suffice it to say that the essential reason for the disagreement was the fear it induced among opponents about even the existence of *maṣlaḥa mursala*, i.e. that such a notion could, hence, permit some *'ulamā'* to formulate rulings without reference to the Qur'ān and the *Sunna*, but rather through exclusive and absolutely free rational elaboration and all this in the name of some remote hardship. These were the main arguments of the *Ẓāhirī* school as well as numerous Shāfi'ī and even Mālikī *'ulamā'* who did not recognise *maṣlaḥa mursala* – given that it does not refer to the sources – as a proof: instead, they considered it specious (*wahmiyya*) and invalid for legislation. It was the same instinctive fear of a purely rational and disconnected approach to the Law that pushed al-Ghazālī to confine the seeking of *maṣlaḥa* to the application of *qiyās* (analogy) which, by its nature, requires a very close link to the text in order to extract the cause (*'illa*) by which the reasoning for the analogy is based.

These fears were in fact well-founded, for in the course of history some *'ulamā'*, in the name of *maṣlaḥa*, have stipulated strange rulings and, sometimes, have completely modified and disturbed the mode and requirements of use of the legal instruments within the Islamic framework. This was the case of the well-known Ḥanbali jurist Najm ad-Dīn at-Ṭūfī in the 14th century. He eventually gave preference to *maṣlaḥa* over the texts of the Qur'ān and the *Sunna*, so long as, according to Mahmassānī, "public interest does not require otherwise".[61] Nowadays, we are also witnessing strange modern Islamic rulings, the result being modern *maṣlaḥa* which clearly contradicts the sources. The notion of *maṣlaḥa mursala* seems, hence, to allow for all kinds of odd behaviour, along with the most dubious, financial commitments or bank investments for it is said that they preserve, or would, or should, preserve the public interest.

This kind of excess was not to be found among the majority of proponents who considered *maṣlaḥa mursala* as an authentic and legitimate source of legislation. They were of the opinion that the formulation of Islamic rulings must be made in light of and in accordance with the Qur'ān and the *Sunna* and, moreover, only under demanding conditions (and this, even if *maṣlaḥa mursala* is to be considered as an independent source when no text is available). A close study of the different opinions for and against *maṣlaḥa mursala* shows that the *'ulamā'* agreed on many major points and particularly if we consider the conditions stipulated by its proponents among whom we find, in the first rank, the *'ālim* of Granada, ash-Shāṭibī. We find in these works a set of conditions and specifications regarding the recognition of public interest as a reliable legal source which restricts and prevents the *'ulamā'* making unwarranted use of *maṣlaḥa*. Without entering into too many details, we can sum up the three main conditions which are generally recognised if, of course, there is no text available:

1. The analysis and the identification have to be very close in order to be certain that we are facing a genuine *maṣlaḥa* (*ḥaqīqiyya*) and not merely an apparent or specious one (*wahmiyya*). The *'ālim* must reach a high level of certitude that, by formulating a ruling, this will, in respect of the Islamic framework, remove hardship and not, on the contrary, accrue harm.

2. The *maṣlaḥa* must be general (*kulliyya*) and provide benefit to the people and society as a whole and not only to a group, class or an individual.
3. The *maṣlaḥa* must not be in contradiction or conflict with a text from the Qur'ān or the authentic *Sunna*. In such a case, it can no longer be considered as a *maṣlaḥa mursala* but as *maṣlaḥa mulgha*.[62]

These three conditions[63] give us the outlines by which we have to understand the concept of *maṣlaḥa*, public interest, within Islamic Law. What is clear, first, is the supremacy of the Qur'ān and the *Sunna* over any other reference and juridical instrument. Yūsuf al-Qarḍāwī[64] reminds us aptly, following the statements of al-Ghazālī, Ibn al-Qayyim and ash-Shāṭibī, that all that is in the Qur'ān and the *Sunna* is, *per se*, in accordance with human interest, at large, for the Creator knows, and wants, what is best for human beings and He indicates to them how they must implement it. God says in the Qur'ān about the Revealed Message that it:

> *... enjoins upon them the doing of what is right, and forbids them the doing of what is wrong, and makes lawful to them the good things of life and forbids them the bad things, and lifts from them burdens and the shackles that were upon them (aforetime).*[65]
>
> *O mankind! There has now come unto you an admonition from your Sustainer, and a cure for all (the ills) that may be in men's hearts, and guidance and grace unto all who believe (in Him).*[66]

We find the fact of preference for the good of mankind in the first Revelation regarding intoxicants (this is among three leading to its definitive prohibition):

> *They will ask you about intoxicants and games of chance. Say: "In both there is great evil as well as some benefit for men; but the evil which they cause is greater than the benefit which they bring."*[67]

Ibn al-Qayyim al-Jawziyya summarised this state of affairs as follows:

"The principles and the bases of the *Sharīʿa* concerning the rulings and human interest in this life and the Hereafter are all (founded) on justice, grace, human good, wisdom. Every situation which moves from justice to tyranny, from grace to hardship, from goodness to corruption, from wisdom to absurdity, has nothing to do with the *Sharīʿa*, even if this is presented through allegorical interpretation (*taʿwīl*). For the *Sharīʿa* is God's justice among His servants, God's grace among His creatures, His shadow on His earth, and His wisdom which proves His own existence as well as, and this is the best evidence, the authenticity of His Prophet."[68]

Seeking human *maṣlaḥa*, for this life and the Hereafter, is at the essence of Islamic commands and prohibitions. If the latter are clearly stated (*qaṭʿī ad-dalāla wath-thubūt*)[69] in the Qur'ān and/or the *Sunna*, they should be respected and implemented in light of the overall understanding of *maqāṣid ash-Sharīʿa* (the objectives of Islamic teaching):[70] they are – and represent – the revealed *maṣlaḥa* provided by the Creator to His creature so that he could be guided towards the good.

Nevertheless, as we have discussed above, there is sometimes a *silence* in the sources. Facing new situations and problems, the *ʿulamā'* can not always find specified answers in the Qur'ān and the *Sunna*; thus, guided by Revelation and the example of the Prophet, they have to formulate rulings which must protect people's interests without betraying the references. These interests are called *maṣāliḥ mursala* and require a total and permanent involvement of the *ʿulamā'* in order to allow Muslims to live as Muslims in any time and at any place and to preserve them from an overwhelming burden, since God says:

> *God wills that you shall have ease, and does not will you to suffer hardship.*[71]

This is exactly what the Companions did, starting with Abū Bakr and ʿUmar, in every new situation. Al-Qarḍāwī says:

"This is the field of what was known by the *uṣūliyyīn*[72] as *al-maṣāliḥ al-mursala*, i.e. those for which there is no specific text in the Qur'ān and the *Sunna* to support or nullify them. Both the rules based on the sources or extracted from them and the action of the guided Caliphates as well as the Companions are an evidence of the accuracy of those whose schools of thought referred to *maṣlaḥa* (*mursala*) and recognised it as a proof."[73]

This is the framework within which we have to consider the notion of *maṣlaḥa*. It has been a controversial concept not least because of the lack of clarity with respect to its definition and the strict and demanding conditions of its application. Sometimes, it has been used excessively by *ʿulamāʾ* trying to justify any modern ruling or progress in the name of *maṣlaḥa*. We have seen that this concept is very specific – in its definition, level, type and condition – and it requires from the *ʿulamāʾ* a constant reference to the sources so as to permit them to formulate rulings in accordance with the revealed Message even if there is no text available. They must exert themselves – through a deep, difficult and detailed study – so as to provide the Muslim community with new rational rulings directed by Revelation. This is exactly the meaning of *ijtihād* which is both the source and the juridical instrument permitting dynamism within Islamic jurisprudence.

## E. *Ijtihād* and *Fatwā*

### *1. Definition and classification*

We have already explained[74] that the two chief sources of Islamic jurisprudence are the Qur'ān and the *Sunna* and that the Prophet, sending Muʿādh to Yemen, approved his statement "to exert (himself) to form (his) own judgement" in cases where there was no text available in the Qur'ān and the *Sunna*. This self-exertion by the *ʿālim* (jurist) in order to understand the source, to extract rules or, in the absence of clear textual evidence, to formulate independent rulings, is called *ijtihād*. The definition proposed by Hashim Kamali is instructive:

"*Ijtihād* is defined as the total expenditure of effort made by a jurist in order to infer, with a degree of probability, the rules of *Sharīʿa* from their detailed evidence in the sources. Some *ʿulamāʾ* have defined *ijtihād* as the application by a jurist of all his faculties either in inferring the rules of *Sharīʿa* from their sources or in implementing such rules and applying them to particular issues. *Ijtihād* essentially consists of an inference (*istinbāṭ*) that amounts to a probability (*ẓann*), thereby excluding the extraction of a ruling from a clear text."[75]

Like *maṣlaḥa*, the juridical instrument of *ijtihād* has been used for justifying every kind of new ruling. Thus, Hashim Kamali aptly recalls the general principle (on which there is unanimous agreement among the *ʿulamāʾ*) that there is no *ijtihād* where there is a clear text in the sources (*lā ijtihāda maʿan-naṣṣ*). This means that when there exists a plain Qur'ānic verse whose meaning is evident and cannot be subject to speculation or interpretation (*qaṭʿī*), there is no possible *ijtihād*. Similarly, if the jurist finds an authenticated *ḥadīth* (*mutawātir, qaṭʿī ath-thubūt*)[76] whose content is also definitive and free from obscurity, he has to refer to it and, hence, there is no need to exercise *ijtihād*.

In fact, these clear texts, both authenticated and explicit, represent – even though they are not numerous – the *immutable* foundations, the fixed principles on which the *Sharīʿa* relies, to which the jurist has to refer and from which he is able to analyse, comment and explain the speculative text (*ẓannī*) and from which he should also formulate, within a dynamic process, new rulings when his community is facing new situations. The laws or rulings provided by those clear texts form a specific framework called *al-maʿlūm min ad-dīn biḍ-ḍarūra*, meaning that they partake of the fundamental essence of Islamic jurisprudence and that they lead, if rejected, to the negation of Islam (*kufr*).

Nevertheless, the great majority of the Qur'ānic verses and the Prophet's traditions are not of this very strict nature. The Qur'ān is authenticated *per se* (*qaṭʿī ath-thubūt*) but the majority of verses containing legal rulings (*āyāt al-aḥkām*) are subject to analysis, commentaries and interpretations (*ẓannī*) as is the case for *aḥādīth* which are for the most part open to speculation regarding both their authenticity (*thubūt*) and their meaning (*dalāla*). This means that the *fuqahāʾ* (jurists) have had, and still have, an important and imperative function in the formulation of the laws qualified as Islamic. In particular, through their *ijtihād* applied at different levels:

with respect to the understanding of a specific text (in light of the whole Islamic juridical framework), to the classification of the texts according to their clarity or their nature (*qaṭʿī* or *ẓannī*; *ẓāhir* – manifest – or *naṣṣ* – explicit, *khāṣṣ* – specific – or *ʿām* – general, etc.) or to the stipulation of rulings where there is no text at all. *Ijtihād* as a whole (as both a source and a legal instrument), has in fact been considered by many *ʿulamāʾ* as the third chief source of the *Sharīʿa* in which one will find *ijmāʿ* (*ijtihād jamāʿī*), *qiyās* (*ijtihād fardī*), *istiṣlāḥ* and *istiḥsān* along with all the known subdivisions among the so-called supplementary sources of the *Sharīʿa*. Hisham Kamali again aptly remarks:

"The various sources of Islamic law that feature next to the Qur'ān and *Sunna* are all manifestations of *ijtihād*, albeit with differences that are largely procedural in character. In this way, consensus of opinion, analogy, juristic preference, considerations of public interest (*maṣlaḥa*), etc., are all inter-related not only under the mean heading of *ijtihād*, but via the Qur'ān and the *Sunna*."[77]

Al-Ghazālī, ash-Shāṭibī, Ibn al-Qayyim al-Jawziyya and more recently al-Khallāf and Abū Zahra referred to this kind of classification by emphasising the importance of *ijtihād* as the third source of Islamic jurisprudence for it contains all the judicial instruments used through human reasoning and self-exertion. *Ijtihād* is, in fact, a rational elaboration of laws either based on the sources or stipulated in their light. Thus, even *ijmāʿ* (consensus) is the product of a collective human and rational elaboration and as such we can suppose, even though it is unlikely or very rare, that a legal decision taken through *ijmāʿ* eventually becomes unsuitable and has to be reconsidered. Professor Muhammad Hamidullah, referring to the Ḥanbalī school of law says:

"The opinion of a jurist can, however, be rejected by another jurist who can offer his own opinion instead. This applies not only to individual opinion or an inference but also covers collective opinion. At least the Ḥanafī school of law accepts that a new consensus can cancel an old consensus. Suppose there is a consensus on a certain issue. We accept its authority but it does not mean that no one can oppose it till eternity. If someone has the courage to oppose it with due respect and reason, and if he can persuade the jurist to accept his point of view, a new consensus comes into being. The new consensus abrogates the old one. This principle has been propounded by the famous Ḥanafī jurist, Abū al-Yusr al-Bazdāwī in his book *Uṣūl al-Fiqh* (Principles of Jurisprudence). Al-Bazdāwī belongs to the fourth and fifth century of the *Hijra*. This work is a great contribution to Islamic jurisprudence. It is on account of his statement that we can say that consensus cannot become a source of difficulty for us. If a consensus is reached on some issue and it is found subsequently to be unsuitable the possibility remains that we may change it through reasoning and create a new one cancelling the old consensus."[78]

This analysis recalls one important principle within the field of *uṣūl al-fiqh*, that is that the Qur'ān and the *Sunna* are the only indisputable sources in which the verses and the *aḥādīth* dealing with rulings (*āyāt wa aḥādīth al-aḥkām*)[79] are divided into two main levels: the *qaṭʿī* (definitive) which is clear in itself and the *ẓannī* (subject to speculation and interpretation) which requires a close study of the considered texts by the *ʿulamā'* so that they are able to infer the appropriate rulings to be extracted from the sources. The aim of this kind of *ijtihād* (with the *ẓannī* texts available), sometimes called *bayānī* (explanatory *ijtihād*), is to analyse the text (*naṣṣ*), to extract a ruling and its *ʿilla* (the effective cause of this specific ruling) in order to permit both an adequate understanding of the text and possible analogic reasoning (*qiyās*) in light of its historical context. This has been subjected to many diverse sub-divisions according to the different opinions of the *ʿulamā'*.

There exists another kind of *ijtihād* when there is no text available. Here also we face numerous sub-divisions due to the diversity among the *ʿulamā'* and the compilations of works and commentaries throughout history. At least three types can be roughly identified: *ijtihād qiyāsī* when it is done through analogical reasoning which takes into account the effective cause (*ʿilla*) of a ruling extracted from the sources; *ijtihād ẓannī*, in the case of an impossible reference to a known effective cause; the latter is often linked to *ijtihād istiṣlāḥī*, based on *maṣlaḥa*, and seeks to deduce the *aḥkām* in light of the overall purpose of the *Sharīʿa*. There is no unanimity among the *ʿulamā'* regarding a specific classification within the field of *ijtihād* for they did not even agree on its definition and mode of implementation.

Another distinction is made as to the degree of *ijtihād*, i.e. whether it is absolute (*muṭlaq*) or limited (*muqayyad*). The former, also called *ijtihād fī ash-shar*ʿ, relies on the capacity of the *mujtahid* (an *ʿālim* who can exercise *ijtihād*) to extract and formulate rulings of his own through an immediate study of the sources. The latter, called limited *ijtihād* or *ijtihād madhhabī* is, on the contrary, confined to a particular school and the *mujtahid* is to formulate rulings in accordance with the rules of a given *madhhab* (school of law).[80]

## 2. The conditions (ash-shurūṭ) of ijtihād

The framework we have presented of *ijtihād*'s definition and classification was taken into account by the *ʿulamāʾ* when they determined the conditions of *ijtihād*. To analyse and classify the latter, they focused their attention on the required qualities an *ʿālim* must possess in order to exercise a genuine and reliable *ijtihād*, to become a *mujtahid*. As for other classifications, many divergent conditions were formulated by the *ʿulamāʾ* according to their respective views on juridical instruments, the applicability of the laws or, simply, the priorities in their implementation.

Before going further in the presentation of the necessary conditions to be a *mujtahid* it seems useful here to refer to the concise opinion of ash-Shāṭibī who distinguishes between the very nature of *ijtihād* and its instruments. His overall view, in this sense, is a clarification for he encapsulates all the conditions under two main headings. Thus, according to him, "the degree of *ijtihād* has been attained when two qualities are present:

1. A deep understanding of the objective (*maqāsid*) of the *Sharīʿa*.
2. A real mastery of the different methods of deduction and extraction (*istinbāṭ*) based on knowledge and understanding."[81]

The "five essential principles" (*aḍ-ḍarūriyyāt al-khamsa*) we have already quoted (Religion, life, intellect, lineage and property), along with the necessary distinction that exists between essentials (*ḍarūrī*), complementary (*ḥājī*) and embellishments (*taḥsīnī*), form the framework given by the Lawgiver to direct the researches of the *mujtahid*, and, as such, they represent the fundamental reference. The *mujtahid* must also know which instruments[82] he can resort to among the general maxims of *fiqh*, *qiyās*, *istiḥsān* and so forth.

From Abū al-Husayn al-Baṣrī and his book *al-Muʿtamad fī Uṣūl al-Fiqh* (11th century) to Ibn al-Qayyim al-Jawziyya with his *Iʿlām al-Muwāqqiʿīn ʿan Rabb al-ʿĀlamīn* (14th century), many *ʿulamā'* proposed different classifications of the required qualities and conditions which permit an *ʿālim* to be considered a *mujtahid*. Some thought that a knowledge of Arabic was the first condition,[83] others that it was knowledge of the verses and the *aḥādīth* regarding legal issues which first had to be brought to the fore. Notwithstanding all these variations, which in fact are largely procedural for their respective conditions overlap, we can synthesise the works of the *ʿulamā'* in this field as follows. The *mujtahid* must attain:

1. A knowledge of Arabic to the extent that it enables him to correctly understand the Qur'ān and the *Sunna* and, especially, the verses and *aḥādīth* containing rulings (*ayāt* and *aḥādīth al-aḥkām*).

2. A knowledge of Qur'ānic and *Ḥadīth* sciences in order to know how to understand and identify the evidences within the text (*adilla*) and, moreover, to infer and extract rulings.

3. A deep comprehension of the *maqāṣid al-Sharīʿa*, their classification and the priorities they subsequently bring to the fore.

4. A knowledge of the questions on which there was *ijmāʿ*: this requires knowledge of the works on secondary questions (*furūʿ*).

5. A knowledge of the principles of analogical reasoning (*qiyās*) along with its methodology (the causes – *ʿilal* or circumstances – *asbāb* of a specific ruling, conditions – *shurūṭ* etc.).

6. A knowledge of his historical, social and political context. That is, the situation of the people around him (*aḥwāl an-nās*) and the state of their affairs, their traditions, customs, and the like.
7. Recognition of his competency, honesty, reliability and uprightness.[84]

As we have already mentioned, many other conditions, in different orders, have been proposed, but these seven points more or less gather together the most important prerequisites of a *mujtahid*.[85]

Some *ʿulamāʾ* consider that these conditions and qualifications are so high and demanding that it has not been possible to reach such a level after the era of the great *ʿulamāʾ*, roughly during the 9th century. This is why they say that the "gates of *ijtihād*" have been definitely closed since this flowering epoch. Other *ʿulamāʾ*, the great majority, are of the opinion that the practice of *ijtihād* has been partly abandoned because of historical circumstances which have either pushed political leaders or the *ʿulamāʾ* themselves to declare that hence there is no need to make *ijtihād*.[86] As such, the gates of *ijtihād* have never been closed for no *ʿālim* would have had the right to take such a decision in the name of Islam, i.e. it is an anti-Islamic statement by its very nature since *ijtihād*, being the third source of Islamic jurisprudence, is *farḍ kifāya*, a collective obligation. All admit that these conditions are demanding and that they are still required to permit a qualified *ijtihād* but they state that such qualifications have never been beyond the reach of the *ʿulamāʾ* during the later eras up to our own contemporary one. Progress within the field of *aḥādīth* authentication coupled with easier access to reference books and computerised classifications facilitate the work of the *mujtahid* today, making it more effective. Therefore, the Muslim community, through its *ʿulamāʾ*, still has to fulfil this fundamental duty today. It also requires that they find the appropriate form to implement it in our contemporary context, this because of the complexity of many sciences such as medicine, technology, economics and the social sciences, etc.[87] *Ijtihād* remains the most important instrument in the hands of the *ʿulamāʾ* to achieve the universal vocation of Islam through a constant dynamic of adaptation in light of the era and its context.

### *3. What is a fatwā?*

To understand the very meaning of what a *fatwā* is, it is necessary to bear in mind the entire substance of our above analysis, for a *fatwā* is a part, an element and, more specifically, a juridical instrument which has to be apprehended in the context of Islamic jurisprudence as a whole. *Fatwā* (pl. *fatāwā*) literally means religious ruling, a verdict or as ash-Shāṭibī defines it: "An answer to a legal question given by an expert *(muftī)*, by way of words, action or approval."[88] Therefore, a *fatwā* first has to be based on the sources and, second, on the legal inferences and extractions made by the *mujtahidīn*[89] through their exercise of *ijtihād* if the sources are not definite and clear (*ẓannī*) or if there is no text available.

The place of the *mujtahid* and the *muftī*, in fact, are of major importance. Ash-Shāṭibī says:

"The *muftī*,[90] within the community, stands in for the Prophet. There are many evidences supporting that (statement): first, there is the proof of the *ḥadīth*: 'Verily, the *ʿulamā'* are the heirs of the Prophets, and what is inherited through the Prophets is not money (*lā dināran wa lā dirham*) but knowledge (*ʿilm*).' Second, he (the *muftī*) is the means to convey the rulings (*aḥkām*) according to what he (the Prophet) said: 'The one who witnesses among you must transmit (what he witnesses) to the absent' and 'convey from me even if it is one verse only' ... And if it is so then this means that he (the *muftī*) stands in for the Prophet. Third, the *muftī* is a kind of lawgiver for what he bears from the *Sharīʿa* is either taken (as stipulated) from the Lawgiver (through the Revelation or the *Sunna*) or inferred, extracted from the sources. As Regards the former he is but a conveyor whereas in the latter he stands in for the Prophet by stipulating rulings. To formulate rulings is the function of the lawgiver. Thus, if the function of the *mujtahid* is to formulate rulings according to his opinion and his efforts, then it is possible to say that, in this way, he is a lawgiver who must be respected and followed: we have to act in accordance with the rulings he formulates and that is vicegerency (*khilāfa*) in its genuine implementation ..."[91]

Ash-Shāṭibī emphasises the importance of the *mujtahid* who stands in for the Prophet in the Muslim community after Muḥammad's death. As such, the *mujtahid* or the *muftī* represent the continuity of knowledge (*ʿilm*) directed by the two sources so as to allow its fair implementation throughout history. Ash-Shāṭibī establishes a distinction between clear and definitive evidences (taken as stipulated in the sources) and those which require inference and deduction and which make the *mujtahid* similar to a lawgiver (even if he must seek the guidance of God, the ultimate Lawgiver, and follow the Prophet's example). Ash-Shāṭibī's distinction has the great merit of bringing to the fore the two different degrees of *fatāwā*:

1. Asked about legal topics, the *mujtahid* will sometimes find a clear answer in the Qur'ān and the *Sunna* since a plain text exists. The *fatwā*, here, consists in a quotation, a reminder of the authoritative proof.

2. If there is a text subject to interpretation or if no text is available, the *muftī* is to give a specific answer in light both of the objectives of the *Sharīʿa* and the situation of his interlocutor(s). The *muftī* plays, as mentioned by ash-Shāṭibī, the true role of vicegerent who should provide his fellow humans with a legal decision. The more the question relates to an individual or a very specific case the more it should be precise, clear and accurate. As such a *fatwā* is hardly "transferable" for it is a legal decision given (in accordance with the sources, the *maṣlaḥa* and the context) to a clear question set out in a specific context. This is, in fact, the exact meaning, within the field of law, of jurisprudence.

Many questions have arisen in the course of history regarding the diversity of *fatāwā*. For example, if Islam is one, how is it possible to have different legal decisions for the same legal question? The *ʿulamā'* have been unanimous in saying that if the geographical or historical contexts are different, this means that it is no longer the same question for it should be considered in relation to its environment. Thus, the qualified answers should, by their nature, be diverse following the example of ash-Shāfiʿī who modified some of his juridical decisions after moving from Baghdad to Cairo. Then, even though Islam is one, *fatāwā*, in their diversity and sometimes in their contradictions, still remain *Islamic* and authoritative.

This kind of divergence is understood, admitted and respected whereas the problem of disagreement between the *ʿulamāʾ*, when a similar legal question has been asked, has provoked endless debates. Is this possible within religious matters and if so, how can Islam, hence, have a unifying quality for Muslims? Two essential positions on this have been taken by the great majority of *ʿulamāʾ*:

1. There is no divergence of opinion concerning the principles, the fundamentals (*uṣūl*), of Islamic Law. There is a consensus among *ʿulamāʾ* that these principles are the essence, the references and the milestones for Islamic jurisprudence. However, it is not possible to avoid differences of opinion in matters relating to secondary questions (*furūʿ*), for a legal decision on these is determined and influenced by many elements: the *ʿulamāʾ*'s knowledge, understanding, ability to infer and extract rulings which, through their varying competences, leads to different interpretations and opinions. This was true of the Companions even during the time of the Prophet and, according to the *ʿulamāʾ* these divergences have to be recognised and respected within the limits of what is known to be the fundamentals of Islam.

2. From the previous agreement a question naturally arises: If there are different acceptable legal opinions for one and the same problem (even if secondary – *farʿ*), does this mean that all *fatāwā* are of the same value or are they all correct? If so, this would lead us to admit that two different opinions can be true at the same time, in the same place, regarding the same person, and this is rationally impossible to concede. The majority of *ʿulamāʾ*, and among them the four leading *Imāms*, are of the opinion that only one of the several

> opposing views on a particular issue may be said to be correct. This is clear from the Qur'ān through the story of David and Solomon who had to judge the same case, and despite the fact that they were both gifted with discretion and knowledge, it appears that Solomon's opinion was the correct one: "*We made Solomon understand it.*"[92] This position is also supported by the *ḥadīth* we have already quoted concerning the reward of the *mujtahid*: he gains two rewards if he is correct and only one if he is wrong, his effort and sincerity to seek the Truth having been taken into account by God. Thus, acceptance of the diversity of legal opinions regarding precise questions (when they are stated in the same context, at the same time and for the same community or individual) by no means leads us to suppose that there are many truths and that all these opinions are of the same value and accuracy. In fact there is only one Truth that all the *ʿulamāʾ* should try to find out, and for this effort they will be rewarded. As long as there is no definitive evidence relating to the studied problem, every Muslim has to follow the opinion whose evidence and strength appear, after reflection and analysis, the more obvious and convincing in his/her eyes.

Upholding the Revealed Book and the example of the Prophet, which are for Muslims the sources of Truth, they have to do their best to look for Truth when the texts are not clear or simply missing. In fact, the meaning and content of the vicegerency given to mankind by God reaches its peak and is achieved when the *ʿulamāʾ* continuously and tirelessly exert themselves to find the most accurate decision, the one which is closest to the Truth. Thus, the *ʿulamāʾ*, *mujtahidīn* and *muftī*, should be determined, demanding and confident about their own decisions but remain modest and calm to face and accept the necessary and inevitable plurality of views. Ash-Shāfiʿī aptly said, speaking about the state of mind which should characterise the *ʿulamāʾ*'s attitude: "(In our eyes) our opinion is correct but could yet contain error; while we consider the opinion of our opponents as wrong but it could yet be right."[93]

## 4. *Prospects for a contemporary ijtihād*

Since the 14th century, with Ibn Taymiyya, and in a more pronounced way over the last two centuries, calls to restore *ijtihād* have increased, becoming a *leitmotiv* among the *ʿulamāʾ*. These latter, along with scientists, following in the footsteps of Ibn Taymiyya and his disciple Ibn al-Qayyim, have become aware that without the instrument of *ijtihād* Muslims can never manage to face the challenges of their era. Within the religious, scientific, political, economic or social fields, it is no longer conceivable to remain stuck with the juridical contributions of the *ʿulamāʾ* of the 10th or 11th centuries. The *Fiqh* of *muʿāmalāt* (social and public affairs), being the rational, analytical and contextualised application of Islamic global rules relying on sources, needed to be rethought and adapted. This process, in fact, was not the simple expression of a desire to be modern according to the Western criteria but rather a deep feeling that it was necessary to refind again the genuine spirit of Islamic jurisprudence.

If Islam is a universal Message, appropriate to all places over all times, then this should be shown, proved and expressed through a permanent reflection going and coming from the sources to reality and from reality to the sources. This process should be witnessed in every time, everywhere so that the application of the Islamic law remains faithful to *maqāsid ash-Sharīʿa* (the objectives). With ash-Shawkānī, then al-Afghānī, al-Kawākibī, ʿAbduh, Riḍā, an-Nursī, Ibn Bādis, Iqbāl, al-Mawdūdī, al-Bannā and Bennabi, more and more voices have been heard calling for a new *ijtihād* and, consequently, applying it when they faced new situations or problems. This movement, born more than 200 years ago, has provoked consistent disruption within the traditional religious curricula in the great Islamic universities of the Muslim world. Even if the improvements are not so visible, one can witness important changes since Muḥammad ʿAbduh expressed deep criticism against the "old, fusty and useless teaching of al-Azhar" for instance. "If today I have some knowledge that can be mentioned, it is only due to my efforts, during more than ten years, to try to clean up my mind from the dirt and rubbish al-Azhar put into it. So far, I have not been able to reach the cleanliness I wished for."[94]

ʿAbduh's main objective was to modify the religious studies curriculum at al-Azhar University and, at the same time, to add new disciplines such as geography or history to the programme. He was against the way of teaching and learning within "a great institution" he still respected but which needed, according to him, profound reform: above all, he was very critical about knowledge acquired "by heart" and assessed as such without any concern for real understanding. The tradition of memorising, he argued, if it had had some benefit, was no more able to fit our modern era for which we need, in addition to the religious matter, analytical knowledge, comprehension and, moreover, contextualisation.

Many later *ʿulamāʾ* felt the same lacuna and called for similar reform: Rāshid Riḍā, Muḥammad Abū Zahra, Ḥassan Aḥmad Khallāf, and more recently Muḥammad al-Ghazālī and Yūsuf al-Qarḍāwī.[95] Throughout the world, this call was also echoed: a revival of the Islamic sciences and a reform of religious education was, and still is, imperative in order that Muslims respect their sources and, at the same time, live up to their age. The problem still remains a question of balance: as we have said above, there are some immutable principles in Islam and many rulings which are subject to change: the *ʿulamāʾ* are bound to the former in order to be able to formulate the latter. So how do we implement this process today? What should we retain from the work of the earlier *ʿulamāʾ*? What shall be the shape of the Islamic framework in our century? Numerous contributions have been made in this respect during the last 50 years and there is a profusion of debates, discussions and responses concerning the current problems faced by the Muslim community.

Yūsuf al-Qarḍāwī, who attends many meetings dealing with the problems of our modern life and the formulation of appropriate Islamic solutions, has tried to fix some of the rules which are necessary for the application of adequate *ijtihād* today. He has written extensively on this matter and more specifically in his book, *Contemporary Ijtihād, between Regulation and Disintegration*.[96] In this book, he reminds us of the principal conditions of *ijtihād*, both intrinsically and in light of our contemporary situation. He specifies three aspects which, according to him, characterise *ijtihād* today:

1. ***Selective ijtihād based on preference.***[97] Says al-Qarḍāwī, "What do we mean by 'selective *ijtihād*'?: it is the choice of one of the inherited legal opinions from our wide Islamic juridical legacy in order to stipulate rulings on it or to judge through it. This legal opinion is chosen as a preference from amongst other opinions and statements. We do not agree with those who say we could equally choose among any inherited legal opinion truly stipulated by the later *mujtahidīn* without looking for evidence (*dalīl*), especially if (this opinion) is linked with one of the followed schools of law. In fact, this kind of attitude is but pure imitation (*taqlīd*) and has nothing to do with the *ijtihād* we are calling for. It is but submitting ourselves to a statement which is not infallible, (and moreover) without proof ... On the contrary, what we are calling for here is to assess and compare the different legal opinions and to revise their respective evidence based on the sources or on *ijtihād* so that, in the end, we can choose the one which seems to us the stronger proof and a preferable evidence according to the numerous parameters of preference. Among the latter is that the legal statement has to fit our era, to consider people, to be the closest possible to the *Sharīʿa* and the most appropriate for implementing the objectives of Islamic teaching, serving the interests of mankind and protecting them from evil."[98]

   This means that the *ʿulamāʾ* of today have to reconsider all the opinions of the previous *mujtahidīn* in the course of history so that they can assess their contributions and so choose the most appropriate one according to its authenticity and contemporary context. Thus, our inherited Islamic rulings are not all of the same value even if they were considered as qualified by Muslims at a certain moment in history. All this legal patrimony should be closely assessed in view of our new scientific criteria (for instance, our knowledge regarding *ḥadīth* authentication is more precise today) and our contemporary understanding (regarding recent researches dealing with social, political or economic issues). Al-Qarḍāwī aptly refutes the idea, or the simplistic conclusion, that if it had been stated and accepted once, it is thus a right opinion which ought to be respected for all times. It is part of contemporary *ijtihād*, according to him, to study what we inherited from the classical scholars because none of them were infallible, even the great *ʿulamā'* who founded the diverse schools of thought. To select and to choose is not only imperative, it is an Islamic duty.

Al-Qarḍāwī gives many examples in this respect, especially regarding the situation of Muslim women. If it is understandable that some *ʿulamā'*, such as ash-Shāfiʿī, Mālik, Ibn Ḥanbal and a great number of their followers, stipulated restrictive rulings concerning women's rights (visiting the mosque, marriage, etc.) in light of their social context, we are, however, asked to consider their opinion as well as their evidence and even to call the former into question if they do not take into account all the texts in the sources or if they do not fit our environment. According to al-Qarḍāwī, the statements of Abū Ḥanīfa are more appropriate today and should be selected and applied: for instance, as regards relying on Qur'ānic verses and *aḥādīth*, he is of the opinion that there are no valid restrictions in allowing women to go to mosques (to pray, to learn or simply to attend meetings) and that the agreement of the girl must be obtained to permit an Islamically legalised marriage.

2. ***New rulings based on original analyses.***[99] Al-Qarḍāwī says: "What do we mean by *original ijtihād* (*ijtihād inshā'ī*)?: it is the inference and extraction of a new ruling regarding a specific legal question that has never been stipulated by previous *ʿulamā'*; so was the legal question an old or a new one? ... The legal question subject to *ijtihād* and about which there were divergences between previous *fuqahā'* presents at least two opinions and it is possible that a third opinion appears afterwards; if it is possible to have a divergence between three then it is possible to have it

between four, and so on ... Yet, the majority of legal questions which the *original ijtihād* has to deal with are of a new nature, unknown to our predecessors. The question had maybe not materalised during their era or in a less accurate aspect and this did not push the *faqīh* to look for a solution through a new *ijtihād*."[100]

Al-Qarḍāwī gives some examples of this kind of *ijtihād* in economics (*zakāt*, heritage and the like) and within scientific and technological progress (photography, abortion and the like),[101] thus demonstrating that Muslims need specific answers to new problems which the previous *'ulamā'* did not face.

3. ***The necessity for collective ijtihād (ijtihād jamā'ī).*** It happens, says al-Qarḍāwī, that depending on the subject, contemporary *ijtihād* has to mix selection and original analyses and that the *fuqahā'* of today should master a wide range of religious knowledge which is, *per se*, very demanding. At the same time, the legal questions become more and more complex for they require specific competences and specialisations in science, technology, medicine and economics, etc. It is quite impossible then to master both the religious references and the scientific knowledge: it is imperative today to acquire a "double vision" constituted, on the one hand, by the sources and the contributions of the *'ulamā'* and, on the other, by an appropriate and deep knowledge of our time, our environment as well as the diversity of scientific matters. This is too heavy a burden for one person and contemporary *ijtihād* cannot be effective without the constitution of councils or forums of *'ulamā'* and secular scholars or specialists in different disciplines such as those we have already mentioned.

Al-Qarḍāwī aptly states: "It is necessary, as regards new, important problems, not to rely on individual *ijtihād* only but to move from individual to collective *ijtihād* in which there is consultation between scholars about one determined problem and (this should be done) especially for questions which are of general interest. Collective opinion is nearer

> to the truth than individual opinion, no matter how wide the knowledge of the latter is."[102] He adds that that is "the grace of consultation" (*shūrā*) whose outcomes can be guaranteed if, and only if, "absolute freedom is assured" to pursue the researches in an appropriate atmosphere.
>
> Such forums are already constituted in many Arab or Islamic countries and recently a "European Council for Islamic Rulings and Researches" has been founded in London.[103] The main objective is to create a platform where legal responses are given to Muslims living in a new world, with new legal questions and ethical problems.

Selection, new Islamic rulings and collective decisions are the three essential aspects of contemporary *ijtihād* according to al-Qarḍāwī. Many *'ulamā'* have been of the same opinion for the last 50 years, especially when it appeared that the Islamic countries must refind their religious and intellectual dynamism if they are to face the fantastic changes the world is witnessing in the social, political, economic and technological domains. In other words, they were asked to give their own Islamic responses to the challenge of modernity. The necessity of a thorough revival of *ijtihād* was felt everywhere in the Islamic world and numerous initiatives have been taken to fulfil this objective. There are a considerable number of selected, new and collective rulings which have been stipulated by the contemporary *'ulamā'* regarding medical, financial and economic issues, along with specialists in these respective fields. We will discuss some of these contributions below but we can already say here that the existence of all these councils and forums is sufficient proof that Islamic laws are not static and, even if they still refer to revealed and absolute principles, the room for manoeuvre supported by intellectual researches and adaptations is wide and, in fact, very demanding.

Over the last 20 years a new awareness has arisen within the Muslim communities of the West. During the 1960s and 1970s, the migrants arrived with the idea of returning to their country of origin as soon as they had earned sufficient money, but it became difficult, and often impossible, to achieve this aim. Their sons and daughters were born in a new country, in a new environment, with a new state of mind. They were from "here", the country their parents had immigrated to became their country, they were "at home". This fundamental change quickly brought about a set of questions which needed to be answered imperatively. Early in Islamic history, some *ʿulamāʾ* drew a specific geography of the world, distinguishing *dār al-Islām* (the abode of Islam) from those which were not under Islamic rule called *dār al-ḥarb* (the abode of war)[104] stating that it was not possible for Muslims to live in *dār al-ḥarb* except under some mitigating circumstances. What bearing does this have on those Muslims who came to work and are now living in the West with their families? What about their children and their nationality? Can they take the nationality of their new Western country, can they be true, genuine and complete citizens, giving allegiance – through the national constitution – to a non-Islamic country? We could add to these questions another long list made up of strictly religious topics as well as social, economic, political and scientific problems. Consequently, it became apparent that the contemporary development of *ijtihād* should face this new state of affairs, namely the specific situation of Muslim minorities in a non-Islamic country. In other words, in light of Islamic references, with all the juridical Islamic instruments and in accordance with the *maṣlaḥa* (public interest), the *ʿulamāʾ* have had to say whether it is possible to be a European Muslim or not. The last two decades have witnessed countless contributions to this debate.

## F. Priorities and Steps

It is important, when speaking about the new situations facing Muslims in general and those within Western countries in particular, to bear in mind the overall framework of Islamic references we have outlined above in order to avoid confusing the principles and the actions which need to be implemented. The subject is a sensitive one for we are not only dealing with legal questions but also with the detailed building-up of a balanced Islamic identity in a world of constant change.

In our description of the function as well as the specific typology and articulation of Islamic sciences and of the essential difference between the global and absolute principles of the *Sharīʿa* (based on the Qur'ān and the *Sunna*) and the dynamic thought required for their faithful juridical application – which is called *Fiqh*, jurisprudence – our intention was to clarify the landscape within which Muslims are able to provide answers to some fundamental contemporary problems and, by so doing, constitute an Islamic concept of modernity.

This is especially necessary when we are dealing with the very specific situation of Muslim minorities in Western countries for the essential questions are intertwined with emotion, feeling, fear and other psychological and social inferences which often make it difficult to identify the exact and objective nature of the problems themselves. The simple and natural contrast between the first generation of Muslim immigrants who tried to protect their religious identity by being as discreet and invisible as possible and the increasing number of their children who have become assertive and self confident about their rights (for they understand that they are at home in the West) has brought about a fundamental disruption in the thought of some prominent *ʿulamā'* who considered, only 15 or 20 years ago, that to come back home (meaning returning to Muslim countries) was the only solution to the seemingly inextricable religious and legal problems arising from living as Muslims in the West. Thus, their rulings were often influenced by other considerations which had little to do with the strict Islamic legal framework. Furthermore, the fear of a total loss of Islamic references or of a total assimilation of young Muslims into the indigenous Western culture, added to the reactive, and sometimes conflicting, posture of Muslim immigrants themselves. Hence many *ʿulamā'* found themselves referring to the *Fiqh* contributions of their predecessors so as to establish and confirm, *a posteriori*, that a Muslim could by no means consider him or herself as part of a non-Islamic society.

Such changes over the last two decades, and especially with the maturity of second and third generation Muslims who have no intention of leaving Western countries, has forced the *ʿulamā'* to rethink the matter and to return to the sources in an attempt to provide Muslim communities with an appropriate Islamic framework and a set of specific and adequate rulings fitting their new situation. This state of affairs has obliged these *'ulamā'* to purify and purge their references to the Islamic sources from all secondary interferences resulting from the crisis in identity and the change in values which has accompanied the process of settlement and adaptation of Muslims in Europe. They have had to precisely fix the priorities within the Islamic legal framework (and the ethical values which ensue therefrom) and the steps that have to be followed in Western countries to allow Muslims to live in peace and serenity as well as coexist within society and respect the rules chosen by its majority. We are still witnessing this fundamental process today, the dynamics of which started about 15 years ago and which will continue for some time as changes are constant and the problems more and more complex.

It is, in fact, a new, positive and constructive posture which relies on a fine comprehension of Islam's priorities, a clear vision of what is absolute, definitively fixed and what is subject to change and adaptation and, finally, on an appropriate understanding of the Western environment. The objective being to shape a European-Islamic identity out of the crisis. Before disputing the secondary aspects of Islamic legislation, it was thus imperative to protect the five elements constituting *maqāṣid ash-Sharī'a*: namely, Religion, life, intellect, lineage and property. As we saw above, within each of these fields there are priorities and secondary matters (*ḍarūriyyāt, ḥājiyyāt, taḥsinīyāt*) and, in view of the Western context, they have to be referred to and/or specified so that the path Muslims must follow if they are to remain faithful to their Religion is clearly drawn.[105]

Our new European context requires that we stipulate *fatāwā* within the framework and in light of European legislation. In each situation, we must measure the latitude offered by national legislation in order to define an orientation which will enable us, while remaining within the limits of the constitution of one country or another, to come as close as possible to respecting Islamic prescriptions. In cases of constraints as to the implementation of law, the degrees of compatibility or possibly the explicit or implicit conflicts must be measured in order to formulate the terms and the stages of the adaptation of Islamic references: the reference to public interest, the principle of flexibility and the formulation of specific *fatāwā* will fully play their part in this field. This shows how urgent it is to carry out intensive and specialised research concerning the law in each European country, in order to produce a *fiqh* fitting the new legal circumstances.[106] The rule is respect of the national legal framework[107] and the will, for each apparently contentious point of law, to look for the solution which, from an Islamic point of view, will be the most satisfactory, or at all events the least bad (*akhaf aḍ-ḍararayn*). In many sectors of law, one will realise that this contradiction (between the constitution and Islamic fundamentals) is only apparent and that the latitude offered by national legislation leaves the Muslim with surprising possibilities for adaptation (in particular concerning contracts and their conditions). The actual areas of constraint (*darūrāt*) will appear in the course of this research and will require that we stipulate specific legal rulings to the exact measure of each limitation.[108]

To protect the Islamic Faith and spirituality, to permit a real, worthy and permanent practice of Islam without constraint, to promote and defend the family and the values linked with it, to assure both religious and secular education, to offer Muslims the legal means of working and earning the money which enables them to become independent and no longer a burden on society represent the most basic priorities for which solutions must be found as soon as possible. This means that it is important to work concomitantly across many different fields: religious, social and educational but also to be involved in politics and economics, to defend the rights of citizens in general and of Muslims in particular concerning freedom, work, trade, and the like. To promote and to advocate such involvement in Western society is not only new, and thus difficult, but also necessitates that some sensitive legal questions and ethical issues receive, as essential prerequisites, clear answers and solutions. In the first rank of these is the problem of the Islamic lawfulness of a Muslim living in a non-Islamic country (and, if it is lawful, to what extent). There follows a series of other very important issues which we will try to deal with in Part Two.

## Notes

1 *al-Ijtihād al-muṭlaq* refers to the juridical rulings (*fatāwā*) given in light of the Qur'ān and the *Sunna* and it further requires that those suitably qualified also gain the recognition of the *'ulamā'* of the Muslim community. *al-Ijtihād al-muqayyad* (also called *ijtihād madhhabī*) which has been the most widespread over the seven centuries, are the juridical rulings given in accordance with a specific school of thought (*madhhab*).

2 Qur'ān 15: 9.

3 Qur'ān 67: 2.

4 Qur'ān 5: 48.

5 These subjects were the main content of the Makkan Revelations, between 610 and 622 CE.

6 There are different opinions among the *'ulamā'* concerning the number of legal verses (*āyāt al-aḥkām*): Abū Hāmid al-Ghazālī, for instance, estimated them at 500 and ash-Shawkānī, in his comments on al-Ghazālī's work, considered such calculations to be hypothetical. See 'Abd al-Wahhāb Khallāf, *'Ilm Uṣūl al-Fiqh* (Dār al-Qalam, Kuwait, 1978).

7 The Qur'ān and the *Sunna* are the two Islamic sources unanimously recognised by the *'ulamā'* of all schools of thought. *Ijmā'* (consensus of opinion) and *qiyās* (analogical deduction), even if clear are the third and fourth sources respectively: they are the subject of discussion and argument so as to determine their exact field and limits of application. This has led some *'ulamā'* to consider these two juridical instruments as a part of *al-ijtihād* which is so understood to be the third global source: they call *ijmā'*, *ijtihād jamā'ī* (collective *ijtihād*) and *qiyās*, *ijtihād fardī* (individual *ijtihād*). See 'Alī Ḥassab-Allāh, *Uṣūl al-Tashrī' al-Islāmī* (Roots of Islamic Jurisprudence), (Dār al-Ma'ārif, le Caire, 1985), Chapter 3. This is in accordance with the position of the four *'ulamā'* who are known to be the historical references of the major *Sunnī* schools of thought existing today; they permanently referred their students to the Qur'ān and the *Sunna*, considering them as the exclusive sources and parameters for Islamic judgement. Many of their statements have been recorded, such as: "If I have made a ruling which contradicts God's Book or the Messenger's *ḥadīth*, reject my ruling" said by Abū Ḥanīfa. Mālik once stated: "Verily I am only a man, I err and am at times correct; so thoroughly investigate my opinions, then take whatever agrees with the Book and the *Sunna*, and reject whatever contradicts them." Ibn Ḥanbal emphasised the same: "Do not blindly follow my rulings, those of Mālik, ash-Shāfi'ī, al-Awzā'ī, or ath-Thawrī. Take (your rulings) from whence they took theirs," i.e. the Qur'ān and the *Sunna*. These statements make it clear that the Qur'ān and the *Sunna* were their principal sources and, at the same time, they prevent us from blindly following the *'ulamā'* and their rulings (*taqlīd*). For a good summary of this issue, see Abū Amina Bilal Philips, *The Evolution of Fiqh, Islamic Law and Madhhab* (Tawheed Publications, Riyadh, 1990), pp. 117–28.

8 The rulings concerning the field of worship (*'ibādāt*) within Islamic Law (*Fiqh*) are, of course, mostly determined and fixed. It is in the field of *al-mu'āmalāt* (social affairs) that the permanent work of adaptation has to be

done in order to formulate Islamic answers to new problems, for example on the economics, technology, medicine and the like.

9 Qur'ān 16: 116.

10 Qur'ān 2: 168–9. "*To attribute unto God something of which you have no knowledge*" refers, according to some commentators, to "an arbitrary attribution to God of commandments or prohibitions of what has been clearly ordained by Him" (Zamakhsharī). See Muḥammad Asad, *The Message of the Qur'ān* (Dār al-Andalus, Gibraltar, 1980), p. 34.

11 Qur'ān 2: 29.

12 Qur'ān 31: 20.

13 *Ḥadīth* (Dāraqutnī, Tirmidhī, Ibn Māja and Ḥākim).

14 Qur'ān 2: 35–7.

15 Qur'ān 2: 286.

16 Qur'ān 17: 15.

17 Qur'ān 67: 2.

18 This relates to social affairs (*mu'āmalāt*): as regards codified worship (*'ibādāt*), the rule is exactly the opposite: what is not clearly prescribed is forbidden.

19 Yūsuf al-Qarḍāwī, *Al-Ḥalāl wal-Ḥarām* (Cairo, 1991), 20th edition, pp. 19–22. See also Sa'īd Ramaḍān, *Islamic Law, Its Scope and Equity* (Geneva, 1970), 2nd edition, pp. 64–73.

20 *Ḥadīth* (Bukhārī and Muslim).

21 Using this concept, as also other elements of the Islamic Faith, it becomes easy to understand that there is no idea of original sin in the Islamic reference.

22 In Arabic, *al-aḥkām at-taklīfiyya*.

23 Qur'ān 24: 41–4.

24 Qur'ān 17: 44.

25 Qur'ān 7: 172.

26 Qur'ān 30: 30.

27 *Ḥadīth* (Bukhārī and Muslim).

28 Qur'ān 2: 187.

29 Qur'ān 2: 284.

30 *Ḥadīth* (Bukhārī and Muslim). The Prophet, with this statement, confirmed the saying of Salmān Abū Dardā': "You have duties towards God, you have duties towards yourself, you have duties towards your wife: give everyone his own." There are other versions of these *aḥādīth* in Bukhārī and Muslim.

31 Literally, "pens have been lifted". *Ḥadīth* (Bukhārī and Muslim).

32 Qur'ān 2: 43.

33 Qur'ān 17: 32.

34 There are, of course, many other types of formulations which lead to their classification into these two types.

35 Qur'ān 2: 185.

36 The *'ulamā'* of *uṣūl al-fiqh* and the *fuqahā'* themselves must study these kinds of variations in the moral value of an act depending on the context: for instance, in certain circumstances, an act previously considered as permitted, *mubāḥ*, could become *makrūh*, reprehensible, or even *ḥarām*, forbidden. This could happen, of course, in the opposite sense: a forbidden action could become permitted, *mubāḥ*, or *mustaḥab*, or even *wājib*. With for instance, the obligation of eating pork in a period of starvation if it avoids death.

37 In this respect, the *fuqahā'* of *al-uṣūl* have formulated a principle: What leads to prohibition is prohibited.
38 We have said above that the *Sunna* sometimes stipulates juridical rulings which are not in the Qur'ān. This is very rare and, moreover, these few rulings do not go outside the general frame or direction prescribed by the Qur'ān.
39 Qur'ān 4: 48.
40 Ash-Shāfi'ī, *al-Um* (Al-Amiriyya, Cairo, 7 Volumes, 1926), Vol. 7, p. 317.
41 See al-Qarḍāwī, *Al-Ḥalāl wal-Ḥarām*, op. cit., pp. 24–5.
42 *Ḥadīth* (Muslim, Aḥmad and Abū Dāwūd).
43 Qur'ān 5: 87–8.
44 Qur'ān 6: 119.
45 Qur'ān 16: 88.
46 Qur'ān 5: 101–2.
47 See this expression already quoted, Qur'ān 5: 3.
48 *Ḥadīth* (Dāraqutnī, Tirmidhī, Ibn Māja and Ḥākim).
49 See Muḥammad Iqbāl, *The Reconstruction of Religious Thought in Islam* (New Delhi, 1990). Chapter Six, 'The Principle of Movement in the Structure of Islam', addresses *ijtihād*.
50 Ibn Ḥazm – and his school of thought the *Ẓāhirī* – went far in this way, saying that Islamic Law is no more than the clear injunctions of the evident (*ẓāhir*) meaning of the Qur'ānic and Prophetic words. Even if scholars have to stipulate specific or additional legislation – which is natural and necessary due to the evolution of time – it must be clear that they are not part of the *Sharī'a*, which is exclusively composed of the Qur'ān and the authentic *Sunna*. This point of view is interesting for it makes clear the difference between the sources, bearing absolute teaching and rulings, and the human contribution, always necessary and imperative, but yet temporary, limited, and, above all, human and subject to error. See Ibn Ḥazm, *al-Muḥallā* (Cairo, 1975), Vol. I, p. 56 ff.
51 *Istiṣlāḥ* is the tenth form of the root *ṣa-lu-ḥa*, which is the same as *maṣlaḥa*.
52 Abū Hāmid al-Ghazālī, *al-Mustaṣfā min 'Ilm al-Uṣūl* (Muthanna, Baghdad, 1970).
53 See *Al-Mustaṣfā min 'Ilm al-Uṣūl*, Volume I, pp. 286–7. See also the interesting book written by Muhammad Khalid Masud, *Shatibi's Philosophy of Islamic Law* (Islamic Research Institute, Islamabad, 1995), pp. 139–40.
54 Apart from the *'ulamā'* of the *Ẓāhirī* school who did not recognise *per se* the concept of *maqāṣid*.
55 *Al-Maṣāliḥ aḍ-ḍarūriyyāt* are those on which the lives of people depend as well as the protection of their meaning as worshippers of God.
56 *Al-Maṣāliḥ al-ḥājiyyāt* are those which deal with hard situations. We find in this field the rules concerning, for instance, the sick, the elderly or the concessions (*rukhas*) in Prayer, fasting and so on.
57 *Al-Maṣāliḥ al-taḥsīniyyāt* are concerned, for example, with the observance of cleanliness and moral virtues which permit an improvement in worship and a way of reaching what is desirable.
58 This was the opinion of Ibn Ḥazm for whom there was no need to speak of *istiṣlāḥ* for the *Sharī'a* itself and all its rulings are based on *maṣaliḥ* which are both the content and the aim of the Revealed Laws.

59 Ash-Shāṭibī explains, in the course of his study *al-I'tiṣām*, that the two sources of Islam are the Qur'ān and the *Sunna* whose rulings are founded on *maṣlaḥa* (he agrees on this point with Ibn Ḥazm) but it is clear that we have to refer to our reason when the evidence of the texts are missing (this is in fact, according to ash-Shāṭibī, what has been done through *ijmā'* or *qiyās*). Thus, when the text remains silent, the *maṣlaḥa* is the reference and acts as an independent source in light of the Qur'ān and the *Sunna*.

60 This is the opinion of al-Ghazālī who, in subordinating the method of reasoning by *maṣlaḥa* to *qiyās*, linked the sources in order to avoid a purely rational formulation far from abiding by the sources.

61 Subḥī Rajab Mahmassānī, *Falsafah at-Tashri' fil-Islam* (E.J. Brill, Leiden, 1961), p. 117. Quoted by Mohammad Hashim Kamali, *Principles of Islamic Jurisprudence* (Cambridge, UK, 1991), p. 276.

62 This is the case when some *'ulamā'* have tried to justify usury and bank interest (*ribā*) in the name of public interest. There is no *maṣlaḥa mursala* here for the evidences from the Qur'ān (*qaṭ'ī ath-thubūt wa qaṭ'ī ad-dalāla*) and the *Sunna* (*ẓanni ath-thubūt wa qaṭ'ī ad-dalāla*) are clear and indisputable.

63 There are many other secondary conditions (as for the *maṣlaḥa* to be rational – *ma'qula* – for Mālik or essential – *ḍarūriyya* – for al-Ghazālī, etc.). For more details and in-depth studies, see the specialised books already mentioned of ash-Shāṭibī (*al-I'tiṣām*) Khallāf, Ḥassab-Allāh and Kamali.

64 Yūsuf al-Qarḍāwī, *al-Ijtihād al-Mu'āṣir, Bayn al-Inḍibāṭ wal-Infirāṭ* (Dar al-Tawzī' wan-Nashr al-Islamiyyāt, 1993), pp. 66–7.

65 Qur'ān 7: 157.

66 Qur'ān 10: 57.

67 Qur'ān 2: 219.

68 Ibn al-Qayyim al-Jawziyya, *I'lām al-Muwaqqi'īn 'an Rabb al-'Ālamīn* (Cairo, nd) ,Vol. 3, p. 1.

69 We will discuss the different levels of clarity in the next section relating to the question of *ijtihād*.

70 The *'ulamā'* are in agreement that there is no *ijtihād* (hence, no *maṣlaḥa, istiṣlāḥ, qiyās, istiḥsān* and no need for *ijmā'*) in respect of *'ibādāt* (devotional matters) whose prescriptions and modes are known through Revelation and have to be implemented as they have been revealed to and taught and explained by the Prophet. Similarly, when there exist clear and specified injunctions within the sources (only a few prescriptions are of this nature), they must be applied (without neglecting, of course, the overview of Islamic jurisprudence's objectives and the social situation as we are experiencing it).

71 Qur'ān 2: 185.

72 Scholars who study the principles of Islamic jurisprudence.

73 Yūsuf al-Qarḍāwī, *al-Ijtihād al-Mu'āṣir, Bayn al-Inḍibāṭ wal-Infirāṭ*, op. cit., pp. 68–9.

74 See Part I above and more especially the section "The Birth of Islamic Sciences".

75 Muhammad Khalid Masud, *Shatibi's Philosophy of Islamic Law*, op. cit. p. 367.

76 According to the classification made by the *'ulamā' al-ḥadīth, al-ḥadīth al-mutawātir* is of the highest authenticity. One of the conditions of its

acceptability as *mutawaṭir* is to have numerous transmitters at each level of its chain of transmission (there are different opinions concerning the required number). Aṣ-Ṣuyūṭī said "at least ten". See Aṣ-Ṣuyūṭī, *Tadrīb ar-Rāwī fi Sharḥ Taqrīb an-Nawawī*, ed. Al-Latīf (Cairo, 1960) and Mahmūd at-Taḥḥān, *Taysīr Muṣṭalaḥ al-Ḥadīth* (Beirut, 1985). There are only a few *aḥādīth* of this nature considered as *qaṭ'ī ath-thubūt*: the content, moreover, must be completely clear to avoid *ijtihād*.

77 Muhammad Khalid Masud, *Shatibi's Philosophy of Islamic Law*, op. cit. p. 366.

78 Muhammad Hamidullah, *The Emergence of Islam*, edited and translated by Afzal Iqbal (Islamic Research Institute, Islamabad, 1993), p. 97.

79 There are different opinions among the *'ulamā'* regarding the number of such *āyāt* and *aḥādīth*. For instance, al-Ghazālī or Ibn al-'Arabī counted 500 verses whereas 'Abd al-Wahhāb Khallāf counted about 228. Al-Shawkānī, however, was of the opinion that such calculations are not definitive for some verses could be interpreted differently according to the *'ālim* or the context. The same statement could be made concerning the *aḥādīth al-aḥkām* even though Ibn Ḥanbal was supposed to have said that there are about 1,200 *aḥādīth* of this category. See al-Shawkānī, *al-Qawl al-Mufīd fil-Ijtihād wat-Taqlīd* (Cairo, 1975), Chapter Two and 'Abd al-Wahhāb Khallāf, *'Ilm Uṣūl al-Fiqh*, 7th ed. (Cairo, 1956), pp. 34–5.

80 Many other detailed classifications within the field of *ijtihād* exist but such a study is beyond the scope of our presentation. They are known by specialists of *uṣūl al-fiqh* and are the subject of much argument and controversy between the *'ulamā'*. This is the case, for instance, with the problem of the divisibility of *ijtihād* (*tajzi'a*) about which many pages of argumentation have been written. It is a very theoretical, and in fact secondary, issue. We will discuss the question of *ijtihād fardī* (individual) and *jamā'ī* (collective) below.

81 Ash-Shāṭibī, *al-Muwāfaqāt fī Uṣūl al-Sharī'a* (Dār al-Ma'rifat, Lebanon, new edition, 1996), Vol. 4, the Chapter on 'Conditions of Ijtihād', p. 477 ff.

82 This is how ash-Shāṭibī himself describes the second quality: after saying that the first is the objective, he adds "the second (is) the instrument". Cf. ibid. p. 478.

83 Ash-Shāṭibī, for instance, was very demanding in this field: he thought that a person who did not possess a deep knowledge of the Arabic language could not reach the true degree of *ijtihād*. Cf. *al-Muwāfaqāt fī Uṣūl al-Sharī'a*, op. cit., Vol. 4, p. 590 ff.

84 That recognition should be both by other scholars and the Muslim community.

85 The *'ulamā'* have prescribed different conditions for the *mujtahid muṭlaq* (absolute) and the *mujtahid muqayyad* (limited) who infer rulings within the framework of a specific school of law. The conditions are, of course, less demanding for the latter and knowledge of the rules of inference linked to the school of law is additional.

86 For a detailed analysis of historical causes, see Muḥammad Iqbāl, *The Reconstruction of Islamic Thought* (Ashraf, Lahore, 1951), pp. 149–52.

87 We shall discuss this point below when examining the conditions relating to contemporary *ijtihād*.

88 Ash-Shāṭibī, *al-Muwāfaqāt fī Uṣūl al-Sharī'a*, op. cit., Vol. 4, pp. 595–602.

89 The *'ulamā'* have very often used the two terms *mujtahid* and *muftī* synonymously. Nevertheless, these two functions are not exactly of the same nature, nor of the same degree, even though their respective fields overlap. The *mujtahid* works on the sources and tries to infer and deduce legal rulings, whereas the *muftī* has to provide his interlocutor – be it an individual or a community – with specific answers and, as such, he works downstream from the *mujtahid*. He must possess most of the qualities we have mentioned above except if his *fatāwā* concern some specific topics (*juz'ī*) – we will discuss below the different degrees of *fatāwā*.

90 In all the explanations to come, ash-Shāṭibī classes the *muftī* as *mujtahid* and vice versa.

91 Ash-Shāṭibī, *al-Muwāfaqāt fī Uṣūl al-Sharī'a*, op. cit., Vol. 4, pp. 595–6.

92 Qur'ān 21: 79.

93 Ash-Shāfi'ī, *ar-Risāla*, p. 128.

94 Quoted by Muḥammad 'Imāra, *al-Imām Mūhammad Abduh, Mujaddid ad-Dunya bi Tajdīd ad-Dīn* (Dar ash-Shurūq, Cairo, second edition, 1988), pp. 55–6. Muhammad 'Abduh was still a member of the Administrative Council of al-Azhar when he made this statement.

95 The list could be longer, of course, but we mention here only the most well-known *'ulamā'* who called for reform having been educated at al-Azhar.

96 Yūsuf al-Qarḍāwī, *al-Ijtihād al-Mu'āṣir, Bayn al-Inḍibāṭ wal-Infirāṭ*, op. cit.

97 *Ijtihād tarjīhī intiqā'ī.*

98 Yūsuf al-Qarḍāwī, *al-Ijtihād al-Mu'āṣir, Bayn al-Indibāṭ wal-Infirāṭ*, op. cit., p. 20.

99 *Ijtihād ibdā'ī inshā'ī.*

100 Yūsuf al-Qarḍāwī, *al-Ijtihād al-Mu'āṣir, Bayn al-Indibāṭ wal-Infirāṭ*, op. cit., p. 34.

101 Al-Qarḍāwī even speaks about *iḥrām* (the state of purification of those who are going to perform the lesser – *'Umra* – and the greater – *Ḥajj* – Pilgrimage). Quoting ash-Shaykh 'Abd Allah Ibn Zayd al-Maḥmūd, Chairman of the Islamic Courts in Qatar, who stated that travellers by plane are allowed to be in a state of *iḥrām* from Jeddah and that it is not necessary to be so from the departure town or in the plane, Al-Qarḍāwī adds that he has found some *'ulamā'* of the Mālikī school of law who permitted the delay of *iḥrām* for pilgrims arriving by boat. See ibid., p. 35.

102 Yūsuf al-Qarḍāwī, op. cit., pp. 97–9. The International Organisation of Islamic Medicine, with its "Code of Islamic Ethics" (*ad-Dustūr al-Islamiyya lil-Mihna at-Ṭibbiyya*), arrives at the same conclusion concerning medical practice: "The Medical Profession has the right – and owes the duty – of effective participation in the formulation and issuing of religious verdicts concerning the lawfulness or otherwise of unprecedented outcomes of current and future advances in biological science. The verdict should be reached together with Muslim specialists in jurisprudence and Muslim specialists in biosciences. Single-sided opinions have always suffered from

a lack of comprehension of technical or legal aspects." International Organisation of Islamic Medicine, Kuwait Document, First International Conference on Islamic Medicine, January 1981.

103 Numerous *'ulamā'* – from the Arab world and from Europe – attended the constitutive meeting of this Council on 30th March 1997. Shaykh Yūsuf al-Qarḍāwī, unanimously elected President, and Shaykh Muḥammad Sa'īd Bazankshī, General Secretary, along with about 30 other *'ulamā'*, will try to give legal responses to some specific questions Muslims living in Europe are facing.

104 There were of course a lot of other designations, such as *dār al-amn* (the abode of security) or *dār al-'ahd* (the abode of contract), which squared with the specific state of relations between the Islamic government and its neighbouring countries. Still, the two antithetical appellations *dār al-Islām* and *dār al-ḥarb* were to be the more widely used and known among both the *'ulamā'* and the average populace. We shall discuss their meaning, scope and current relevance below.

105 Especially in time of crisis when some secondary religious questions seem to be considered as a matter of life or death ... Some, for example, make a big issue of *ḥalāl* food while they still do not perform Prayer. Others are totally absorbed in very detailed issues of *Fiqh* – and sometimes harshly sectarian in their opinion – as if nothing else was important within the Muslim community they are living in.

106 In light of our analysis, and while remaining faithful to the principles set forth above, we will have to go so far as to conceive differentiated implementations of *fiqh* within Europe itself, according to the countries and their respective constitutions. There will of course be similarities over most questions, but specific *fatāwā* will necessarily be stipulated when, for instance, one particular point of law is present in one country but not in another (this may concern marriage, food, animal slaughter, military service or any other point of detail).

107 We shall come back to this in Part Two.

108 This is another principle of *uṣūl*: constraint must be determined to its exact measure.

# Part Two

# Sensitive Questions

## Belonging, Identity, Citizenship

### Introduction

#### *1. Difficulties*

A dual phenomena is observable within the Muslim community today: first, the difficulties linked with immigration (for the first generation) have provoked the kind of reactive attitude discussed in Part I. This has brought about, along with a natural desire to protect the Muslim identity, a tendency to exaggerate the importance of some issues which face Muslims in the West. Food, mosques, cemeteries and very detailed points of *Fiqh* have occupied many peoples' minds and have displaced the fundamentals of Islam and its essential teachings which go beyond the problems and contingencies of a specific moment and place in human history. Second, the European perception of this new presence – often considered as a *problem* – has been assimilated into Muslim minds. It is as if – through the prism of current social difficulties in the West, modern sociological analysis and the media – they have been colonised by the idea, the *obvious* fact, the *indisputable* evidence that Islam *is* a problem in the West and that Muslims *have* problems with progress, democracy and modernity. Thus, in upholding this vision, voluntarily or not, there are but two possible choices left: becoming the least visible possible in order not to let any Islamic feature appear in our day-to-day life, or spending our whole time in explaining *what Islam is not* and/or conscientiously answering all criticisms about the obvious Islamic discrimination against women, the inherent violence of *jihād*, the inhuman laws of the *Sharīʿa*, the well-known anti-democratic tendency of Islam, and so forth. In so doing, the Muslims have often developed a perverted concept of themselves and, consequently, of the Islamic way of life. They have almost forgotten what Islam is *in itself*, what its fundamental and universal Message is, what the Muslim contribution to human civilisation over the course of history has been (within law, science and philosophy): so how can they possibly imagine that they have *something* to offer the West? How can they hope to take an *active* part in European societies and bring about a *positive* influence through peaceful and respectful *coexistence*? Difficult indeed then, is the equation of the Muslim presence in Europe: confined to such considerations Islam is, and will remain, a problem, hence the conclusion that less Islam means less problems. The way forward in this scenario is to become discreet, invisible, or *Muslims without Islam*.

Some changes have, however, occurred over the last 10 to 15 years within the Muslim community and, as we have said, this is due in great part to the growth of second and third generations of Muslims born in the West. Many of these want to re-affirm their identity and live according to Islamic teachings. After a difficult childhood, they have re-discovered their origins as well as their Religion. This process is of great importance in the West and in almost all Western countries there exists a consistent trend among young Muslims towards an affirmation of their Islamic identity and a profound revival of its spirituality and practice. Contrary to widely held beliefs, this phenomenon is not exclusively an expression of opposition to the West but it happens that this re-discovery is a positive affirmation of self-confidence among young Muslims. As such it is a determining factor for the building of the Muslims' future in Europe. There is another aspect which also deserves to be brought to the fore, that is that the youth are coming back to an Islam which is purified from the accidents of its traditional reading. For the more educated, it is no more an Islam of the Moroccan, Algerian or Pakistani countryside but a return to the basics of Islamic teachings through an *immediate* contact with the sources, the Qur'ān and the *Sunna*. This is a fundamental development for it sets the seal on the break-up between, on the one hand, Islam and its actualisation in North Africa or Asia and, on the other, the way it should be thought, adapted and lived in the West. Islam in the West – although its fundamental principles must be known to rely on the Qur'ān and the *Sunna* – should have a specific and appropriate actualisation and this is the message young and not so young Muslims are clearly conveying. If there actually is a will – and this does exist within the Muslim community – to put an end to negative and reactive postures, this clearly means that European Muslims, along with the *'ulamā'*, must face their new reality with a constructive and determined state of mind. This to provide themselves with both a clear direction and a set of plain Islamic rulings allowing them to promote a balanced Islamic identity in the West, one which is confident and part of the future of these societies.

Notwithstanding these improvements, the situation is complex and the picture is not nearly so positive. The appearance of Muslim youth in the Western landscape has also given birth to a new and problematic attitude. Far from their countries of origin, being Muslims in a non-Muslim land, and moreover one which is industrialised, these teenagers, students and now adults, express both an intense desire to be Muslims and a profound need for plain and appropriate Islamic answers and rulings. Because of their background – often they have not had an official religious education and do not speak Arabic – they develop the feeling that they are unable to contribute to the elaboration of the Muslim identity in Europe, thinking, erroneously, that the only appropriate answer is the legal one as if *Fiqh* alone can solve all their problems. We are witnessing, among young European Muslims, the unhealthy development of a complex whereby they discredit themselves and think that the right responses should come from abroad, from great *'ulamā'* residing in Islamic countries.

Some leaders of Muslim organisations, from the first generation or newly arrived as students or political refugees, reinforce the impression that they do not have the ability to formulate Islamic rulings and, consequently, to decide which methodology should be used within the European context. This statement, explicitly or implicitly conveyed, brings about a double simplification and distortion: first, it makes the youth believe that Islamic identity is confined within cold Islamic rulings defining what is lawful and unlawful (*al-ḥalāl wa al-ḥarām*) and this is a misconception. Second, it leads to an infantile and childish process within which the young generations are imprisoned without being able to turn to good advantage what they have experienced by growing and living in a European society, and this is nothing less than a guilty negligence.

This phenomenon is complex and pernicious. If it is clear that Islamic rulings have to be stipulated by a competent *mujtahid*, this should not mean that the rest of the community has nothing to say. Quite the opposite, the formulation of both an Islamic legal frame and a Muslim European identity should be a dialectical process between the community and the *mujtahidīn* in order for the latter to formulate appropriate legal answers to the questions addressed to them in light of their new environment. Furthermore, identity is not just-a-set-of-rulings for, fundamentally, it is a mixture of feelings, emotions, state of mind, cultures, and customs. To approach, understand, and grasp the very essence of an *identity* it is necessary to live it, to live in it, to be part of it and, thus, any *ʿālim* who has to stipulate specific rulings for Muslims in the West should take advantage of the contributions made by many Muslims living there, i.e. they should listen to their questions and problems as they themselves convey them. The participation of the youth in this process is, without doubt, of great importance and, armed with their experience and comprehension of the European environment from within, they ought to formulate appropriate questions so as to permit the *ʿulamāʾ* to give more accurate responses. More than any other group they should think through the different steps of a genuine application of Islamic teaching in view of the Western context and elaborate the content of an overall Islamic education which fits their original situation. Thus, the contribution of Muslims living in the West, especially our youth, is without comparison. Unfortunately, we are still far from reaching such a level; the enriching debate between the Western Muslim community and the *ʿulamāʾ* is still a hope but, here also, things are moving slowly.

## 2. *Prospects*

We are going through both difficult and agitated times. After about 40 years of a new kind of Muslim presence in Europe this is in fact a natural evolution as it is normal to witness some tension among both the indigenous Europeans and the Muslims for positive coexistence needs mutual knowledge and respect, that is to say time and patience.

For the time being, the Muslims must define for themselves which are the essential teachings of Islam and express, delimit and classify which steps are to be followed to apply these teachings. When the social, political and economic problems have such a negative impact on people's lives, it is important to remind ourselves what the foundations of Islam are and not allow ourselves to be drawn into explaining Islam in the tainted light of this difficult environment.

In the West or in the East, in the North or in the South, the essential teaching of Islam is and remains Faith in One God (*tawḥīd*) and in His Messengers and the successive Revelations (*ar-rasā'il as-samawiyya*) ending with Muḥammad and the Qur'ān. Muslims believe that there is a Life after this life and that they will be called to account by God. The Islamic Message is, as that of other Religions, a Message of great and profound spirituality. This is, in fact, what the Muslims want to live by and protect. This spirituality is based on some rules which have to be respected: in the first rank, we find the four practical pillars of Islam: Prayer, the payment of *zakāt*, fasting and Pilgrimage. To perform these codified acts of worship one must live in a safe area, one where freedom of worship is guaranteed and assured. This is the first and inescapable step in any reflection on Islam and Muslims: the Oneness of God, spirituality, worship, respect for such beliefs and the necessary means to perform religious duties with dignity is what Muslims require in their new environments.

Notwithstanding this, there are a number of other issues which should be tackled and discussed in the debate about the Muslim presence in Europe. To give a clear answer about the Islamic legality and conditions for staying in a non-Islamic society is, of course, of great importance but it is still not sufficient: it is also necessary to determine what Muslims' responsibilities and rights towards their new societies are. For, as soon as their Religion is respected and their freedom assured, they become part of society and are asked to act in accordance with the host countries' constitution and law. This has to be clarified for Muslims living in the West: i.e. what does it mean to be part of a Western society? Is there a limit or an exception to respect for the law and the constitution? Is there any discrepancy between respecting Western laws and being faithful to the teachings of the Qur'ān and the *Sunna*? Can a Muslim be a true and trustworthy citizen of a European country or has he or she simply the right to apply for Western nationality? What about schools and education – religious and moral as well as secular and scientific? The present list should be lengthened with other fundamental questions regarding social and economic problems, technology, ethics, culture, sport, and so on.

It would be too difficult to discuss all these subjects in-depth in the present research but at least it is necessary to reflect on these issues which have frequently arisen over the last ten years.

# I

# Where Are We?

## A. Facts and Figures

Few people would have been able to predict, before the Second World War, what would happen during the second half of the century. In fact, we have witnessed much disruption in Europe whereby the social, political, economic, and cultural landscape is no longer the same. The reconstruction of Europe, after long years of war, required a great many cheap labour forces. This, in turn, brought about the first waves of immigration into "Old Europe", especially to Britain and France, and then to Germany (during the 1950s) and other countries.

These waves, followed by others, were to constitute the bulk of the immigrant populations in Western countries. If there was a steady flow of Italian and Spanish workers, the percentage of Muslim Asian (in the case of Britain), North African (in France) or Turks (in Germany) was also important and in less than 15 years (between 1945 and 1960) one could say that Muslim groups or communities had already appeared, at least in the three European countries identified above. This so-called economic immigration was not to stop until the beginning of the 1970s when the need for additional workers dwindled to almost nothing and the European economy showed its first signs of weakness and functional destructuring.

Between 1950 and 1970, the number of Muslim residents in European countries had trebled. Thus, it was no longer a question of a few thousand Muslims that the host nations were having to deal with but rather several hundreds of thousands of Muslims living within their boundaries. Families were established, children were born and the old intention of going back home had become little more than a remote hope. During the 1970s and 1980s a change in the evolution of the Muslim mentality meant that increasingly people believed that their future should be thought and built in the West. Aware of this new situation and pushed by the will to protect their identity, some Muslims began to organise their communities, building more mosques and founding Islamic organisations in order to offer the average person places to pray, gather, learn, and participate in activities, etc.

The situation now pertaining in the 1990s was inconceivable a few decades ago: today, there are between 12 and 15 million Muslims in Western Europe and they are very much part of society – many have taken European nationality – and consequently more visible, due partly to the nature of Islamic worship as also the diverse activities of their organisations. Added to this is the fact that there are numerous converts to Islam who, along with the young generations of Muslims who have now become European, are at home in Europe: they are European citizens; *European and Muslim.*

At least five objective facts can be brought to the fore regarding the reality of the Muslim presence in Europe:

1. There is a revival of Islamic spirituality and practice as well as a feeling of belonging to a religious community amongst a great many young Muslims either born or living in Europe.

2. The number of indigenous European Muslims is increasing either through conversion to Islam or through birth.

3. The number of places of worship have multiplied by four or five times but they are still insufficient and some mosques remain as cellars or warehouses.

4. The number of Islamic organisations in Europe is increasing daily. Some countries (such as France, Britain or Germany) have already recorded more than a thousand official organisations (mosques, centres or diverse Islamic institutions). This same phenomenon is, however, noticeable throughout Europe.

5. At least 80% of Muslims do not practise their religion regularly and do not, for example, perform their daily Prayers. Less than 40% attend the Friday gathering at the mosque. About 70%, however, do fast during the sacred month of Ramaḍān.

This data, roughly reported here, gives us an idea of the reality we are facing in Europe. Furthermore, it is sufficient for us to draw together some fundamental comments and assessments of the current situation of Muslims in Europe. In this respect, three observations deserve pointing out:

1. The fact that after more than 40 years of presence in Europe the Muslims are generally allowed to practise their Religion in peace, to build mosques (even if they sometimes have to face administrative hindrances) and to found Islamic organisations is clear evidence that the various European constitutions and laws respect Islam as a Religion and Muslims as Believers who have the right, as others, to enjoy freedom of worship. This is an indisputable fact and the increasing number of mosques and Islamic centres or institutions supports this assertion.
2. The great majority of Muslims in Europe live in an atmosphere of *security* and *peace* regarding religious matters. We do not have to confuse social, economic and political problems such as unemployment, poverty, exclusion and increases in racism shared by the whole population with what is actually a specific religious discrimination. Occasionally, on a specific issue, one can identify a discriminating decision or a tendentious way of reading the law,[1] but by and large there is no European constitution which is anti-Islamic *per se*. Numerous Muslims have appealed to the law after receiving unfair treatment and very often such cases are decided in their favour. Thus, Muslims have the right to practise, to found organisations, to appeal to the law and, moreover, to decide the appropriate way of solving the problems their religious community is facing.

3. The European context – and generally life in an industrialised and modern society – makes religious duties difficult to perform and respect. Religion, spirituality or any manifestation of Faith have almost completely disappeared from the public face. Many women and men may believe in God but this belief is often passive, having little real effect on their busy lives which are full of work, entertainment and the like. Furthermore, technological developments leave little place for religious involvement and even less for worship and practice. This is a fact for Jews, Christians and Muslims alike: even if there is a visible revival among our youth, or a sincere attachment to some sacred period such as the month of Ramaḍān, harsh reality nonetheless does not allow us to keep alive any kind of illusion. In light of this reality, it appears that Muslims however involved in Islamic institutions have to provide their community with education, courses, lectures and all other kinds of activities which will help people remember their Religion and their duties. Our two previous observations show that there is no legal or official hindrance in Europe preventing Muslims from working in this way. It is quite the contrary and if one takes into account and recognises that during the first wave of immigration when the situation was difficult, one also has to be fair enough to admit that the possibilities offered in Europe to carry out and achieve Islamic works – appropriate to the needs of the community – are abundant. Especially when one views this proportionately to the real commitment of the Muslims, men and women alike. There is *peace* and *security* regarding Religion, as we have said, but the Muslims, themselves, do not fulfil their common duties (*farḍ kifāya*) to improve the situation as they have been commanded.

This is, in fact, the European context and we have to take it into account *as it is*, for it is a new reality which requires an appropriate assessment if we want to formulate adequate Islamic concepts and rulings. Millions of Muslims live in Europe, enjoying, for the great majority of them, freedom of worship, organising themselves and acting within the limits of the various constitutions which, also, protect their rights. Notwithstanding this, millions of Muslims have lost contact with either their Religion or their community, and sometimes both. So, what can we call the new context? What is the West in general, and Europe in particular in light of Islamic references? Are the old concepts chosen by our great *'ulamā'* still fit for our situation? Are the antithetic, and bi-polar, appellations *dār al-Islām* and *dār al-ḥarb* appropriate when the world has become a village, with a very complex geo-political configuration and multi-polar areas of power and influence? To answer these questions – which in fact are one, namely *where are we?* – from an Islamic point of view is imperative. This will make clear whether Muslims in Europe have to consider themselves as on foreign soil, as aliens, governed by constraints with only the duty to protect themselves from the aggressive environment or, on the contrary, whether they must be a part of these countries, at home, as true citizens who, within the limits of the laws, should do their best to provide their society with more justice and solidarity, values which are in accordance with the requirements of their Faith, their conscience and their citizenship.

## B. Old Concepts

*Dār al-Islām* and *dār al-ḥarb* are two concepts which cannot be found either in the Qur'ān or in the *Sunna*. They actually do not pertain to the fundamental sources of Islam whose principles are presented for the whole world (*lil-'ālamīn*), over all time and beyond any geographical limitation.

It was the *'ulamā'* who, during the first three centuries of Islam, by considering the state of the world – its geographical divisions, the powers in place through religious belonging and influence as well as the moving game of alliances – started to classify and define the different spaces in and around them. This process was necessary for at least two reasons: first, by marking out the Islamic territories, the *'ulamā'* were able to point out what the essential conditions making a space or a nation Islamic were and what the rulings determining the political and strategic relations with other nations or empires were. Second, it allowed them to establish a clear distinction, as regards legal issues, between the situation of Muslims living inside the Islamic world and those living abroad or those who travelled often such as traders (and who thus required specific rulings).

Studying the Prophet's attitude after the Peace of Ḥudaybiyya (*Sulḥ al-Ḥudaybiyya*), his sending of numerous messengers to kings over the subsequent five years[2] as well as his behaviour with neighbouring countries, classical scholars came to the conclusion that as regards this very specific issue four elements were to be taken into consideration:

1. The population living in the country.
2. The proprietary of the land.
3. The nature of the government.
4. The laws governing the country.

The Prophet – considering himself, in light of Revelation, as a Messenger for the whole world – sent, according to Ibn Hishām, at least nine delegates (over this five-year period) to the people of neighbouring countries who knew nothing about Islam, or whose leaders were ignorant of the reality of the new Religion and who based their rulings on unfair legislation. In two well-known cases the attitude of the leaders towards the Prophet's messengers brought about war (which was neither the objective of these delegations nor the rule for relations with neighbouring nations). The first was against the Byzantines because the Prophet's messenger, Ḥārith ibn 'Umayr, was killed by 'Amr al-Ghassānī, one of the Ministers of the Empire, and the second against the Persians when their chief tore the Qur'ān into pieces in front of the messenger and instructed some of his soldiers to go and bring him back "this Muḥammad alive". Both these reactions were understood as declarations of war. In the majority of other cases, however, the Message was diffused without war nor constraint. The priority was clearly to make the Message of Islam reach the general populace. The leaders, during this era, were the immediate means of fulfilling this objective for Islam is a Message for people before being a guidance addressed to rulers.

Basing their reflections on these data, the *ʿulamāʾ* tried to infer some principles as well as distinguish and categorise what the features of the Islamic space or country were as compared to those of the non-Islamic. From the outset and considering the reality they faced, their overall concept of the world could not have been much different than this bi-polarity. Thus, prior to any kind of contextualised definition, the first fundamental rule with respect to political relations between Muslims and non-Muslims was considered, after examining the Prophet's actions, *to be a state of peace and not a state of war*. The second is that the Prophet *was above all interested in addressing people* and not taking over power. Tradition shows that he always fought rulers because of their killings, betrayals or injustices and that he never fought a population because they refused to convert to Islam. He wanted the latter to choose, with full knowledge of what Islam was, for themselves. Thereafter, he accepted their choice and gave them the right to stay where they were, to practise their Religion and to pay a tax (*jizya*) in return for State protection.

It still remained, however, for the *ʿulamāʾ* to define the two entities *dār al-Islām* and *dār al-ḥarb* in order that Muslims have a clear picture of the geo-political reality of their era. Numerous definitions were proposed by the *ʿulamāʾ*, especially within the four major Sunni schools of law. It is impossible to present here a detailed study of their respective works but it is nonetheless useful to summarise them as follows:

1. *Dār al-Islām* (the abode of Islam):[3] taking into account two of the four elements mentioned above, ad-Dusūqī, from the Mālikī school of law, stated that the abode of Islam must be the ownership of the Muslims on which the Islamic ruling system is applied (even if non-Muslims take it over).[4] Ibn Taymiyya also held this opinion. The *ʿulamāʾ* of the Ḥanafī school, however, put their emphasis on the very specific situation of practising Muslims by asking whether they are in security or not. Thus, according to them, as stated by as-Sarakhsī, the evidence that we are in the abode of Islam is

when the Muslims are safe and feel no fear because of their Religion. For this school, it is a question of security and protection and not a strict question of Islam and *kufr* (non-acceptance of Islam).

2. *Dār al-ḥarb* (the abode of war):[5] many definitions were proposed and there remains much divergence between the *ʿulamāʾ* about what is an adequate definition. Nevertheless, by and large, they agree on the fact that a country is *dār al-ḥarb* when both the ruling system and the government are not Islamic. This appellation, however, does not depend on the type of population (whose majority could be Muslim) but on the laws and the political system. For the Ḥanafī school, contrary to *dār al-Islām*, *dār al-ḥarb* is the country where Muslims are neither protected, safe nor at peace. The existence of the abode of war though does not necessitate a state of war between the two opposing factions.

A close study of these two definitions (even if it is not exhaustive) shows that the parameters on which the recognition of a specific and qualified *dar* is based are not strictly antithetical: the majority of the *ʿulamāʾ* insist on ownership of the land and the application of the Islamic legal system as indices for determining the existence of *dār al-Islām* whereas it is the nature of the government and the legal system which are relevant for determining the abode of war. The emphasis is placed on population in the former and on government in the latter and this hiatus is, in fact, the cause of the profound divergence of opinion among contemporary *ʿulamāʾ* for they all admit that the Islamic legal system (which is the second condition whose application in part facilitates definition of a space) is not nowadays truly or completely applied. Thus, some *ʿulamāʾ* who refer to population are of the opinion that Islamic countries are still to be considered as *dār al-Islām* whereas others, concentrating on governments which clearly do not respect Islamic teaching, state that these countries cannot be called *dār al-Islām* any longer. Such varying stances were very evident among the *ʿulamāʾ* in France in 1992 when Shaykh Mannāʿ al-Qaṭṭān presented his paper on this issue: the latter questioned whether Islamic countries, in which repression, injustice and dictatorship are widespread, were still to be considered as *dār al-Islām*. Abū az-Zarqā' and Yūsuf al-Qarḍāwī took the view that these countries, as a whole, could and should be considered as *dār al-Islām*, albeit imperfectly, and with the hope of reform. The former had thus put his emphasis on government, whilst the latter looked at the situation from the point of view of population: the conclusions though differ greatly.

If, moreover, we take into account the parameters considered by some *'ulamā'* of the Ḥanafī school, i.e. those based on safety and security, the conclusion is not only different but in complete opposition since Muslims are sometimes safer in the West – regarding the free practise of their Religion – than they are in Islamic countries. Thus, this could lead us to conclude, with respect to the parameters of safety and peace, that the appellation *dār al-Islām* is applicable to almost all Western nations whilst it is not the case for the great majority of the Islamic countries where the populations are overwhelmingly Muslim. We do, however, need to be cautious in drawing such distinctions between the West and Islamic countries for as Shaykh Mawlawī says,[6] except for safety parameters, Western countries are not Islamic.

This debate, along with the problems of definition it has brought about, is based on old concepts which seem far removed from our own time. To apply them to contemporary reality as they were thought out more than ten centuries ago appears to be a methodological mistake. In a world which has become a village, where populations are in constant flux and within which we are witnessing a process of increased complexity regarding financial and political power as well as a diversification in strategic alliances and spheres of influence, it is impossible to stick to an old, simple and binary vision of reality. It would be inappropriate and inadequate and could lead to an over simplistic, and indeed blameworthy, perception of our era.

Even the addition of a third concept, introduced by ash-Shāfi'ī, referring to the abode of treaty (*dār al-'ahd*) is insufficient to draw us out of this old binary vision of the world. This appellation brings to the fore that some countries whilst not Islamic from a political point of view, have nonetheless signed peace or collaboration treaties with one or more Islamic nations. Such a treaty could either be temporary or definitive and it seems that *dār al-ʿahd* opens up an interesting avenue for exploration in the current international political scenario. Thus, the existence both of institutions such as the United Nations or the Organisation for African Unity and the numerous treaties between states could be a plain expression and realisation of this very specific state of affairs. This is the opinion of Mannāʿ al-Qaṭṭān who states that, "this is today the appropriate qualification for the majority of countries with respect to their relations with Muslims."[7] It is obvious that this concept sheds original light on our way of considering the world around us, yet a close analysis also shows that this qualification fails to give us an adequate vision of our current situation. In fact, *dār al-ʿahd* acquires specific meaning only in relation to the two other concepts we have discussed above. To define a treaty means that we should know what the nature of the countries is which have agreed on its clauses; thus, to have a clear idea of what *dār al-Islām* is and what it is not. We have already studied the difficulty this identification brings about and it seems that, if we use it to explain our contemporary world, *dār al-ʿahd* becomes a simple *description* of a situation-without-war rather than an appropriate *definition* of a space where Muslims are living. As such it is both interesting and useful, but it is not completely appropriate, and this for at least two reasons:

1. Based on the idea of two virtual entities (*dār al-Islām* and *dār al-ḥarb*) having to come to an agreement, it seems impossible to use such a concept without precaution in our contemporary world. These entities do not have real and defined existences and the treaties, because of intricate political influences and imbalanced power struggles, cannot be considered as expressions of agreement between two or more independent and free governments.

2. To use the same word (*ʿahd*) when referring to both the "treaties" between countries and the relations Muslims have with one state (and its constitution) could lead to a profound shift in meaning. This because the content we are referring

to is by no means of the same nature. In using these three, old concepts, the *'ulamā'* have neglected some important geo-political data which should be taken into consideration inasmuch as they have a great influence on the new world vision we must develop.

Thus, a study of the discussions running among the *'ulamā'* shows that there exists a clear hiatus between the old frames of reference and the current state of affairs (*wāqi'*). Some, place emphasis on the latter, trying to adapt and modify the content of the concepts, whereas others, attached to the legacy of *fiqh* eventually simplify the reality and continue with a binary vision of the world which is no longer appropriate.[8] This demonstrates how uncomfortable and embarrassed they are at both the inadequacy of the conceptual set they have at their disposal and lack of appropriate understanding of the new world political and economic landscape they are facing.

The four elements we identified above, namely, the population living in the country, the proprietary of the land, the nature of the government and the laws governing the country, are no longer pertinent if we want to extract and bring about a right perception of the current situation of Muslims in the world. Three observations ought to be made in this respect:

1. For about 150–170 years, colonisation and, afterwards, political activities confined to supervision provoked great changes in Islamic countries. The alliance of an important number of Muslim leaders with the West and the introduction, step by step, of an alien and Westernised legal system has led to the large-scale modification of the references within Islamic societies themselves. It is not, and will never be, a single and closed world, purified of foreign influence.

2. Economic and political priorities have forced millions of people to leave their countries to look for jobs or security in the West. This process has brought about their settlement in the West: they are now part of these societies whose most

significant features seem to be their diversity and their multi-religious and cultural dimensions. They represent minorities in the West but the children of these second and subsequent generations are, hence, at home. The West, in turn, is now aware that sizeable elements in its population are both completely European and completely Muslim.

3. It is then an era of diversity, complexity and mix which can no longer be encapsulated into a twofold and simplistic vision. Today, it is neither sufficient nor relevant to concentrate on questions which relate to the nature of government, to laws which are enforced or to ownership of the land since the state of the world makes such issues hugely complicated. Instead, we need to return to a deep consideration and assessment of the Muslim people's situation as such throughout the world and avoid having our minds disturbed by questions of definition based on subjects which are either virtual or theoretical, if not unreal.

The internationalisation of today means that our analysis should take into account the realities in which people live. A radical change in our state of mind is needed if we want to face, as we must, the world around us. To be a consistent and balanced Muslim today is difficult because the world around us and the parameters, in the Islamic or in the Western space, are no longer coherent. This means that we are asked to return to the sources of Islamic teachings if we are to know a framework, a guidance or a direction which allows us to face this contemporary situation.

We should, however, remind ourselves constantly of two things: first, that for a Muslim the Islamic teaching, when it is well understood and implemented, is suitable for all places and times and that this is the very meaning of the notion *ʿālamiyya al-Islām* (the world dimension of Islamic teaching). Second, that the concepts of *dār al-Islām, dār al-ḥarb* and *dār al-ʿahd* are not originated either in the Qur'ān or in the *Sunna.* In fact, they were a human attempt, historically dated, to describe the world and to provide the Muslim community with a gauge to measure the world by adapted to their reality. This situation has now completely changed and it is necessary, today, to return to the Qur'ān and the *Sunna* and, in light of our environment, to deepen our analysis so as to develop a new adapted vision of the context and formulate the appropriate rulings therefrom. To reconsider Islamic teachings is a prerequisite.

## C. Fundamental Principles (and Conditions)

At a time when all the old parameters are no longer relevant within society, and when it is difficult to find guidance or solutions in the historical works, it seems necessary to return to the original sources and present clearly what, from an Islamic point of view, the priorities are in a Believer's life, both as an individual and within the community. That is, to define *Who we are* and *What, as Muslims, is expected from us by our Religion.* At first glance, these two questions appear simple, if not simplistic, yet they are capital given the circumstances we are facing: by fixing the general framework of the Islamic identity, beyond the contingencies of a specific area such as Europe, it becomes possible thereafter to determine what, in the European environment, is already fitting and what needs reform and improvement in order to give birth to both a balanced existence and a peaceful coexistence.

In the first part of this study, we tried to demonstrate that the Islamic sciences were but a means, meeting the Muslims' needs to protect their Faith, lives and religious practice. They are instruments through and by which the *'ulamā'* provide the Muslim community with an overall understanding and a legal framework which allows them to be and remain Muslims whatever the circumstances. Similarly, we can say that the environment, no matter what it is, is a space within which the Muslim should find the required milestones permitting him to act in accordance with his belief: as such, the environment is a means through which his identity can exist and flourish.

Thus, by concentrating our analysis on the essential elements of Muslim identity we avoid the methodological mistake of reading that reality through some previously conceived concepts formulated in another time for another context. Our reflection should firstly rely on a classification of these inherent prerequisites of the Muslim's personality and this, secondly, to shed specific light on the social and political European environment. This method, in a sense, is akin to that of some Ḥanafī *'ulamā'* who, as we saw, preferred to define the space (*dār al-Islām* and *dār al-ḥarb*) on the basis of the security of Believers (*amn*) prior to considering the nature of the laws or the government. By doing so they not only considerably modified the parameters and the conditions around which the different abodes were defined, but they were, above all, the precursors of the overall vision of the world we need today.

Before reflecting upon the essential constituents partaking of the Muslim identity,[9] we can identify at least five elements which taken together determine and permit the blossoming of the Muslim personality:

1. *Faith and spirituality*: Islam is, in the first place, a Faith in one God with whom the Believer is linked through a permanent spiritual life. His life should ideally be a complete manifestation of his belief. Thus, whatever the environment, this testimony and life of the heart must be protected and respected. For a Muslim this spiritual life is the very essence of his existence on earth and the *'ulamā'*, in their classification of the five essential *maṣāliḥ*, mentioned, in the first rank, the protection of Faith and the way of life which is naturally linked to its expression (*dīn*).

2. *Practice*: to respect the commands of Religion and to perform the required practices is the logical consequence of the above. This is a matter of freedom of worship, without any doubt, and a man or a woman should have the choice whether to practise. If one chooses to respect their religion or not the religious requirements linked to worship (to pray, fast, pay the *zakāt* and perform the Pilgrimage) one must be allowed to do so without impediment. This also means that the dimension of the community of Faith must be respected (but it does not, of course, bring about the creation of ghettos). There are other recommendations regarding social affairs (*mu'āmalāt*) which have to be respected as well:

marriage, divorce, contracts, trade and so forth. In this respect, every issue must be studied in light of both the Islamic sources and the legal environment so as to find a way to remain faithful to the Islamic teachings and respect the enforced laws. This by no means signifies that Muslims, or any other human being, should be forced to act against their conscience. The secondary issues of Islamic jurisprudence are subject to very specific juridical analysis (as we will see below) and necessitate adapted considerations and solutions.

3. *Protection*: as a human being and as a Believer, a Muslim does not simply ask for acceptance or tolerance in its etymological meaning of suffering the presence of someone because there is no alternative. Along with freedom of Faith and worship, he or she needs a recognition based on protection that, in itself, is based on respect. Freedom of worship, human respect and the social, economic and political protection of one's rights are the three fundamentals of a true recognition of human dignity and integrity. These are the components of what the Ḥanafīs call security in its most profound meaning and which is not confined to the narrow legal field.

4. *Freedom*: the Muslims bear testimony to Islam, which, according to them, was revealed by God to the world through the Revelations of the Qur'ān. As such, freedom of worship should go hand in hand with that of speech and by means of which they are able to present and explain what their Faith, their Religion and their way of life are. This is the meaning of the Qur'ānic expression "*to bear witness before all mankind*" (2: 143), i.e. that the Muslims have to make their Message understandable and known. This is also the significance of another major concept in the Islamic tradition, namely *daʿwa*, a precise translation of which is very difficult given the multiplicity of meanings it conveys. It is altogether presentation, appeal, and invitation. Transmitting the Message of Islam through *daʿwa* must not

be confused with either proselytism or efforts to convert: the duty of the Muslim is to spread the Message and to make it known, no more no less. Whether someone accepts Islam or not is not the Muslim's concern for the inclination of every individual heart depends on God's Will. The notion of *daʿwa* is based on one principle which is the right of every human being to make *a choice based on knowledge* and this is why Muslims are asked to spread the knowledge of Islam among Muslims as well as non-Muslims. The *mu'min* is the one who has *known* and eventually accepts, whereas the *kāfir* is the one who has *known* and then refuses, denies. This notion of *daʿwa* comes close to the idea that we must refuse compulsion according to the verse, "*No compulsion in matters of Religion*" and it establishes a link between two realities: the constraint of force and that of ignorance. Both are firmly rejected.

5. *Participation*: Islamic spirituality finds its complete blossoming through the Believer's action (*ʿamal*) and participation in social affairs. From an Islamic point of view, to believe is to act and this is the meaning of the recurrent Qur'ānic expression: "*Those who attain to Faith and do good works.*" This means that Muslims should be allowed to commit themselves within society and to act in favour of human solidarity. By doing so, they follow the Prophet's recommendation: "The best one among you is the more useful to the people."[10] This also means that Muslims can be engaged in social as well as political and economic activities. All are important elements of their actions and they testify to the sincerity of their Faith before God. This is why, both at local and national levels, their commitment as Muslims and citizens is imperative for it is the sole way of completing and perfecting their Faith and the essential Message of their Religion. The social space, with its laws and its customs, should permit them to attain this.

An analysis of these five elements is of course not exhaustive but it suffices to give us an idea of the essential prerequisites which mould the Muslim identity. They constitute an overall picture of the latter which does not take into account either historical contingencies or social and political factors. The first and greatest responsibility of Muslims is to produce a fair assessment of their religious, social, legal and political European environment in order to know which of the elements mentioned above are already acquired – and to what extent – and which are missing. As soon as the required conditions are present – completely or partially – it becomes the Muslims' responsibility to act either to assure their security or to improve their situation as well as that of society as a whole.

## D. European Societies

The current situation, as well as the cultural and legal background of the various European countries is often very different, hence it is difficult to generalise about the Muslim presence in every European society. A close study of both the respective constitution and the process leading to the recognition and respect of the Islamic presence in each country would be necessary if one wanted to have an appropriate picture of each countries' situation. Such a study should, of course, be done at national level since this would allow the Muslims to rely on an accurate inventory of facts whilst trying to determine their place in the country in question. However, it is still possible at the European level, and without going into too much detail, to bring to the fore some rights which are already protected and respected in most European countries. An analysis of these rights, in light of the prerequisites presented above, will provide us with sufficient information to assess our situation in order to define in an appropriate manner the European space in which millions of Muslims live today.[11] In this respect, it is possible to assert that at least five fundamental rights are secured:

1. *The right to practise Islam*: today, Muslims living in Europe can observe the major Islamic practices. There is no ban on praying, paying *zakāt*, fasting or going on Pilgrimage to Makka. In several cities there are some administrative

problems with regard to building mosques but in general, basic needs are provided. Debates concerning the scarf (*ḥijāb*), cemeteries and *ḥalāl* meat are particularly intense, symptomatic of the tense and nervous social climate in some societies, but they do not lead us to omit what has actually been acquired concerning day-to-day practice.[12] None of this affects the application of the principle of *freedom of worship*; if the rate of daily practise is so low (between 10 and 15% among the whole Muslim population in Europe), it is not because of some kind of prohibition or pressure, but rather for reasons internal to the Muslim communities themselves.

2. *The right to knowledge*: the whole European population enjoys this right. For Muslims, according to one of the most important principles of their Religion, to have access to knowledge is imperative. In European countries, the legal principle of compulsory schooling for all children offers Muslims the means to apply the famous *ḥadīth*: "Seeking knowledge is a duty for all Muslims (male and female)." Muslims have to acknowledge that fellow Muslims do not have this right in a majority of Muslim countries where illiteracy rates sometimes reach 70%.

3. *The right to found organisations*: according to the law, Muslims, as any other people living in Europe, have the right to found associations. The number of these organisations in Europe is considerable, sometimes numbering more than two thousand as in France and up to 120 for the small Muslim community of two hundred thousand living in Switzerland. The situation is the same in almost all countries and this provides clear evidence that nothing prevents Muslims from organising themselves and founding organisations both at local and national level. There are differences, according to the respective law, between purely religious institutions on the one hand, and social or cultural ones on the other, but both types are present and active today without any great hindrance.

4. *The right to autonomous representation*: nothing, within the respective European Constitutions, prevents Muslims from structuring themselves at either local or national level. They are totally free to set up the structures they think most appropriate. There are, of course, multiple State interferences in Islamic affairs (from European as well as overseas countries) and it is obvious that this is not conducive to finding an elementary basis for unity. In fact, this phenomenon is due first to the Muslim's own incapacity to lay down a common framework for an independent council. There are more than 50 national organisations or federations throughout Europe and even at national level these can hardly agree.[13] Nevertheless, legally speaking, the field is open and nothing prevents Muslims from going further in organising themselves as they should.

5. *The right to appeal to the law*: in all affairs concerning religious, administrative or legal problems Muslims have the right to appeal to the judicial power in place and to engage in a legal procedure against decisions seemingly ill-founded or unfair. The State of law (*l'Etat de droit*) is not perfect, of course, but at least it offers important guarantees regarding the defence of individual or organisational rights. Muslims enjoy this right as do all other citizens. The problem, however, is often not a supposed legal deficiency regarding the rights of Muslims in Europe but one of almost complete ignorance or negligence of legal matters by Muslim individuals and institutions: justice would very often have been done in the Muslim's favour if only the latter had taken the time to learn how to proceed. It is only in the last few years that we have seen Muslims in Europe appealing to the courts in defence of their rights. Slowly, they have become aware of the judicial stake.

An assessment of the European arena could be carried out through a comparative analysis of the two sets of points mentioned above: on the one hand, the essential conditions permitting the blossoming of the Muslim personality and, on the other, the five global and fundamental rights already secured in Europe. It appears, then that a great many of the legal conditions we formulated are already fulfilled and that the Muslims – to a large extent – are allowed to live as Muslims in Europe. This is plain in four of the five fields discussed: Muslims can freely practise their religion (the totality of the *'ibādāt* and a part of the *mu'āmalāt*);[14] the laws generally protect their rights as citizens or residents as well as Believers belonging to a minority Religion;[15] they are also free to speak about Islam and to organise religious, social or cultural activities and nothing prevents Muslims from being involved in society or participating in social life at the different levels mentioned. We must emphasise these facts for they give us a more accurate picture of the European reality and permit us to base our hopes for a better future on a true picture of what is already assured.

At the same time, we must not deny that there are some important issues upon which we must reflect insofar as they appear as impediments to a positive and flourishing Muslim existence in Europe. Thus, we should not belittle the difficulty of protecting the life of Faith in modern countries. Spirituality is of great significance in Islam and the neutrality of the public space, within secular societies, has often been confused with a total absence of religiosity. Here, Muslims are not dealing with legislation, laws or rules, the problem is elsewhere and it is both profound and sensitive. It relates to the fundamental question for Muslim communities living as minorities in Europe: namely, how to maintain a spiritual life in a modern – understood as both secular and industrialised – society and, consequently, how to transmit the necessary knowledge which permits genuine freedom of choice. This point leads us to another set of problematic areas such as the question of Islamic education in a secular environment, the function of the family, of mosques or of Islamic organisations, etc. These are fundamental issues rather than insurmountable hindrances and, as such, they throw responsibility back at the Muslims who are asked – with all the opportunities they benefit from in Europe – to face their reality and to act accordingly.

As a minority, the Muslims obviously cannot apply all the global principles and rulings prescribed by the Qur'ān and the *Sunna* in the field of social affairs (*muʿāmalāt*). The specific rulings concerning marriage, death, inheritance, trade, interest, etc. are not in force in Europe whose nations refer to both their respective national constitutions and some international charters ratified through, for instance, the United Nations or the European Council. Muslim communities, according to their references, should apply and respect the rulings of their Religion as much as possible within the framework of the constitution of the country they live in and must at the same time avoid involvement in activities which contradict their Religion. It should be noted here that, to a great extent, the majority of such activities *are not imposed* on Muslims but are rather *legally allowed*: this signifies that they are free, whilst living in Europe, of a considerable number of activities or transactions which are not Islamic. The real problem arises when, in some circumstances, Muslims *must* resort to financial or administrative operations or deals which are at variance with Islamic teachings: every occurrence of this kind should be studied precisely and specifically in order to assess its degree of obligation and, then, an appropriate and adapted ruling formulated.[16]

A third problem should be brought to the fore insofar as it has an impact on the whole question of Muslims in Europe, namely the image of Islam presented via events taking place on the international scene. The political situation pertaining in some Islamic countries, the interests of and sometimes these governments' manipulations shed a very negative light on Muslims living in Europe and keep alive a set of prejudices and biases against Islam and Muslims. It happens that the laws – which normally protect the rights of Muslims – are read, interpreted and used, because of the suspicious atmosphere surrounding them, in a tendentious manner and they become the official and legitimate support of patent discriminations. It would be foolish, today, to neglect this reality just because it is seemingly unquantifiable or not legally identifiable, since it nonetheless represents the daily experience of thousands of

Muslims in Europe who have to deal with the picture upheld by their interlocutors' imaginations. This representation of Islam and Muslims in Europe is a great – and maybe the greatest – difficulty the Muslim communities face today. This phenomenon is sometimes hidden behind the veil of a supposed definitive legal incompatibility which, indeed, does not hold up to any serious analysis. This is why Muslims should be socially involved, at two levels in concomitance: in the legal field, in order to know what the legislation really says and in a deep and consistent dialogue with their indigenous neighbours so that they are able to modify the widespread, and very often negative, image of Islam that they have.

Thus the abode of Europe appears as a space within which Muslims can live in security – according to the definition of the Ḥanafī *ʿulamāʾ* – with some fundamental rights both acquired and protected. As a minority in a non-Muslim environment they are able to practise and to respect the more important rulings of the Islamic teaching. They are obviously not in the historically defined space of *dār al-Islām*, nevertheless there is room for manoeuvre. Some legal issues must be solved and this requires that the Muslims return to their sources in order to stipulate the appropriate Islamic rulings. This is an important task. It is, however, not the only great challenge facing European Muslims: living in a modern and secular society they have to think of their future and find a way of preserving their spirituality, values, and identity. This will assuredly have an impact on *Fiqh* and should be thought and carried out in a European context. In fact, these two tasks are of a different nature: the former is a global assessment and necessitates that the Muslims ponder deeply over their new situation whereas the latter, following this assessment and in its light, should set some appropriate legal rulings permitting Muslims to live as Muslims whilst also protecting their identity. This process must accompany dialogue and social participation so that Muslims are able to change – at least at local level – the poor image of their Religion and spread the knowledge of who they are and what they believe in.

## E. Small Village, Open World

Our world has become a small village and Muslims today are scattered throughout the various continents. Following our present analysis, it still seems necessary to attribute a name to the European space which suits both Islamic sources and our current situation. We have seen that old concepts do not fit our reality either regarding the strict content of the concepts or the conditions of their use. This is, in fact, a completely new situation which has led the contemporary *ʿulamāʾ* to reflect upon the whole issue through the prism of various and diverse considerations which appeared to them as fundamental. Thus, there is no consensus (*ijmāʿ*) on the question of identification, definition and the name of the Western abode as a whole. We can draw here three different overall positions which are respectively the expression of three specific legal opinions – even if not completely contradictory – regarding this issue. They are based, fundamentally, on distinct ways of assessing the current world's state of affairs and convey, as such, important differences in perception as regards the situation of Muslims in the world in general and in the West in particular.

1. Some *ʿulamāʾ* consider that the old concepts of *dār al-Islām* and *dār al-ḥarb* are still effective even if all the respective conditions are not completely fulfilled. Proponents of respect for the *madhāhib* (schools of law), they consider that the contribution of the great *ʿulamāʾ* must by no means be controverted. This vision is hardly supported by *ʿulamāʾ* or thinkers knowing or living in the West: only minority Islamic movements – such as *Ḥizb at-Taḥrīr* (the Liberation Party) in Europe – relate to some *ʿulamāʾ* living in the Middle East or in Asia and claim that the opinions of the ancient *ʿulamāʾ* are to be literally applied.

2. Other *ʿulamāʾ* are of the opinion that considerable changes must be taken into account and that the conditions (*shurūṭ*), mentioned above, allowing us today to define one space as *dār al-Islām* or *dār al-ḥarb* can no longer be applied, for Islamic teachings are not respected within so-called Islamic countries and there exists in any case a real security for

Muslim Believers practising in Europe. According to them, these facts should be stressed in any discussion of the situation of Muslims in Europe. In defining Western countries, they use the Shāfiʿī concepts of *dār al-ʿahd* (the abode of treaty) or *dār al-amn* (the abode of security), stating that these are the most appropriate terms to define our current situation when we are witnessing treatises between nations (directly or through the United Nations) and the fact that fundamental Muslim rights are protected in these Western countries. However, they continue to consider those countries where Muslims are in the majority as *dār al-Islām* even if their governments are illegitimate and dictatorial and even if Islamic teachings and rulings are neglected. Despite this situation, these countries remain part of *dār al-Islām* since their populations have a Muslim majority and their culture, tradition and day-to-day life are still marked by Islamic features. This opinion is supported by numerous *ʿulamā'* among whom we find the well-known Muṣṭafa az-Zarqā, ʿAbdul Fattāḥ Abū Ghudda and Yūsuf al-Qarḍāwī. They stated this opinion during a *Fiqh* seminar held in France, in July 1992, when discussing a paper related to this issue presented by Mannāʿ al-Qaṭṭān who supported this general view.[17]

3. There are other *ʿulamā'*, such as Fayṣal Mawlawī, who consider that these concepts are no longer effective and that, in order to continue to use them, we are compelled to side-step the issue regarding both the concepts and the reality we are facing. Given the fact, unanimously recognised, that these concepts are neither Qur'ānic nor extracted from the *Sunna* and that our world has changed, the *ʿulamā'*, must think of new appellations which are both faithful to the Islamic sources and also fit our current state of affairs. In Mawlawī's booklet, *Al-Usus ash-Sharʿīyya lil-ʿIlāqāt Bayn al-Muslimīn wa Ghayr al-Muslimīn* (Islamic Principles Concerning the Relations Between Muslims and non-Muslims), the author states:

"The attempt to apply this classification to our current situation is to bring forth numerous problems." After reminding us of the conditions required to define *dār al-Islām* and explaining why, in the West, we cannot consider ourselves in *dār al-ḥarb*,[18] he adds:

"We are not, in the West, in the abode of War but we are either in the abode of treaty or in the abode of *daʿwa* to God. If we want to keep the (traditional) *fiqh* classification of the world with the abode of Islam, the abode of War, and the abode of treaty, thus, we are, in the West, in the abode of treaty. If, on the other hand, we state that the old *fiqh* classification is no longer applicable to our current situation – and this is the opinion we prefer – then we say, based on this, that we are in *dār ad-daʿwa* as the Prophet and the Muslims were in Makka before the *Hijra*. Makka was neither *dār al-Islām* nor *dār al-ḥarb* but a *dār ad-daʿwa*[19] and the entire Arabian Peninsula was, in the eyes of Muslims, *dār ad-daʿwa*."[20]

Here, the traditional appellations are discussed – and almost set aside – while a new name is proposed in light of the source – namely the Makkan period – which, in many aspects, fits our reality more closely.

This last position, following the study we have already undertaken, seems to be the most accurate and pertinent for it allows us, beyond the veil of old contextual considerations, to face our reality as it is and to re-read our Islamic sources from a new viewpoint. This is, for instance, what Fayṣal Mawlawī has done, by putting Muslims, in light of their contemporary world, in the situation of the Prophet and the Companions in Makka where, living as a minority, they were asked not only to believe, but also to present and explain their religion to the people and tribes around. Far from replicating the old binary vision, Mawlawī returns to the sources and, in a world which has become a village, reminds Muslims of one of their fundamental duties, that is to call to the Oneness of God, to present their Faith and to invite people to learn what Islam is:

"It is this call which is the basis of our relations with non-Muslims and not fighting or war."[21]

At this time of globalisation and internationalisation, when all nations are subject to a new world order which denies, rejects or forgets God, spirituality and any type of transcendence, Muslims are asked to develop an in-depth understanding of their own belief and Message in and through its universal dimension:

> *And We have sent you only as a grace towards the worlds.*[22]

If, furthermore, the abode in which the Muslims live provides them with security – as does the West – we must then add another essential dimension to the universal character of the Islamic Message, that is the responsibility of Muslims to bear witness to it, by their lives and their actions. Beyond any kind of sectarian and inadequate classification, Muslims have to face, through and within our era of globalisation and the new world order, their responsibilities in order to bear genuine witness to their Faith in the Oneness of God and their values of justice and solidarity on the one hand, and to act accordingly, as individuals or in society on the other.

Wherever a Muslim, saying: "I testify that there is no god but God and that Muḥammad is His Messenger", is in security and is able to perform his/her fundamental religious duties, he/she is *at home* for the Prophet taught us that the whole world is a mosque. This opinion, supported by several reformist *'ulamā'* and thinkers, such as al-Afghānī, 'Abduh, Iqbāl and al-Bannā, today finds a new relevance. This means that Muslims living in Europe, individuals as well as communities, can not only live in Europe but that they uphold a great responsibility for they provide their societies with a testimony based on Faith, spirituality, values, a sense of limits and a permanent human and social commitment.

This perception reverses the one based on old concepts and which inevitably pushed Muslims into adopting a reactive posture as a minority and, as such, led them to determine and protect their minimal rights. If this attitude was understandable during the first decades of Muslim presence in Europe and among the first generation of migrants, it nevertheless should nowadays be overstepped. It is high time to define the responsibilities of Muslims in Europe and to name the space in which we live as the European or Western abode.

Mawlawī proposed the concept of *dār ad-daʿwa* with reference to the Makkan period during which the Muslims, although a minority in a society which rejected the new Revelation (called by him *dār al-kufr*), considered themselves as responsible for bearing witness to their Faith before their peoples and tribes. Similarly one could say, in the current new world order which seems to forget the Creator up to the point of denying His existence and which is based on an exclusive economic logic, that Muslims are facing the same responsibilities, especially in the heart of industrialised societies. Assertive and confident, they have to remind the people around them of God, of spirituality and, regarding social affairs, to work for values and ethics, justice and solidarity. They do not forego their environment but, on the contrary, once in security, they should influence it in a positive way.

From within, we could make this perspective even clearer for the concept of *daʿwa*, although essential, remains pluri-semantic and over-connoted and, as such, difficult to translate.[23] Bearing in mind both our sources and the universal Message and teaching of Islam (*ʿālamiyyat al-Islām*) we could aptly refer to the notion of *shahāda* (attestation, testimony) insofar as it presents two important aspects: the first refers to the *shahāda* each Muslim, to be recognised as such, must pronounce before God and all mankind that "there is no god but God and that Muḥammad is His Messenger" and through which he or she defines his/her identity; the second relates to the Muslims' duty, according to the Qur'ānic prescription, "*to bear witness (to their Faith) before all mankind*".[24] With the notion of *shahāda*, testimony, we can put together the two essential pillars of the Islamic creed: a clear definition of our identity through our belief in the Oneness of God (*tawḥīd*) and in His last Revelation to the Prophet Muḥammad along with a consciousness that we bear the responsibility to recall people to God's presence and to act in such a manner that our presence among people is, in itself, a reminder of the Creator, of spirituality and ethics. This double function of the notion of *shahāda* could be expressed through the six points given below, the first three referring to the identity of the Muslim *per se*, and the last to his role in society:

1. By saying the *shahāda*, the Muslim testifies to his/her Faith and provides a clear picture of his identity: he/she is Muslim, believes in God, His Messengers, the angels, the Revealed Books, destiny and the Day of Judgement. He/she believes that the Islamic teachings are fruits of a Revelation and that he/she is a member of the Islamic *umma* (community).

2. The *shahāda*, as the first of five pillars, is not only closely linked with worship and practise but can be neither true worship nor practise without it. A part of the Muslim identity is the fact of being able (and allowed) to pray, to pay the *zakāt*, to fast or to perform the Pilgrimage. This is clearly stated in the Qur'ān regarding the God-conscious who "*believe in the existence of that which is beyond the reach of human perception, and are constant in Prayer*".[25]

3. More widely, this means that the Muslim has to, or at least should be allowed to, respect the commands and prescriptions of his/her Religion and to act accordingly with what is lawful and unlawful in Islam. He/she should not be forced to act against his/her conscience for this would be a denial of identity.

4. To pronounce the *shahāda* is to act before God with respect for His creation, for *īmān* (Faith) is actually a trust (*amāna*). Relations between human beings are based on respect, trustworthiness and, above all, on an absolute faithfulness to the agreements, contracts or treaties which have been explicitly or tacitly made. The Qur'ān is explicit, "*Every contract shall We ask about*"[26] and the Believers are those "*who are faithful to their trusts and to their pledges*".[27]

5. As a Believer among human beings, the Muslim has to bear witness to this *shahāda* before others. He/she has to present Islam, explain the content of this Faith and the Islamic

teaching as a whole. In every kind of society, and of course in a non-Muslim environment, he/she is a witness, a *shahīd* and this encompasses the notion of *daʿwa*.

6. This *shahāda* is not only a matter of speech. A Muslim is the one who believes and acts consequently and consistently. "*Those who attain to Faith and do good works,*" as we read in the Qur'ān, stresses the fact that the *shahāda* has an inevitable impact on the actions of the Muslim whatever society he/she lives in. To observe the *shahāda* signifies being involved in the society in all fields where need requires it: unemployment, marginalisation, delinquency, etc. This also means being engaged in those processes which could lead to a positive reform of both the institutions and the legal, economic, social and political systems in order to bring about more justice and a real popular participation at grassroots level. "*Behold, God enjoins justice,*"[28] says the Qur'ān, inasmuch as it is the concrete manifestation of the testimony.

Thus, this concept of *shahāda* seems, from our point of view, the most appropriate to convey a global perception of both the identity and the function of Muslims in light of Islamic teachings. It also suits our current situation since it permits us to express and link our identity and social responsibility as Muslims.

At a time when we are witnessing a strong current of globalisation,[29] it is difficult to refer to the notion of *dār* (abode) unless we consider the whole world as an abode. Our world has become a small village and, as such, it is, henceforth, an open world. This is in fact the intuition on which the original appellation proposed by Fayṣal Mawlawī is based and he explains: "In our opinion, the whole earth is a *dār ad-daʿwa*."[30] Consequently, it seems appropriate to stop translating the notion of *dār* in its restrictive meaning of "abode" and to prefer the notion of *space* which, while still referring to geography and environment, more clearly expresses the idea of an *opening to the world*, for Muslim populations are now scattered all over the world. Migration has been important and, in spite of most restrictive regulations, it seems that population movements are to continue: by now, millions of Muslims have settled in the West. Their fate is linked to that of the societies they live in, and it is unthinkable to draw a line of demarcation between them and the "non-Muslims" on the sole considerations of space. In our world, it is no longer a matter of relations between two distinct "abodes". It is rather a question of relations between human beings belonging and referring to different civilisations, religions, cultures and ethics. It is also a question of relations between citizens, in continuous interaction with the social, legal, economic or political framework which structures and directs the space they live in. This complexification process, which is a feature of globalisation, outangles the factors which previously made it possible to define the different "abodes".

One must go still further: the old binary geographical representation, with two juxtaposed worlds which would be *face to face*, in relative balance, no longer has anything to do with the reality of hegemony and areas of influence regarding civilisation, culture, economy, and subsequently of course politics. Westernisation, the legitimate daughter of pluridimensional globalisation, can be far better expressed through the notions of *centre* (the West and its relay capitals in the South) and *periphery* (the rest of the planet), than by the representation of two "abodes" living the reality of a "*con-front*ation". Muslims settled in the West are at the *centre*, at the *heart*, at the *head* of the system which produces the symbolical apparatus of Westernisation. In this very specific space, at the *centre*, and far more exactingly still than at the *periphery*, Muslims must *bear witness*, they must be *witnesses* to what they are and to their own values. Indeed, the whole world is a *land of testimony* but there is a specific space, bearing an incomparable symbolical charge, which is the heart of the whole system and in which millions of Muslims now live. At the centre, more than anywhere else, the axial principle of *shahāda* takes on its full meaning. We could present things as follows:

Chart V: **The Old and New World**

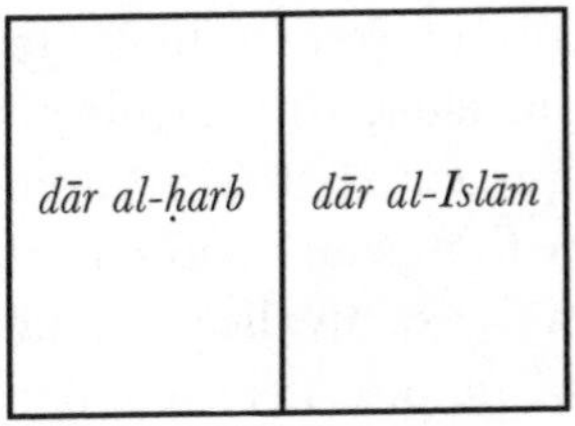


*Old binary representation, face to face*

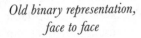

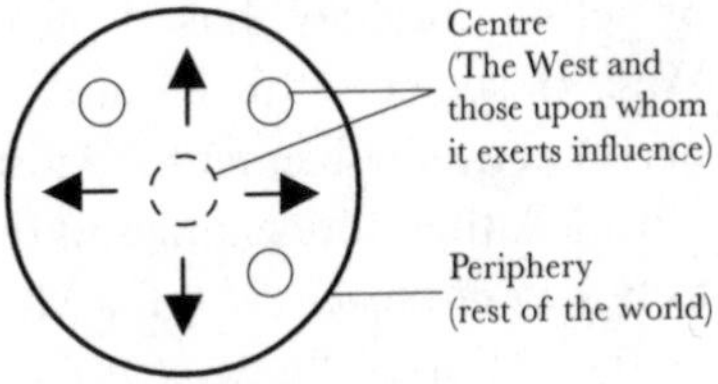


*New representation of the world: centre and periphery*

Such a representation enables us to come out of the logic of conflict. For Muslims, at the heart of the West, what matters is not to fall back into the old bipolar vision by looking for foes, but rather to find partners who will, like them, be determined to select in what Western culture produces in order to promote its positive contributions and to resist its destructive deviations, both on the human and environmental levels. More generally, they will also have to strive to promote authentic religious and cultural pluralism on the international level. Many European and American intellectuals are fighting so that the right of civilisations and cultures to exist might be respected. Before God, and with all men, Muslims must be the *witnesses* involved in this resistance, for justice, for all men whatever their race, their origin or their religion.

The notion of *shahāda* protects and safeguards the essential features of Muslim identity, *per se* and in society: it recalls the permanent bond with God (*rabbāniyya*) and expresses the Muslim's duty to live among people and to bear witness to the scope of the Islamic Message before all mankind, through both acts and speech. This is true in any society, for such is the basis of our relations with others. Called *dār ash-shahāda*, space of testimony, Western countries represent an environment within which Muslims are sent back to the essential teachings of Islam and prompted to ponder over their role: considering themselves as *shuhadā' ʿalan-nās* (witnesses before mankind), as the Qur'ān puts it, should lead them to avoid reactive and overcautious attitudes and to develop a feeling of self-confidence, based on a deep sense of responsibility. In Western societies this should, as we said, go along with a real and permanent involvement for justice. The present approach, "from outside", therefore enables us to define the European environment as a *space of responsibility* for Muslims. This is exactly the meaning of the notion of "*space of testimony*" that we propose here, a notion that totally reverses perspectives: whereas Muslims have, for years, been wondering *whether and how they would be accepted*, the in-depth study and evaluation of the Western environment entrusts them, in light of their Islamic frame of reference, with a most important mission. If they are really with God, then their life must be a *testimony* to a permanent involvement and an infinite self-sacrifice for social justice, the welfare of mankind, the environment, and all forms of solidarity. While they had good reason to remain overcautious, or even hidden, behind the appellations of "abode of war" or "abode of negation" (since they were living "in the wrong place"), Muslims now attain, in the *space of testimony*, the meaning of an essential duty and of an exacting responsibility: to contribute, wherever they are, to promoting good and equity within and through *human brotherhood*. Muslims' outlook must now change from the reality of "protection" alone to that of an authentic "contribution". Muslim men and women are, with so many other human beings, rich with this ethic of giving, and it is this giving which, in the end, will establish their societies' wealth.

## Notes

1 Such as in France concerning the scarf affairs within schools. According to the State Council, to ban girls wearing the scarf (*ḥijāb*) from State schools is a misconception of secularism (*laïcité*) in general and of the French Constitution in particular. Many Administrative Courts have afforded Muslims girls the right to wear the scarf.

2 Between the 6th year of the *Hijra* (*Sulḥ al-Ḥudaybiyya*) and his death in the 10th year.

3 Also called *dār al-'adl* (abode of justice) or *dār at-tawḥīd* (abode of the [belief in] the Oneness of God).

4 By saying that, ad-Dusūqī establishes a difference between Muslims whose presence and number actually express the idea of "ownership of the land" (*al-milkiyyat lil-musliminīn*) and rulers who could be non-Muslims. See the study *Iqāmat al-Muslim fī Balad Ghayr Islāmī* (Muslim Settlement in a Non-Islamic Country) by Shaykh Mannāʿ al-Qaṭṭān (Islamic Foundation for Information, Paris, 1993).

5 Also called *dār al-shirk* (the abode of associationism-polytheism) in contrast with *dār at-tawḥīd*.

6 Fayṣal Mawlawī, *al-Usus ash-Sharʿīyya lil-ʿIlāqāt, Bayn al-Muslimīn wa Ghayr al-Muslimīn* (Islamic Principles Concerning Relations between Muslims and Non-Muslims) edited by the Union of Islamic Organisations in France (UOIF), (Ménilmontant, 1987), pp. 104–5.

7 See *Iqāmat al-Muslim fī Balad Ghayr Islāmī* (Muslim Settlement in a Non-Islamic Country), op. cit., p. 7 ff.

8 This debate is also important because through it the *ʿulamāʾ* have often tried to determine what is the basic principle (*aṣl*) for the settlement of a Muslim. Once *dār al-Islām* has been defined, the principle – *aṣl* – seems to be that Muslims must live in it except for very specific reasons. Coupled with the difficulty of defining the different spaces is of course the other difficulty of determining *aṣl* and this is exactly the question we are currently addressing.

9 We will define what we consider the very element of the Muslim identity to be in the next section.

10 *Ḥadīth* (Bayhaqī).

11 Still it is obvious that it is not only a matter of law. The problems Muslims are facing today have more to do with mentality, bias and sometimes racism than with legal discrimination (which of course does exist). It is, thus, important to distinguish what is due to the law and what to a state of mind so as to determine and define what kind of problems need solving.

12 Neither the scarf nor Muslim sections in cemeteries are related, in France or Switzerland, to real legal problems and the turbulence they bring about in public life is due to the fact that they affect the sensitive and more global question of national identity, both today and in the future. The question thus arises: "What will this identity be if these societies integrate – and identify themselves with these new behaviours and buildings, which are at once so strange and so *visible*".

13 The case of Spain, for instance, is more an exception than the rule.

14 For a definition of these notions see above.

15 There are, of course, considerable differences between the legislations of the various European countries, ranging from an official recognition of the Islamic Religion (as in Belgium since 1974) to only a recognition of races and ethnic groups (as in Britain since 1976). The situation is not perfect and should be improved but European laws, as a whole, protect the population in general and the Muslims in particular against the greatest discriminations. If we witness today so many injustices towards the Muslims, it is due more to the way some people – because of the influence of widespread prejudices against Islam – are reading and applying the laws than to the legislation itself.

16 We shall discuss some of these occurrences later.

17 See the Summary of the Seminar presented and edited by Mutawallī ad-Darsh and the audio cassettes available at The Union of Islamic Organisations in France. See also the study *Iqāmat al-Muslim fī Balad Ghayr Islāmī* (Muslim Settlement in a Non-Islamic Country) by Shaykh Mannāʿ al-Qaṭṭān (Islamic Foundation for Information, Paris, 1993). The position of the latter *ʿulamā'* regarding *dār al-Islām* is slightly different and he is very critical about the current state of affairs within so-called Islamic countries which, in fact, are no longer Islamic, see pp. 11–19.

18 The author brings to the fore three points to support this position: 1. There is no declaration of war stated by an Islamic government; 2. There are treatises between Islamic and Western nations; 3. The Muslims entered Western countries according to these treatises and it is not possible afterwards to unilaterally denounce them after having accepted entry into Western countries. See op. cit., pp. 103–4.

19 *Dār ad-daʿwa*, which means to call to God, to present what is Islam and to transmit its Message.

20 Mawlawī, op. cit., p. 104.

21 Ibid., p. 105.

22 Qur'ān 21: 107.

23 The notion of *daʿwa* is often understood as the expression of the inherent Islamic tendency towards proselytism and the will to convert. This notion conveys the idea of presenting and explaining the Message of Islam for purposes of conversion, but this has to be a free act, one which is between God and the person's own heart.

24 Qur'ān 2: 143.

25 Qur'ān 2: 3.

26 Qur'ān 17: 34.

27 Qur'ān 23: 8.

28 Qur'ān 16: 90.

29 Which is sometimes another name, or a hidden appellation, for the process of Westernization.

30 Mawlawī, op. cit., p. 104.

# II

# Who Are We?

## A. Which Identity? Which Belonging?

The nature of the Muslim identity, *per se* and in the West, has become a piercing question in the debates on Islam in industrialised societies. Defining this identity exactly is difficult because numerous other factors interfere in the analysis. Is there indeed a Muslim identity and, if so, is it of a religious or a cultural nature? Is the Muslim to be defined in the context of the notion of *umma* or could he/she simply be a Muslim citizen of any European nation? To which group or body does he/she belong first, to the *umma* or to the country he/she lives in as a resident or citizen? All these questions are sensitive for, just beneath their apparent surface, we find a fundamental issue, namely knowing whether it is possible for a Muslim to be a genuine European, a true citizen. Therefore, it seems necessary to start our discussion by clarifying what the idea of *umma* represents in the Muslim mind and, then, try to determine what the social and political implications are of being a member of it.

## B. Belonging to the Islamic *Umma*

In the previous section, we explained that the essence of the Muslim personality is the saying of the *shahāda* by which he testifies that he believes in God and in His last Messenger, Muḥammad.[1] Had we to seek the smallest element on which there is agreement among Muslims for a definition of their common identity, we would assuredly find this basic testimony of Faith which, once it is sincerely pronounced, makes one a Muslim.

The *shahāda*, however, is not just a mere statement for it contains an in-depth concept of creation which, itself, initiates a specific way of life for an individual as well as a society. As an individual, this permanent link with God, the remembrance that we belong to Him and that we will return to Him sheds intense light on our own person since we understand that life has a meaning and that everyone will be called to account for their actions. This intimate thought of each act is one of the greatest dimensions of Islamic spirituality which, without any kind of institutionalised mediation, forces every Believer to determine the milestones within his own social life. To believe is, along with remembrance of God's presence, a way of understanding one's life within creation and among people for, from the Islamic point of view, to be with God is to be with human beings. This is the meaning of *tawḥīd* which we discussed in the first part of our study. There are, in Islam, four circles or spaces which, at different levels and with different prerogatives, explain the social scope of Islamic teaching, from the family to the *umma* and, finally, to all mankind.

Immediately after the recognition that there is a Creator, which is the fundamental vertical dimension, a first horizontal space is opened with respect to human relations. The strong assertion of the Oneness of God and His worship is linked, as one of its inherent conditions, with respect for and good behaviour towards one's parents. This first space of social relations, which is based on family bonds, is of the utmost importance to the Muslim. The Qur'ān, in numerous verses, links the reality of *tawḥīd* with respect for parents:

> *Do not set up any other deity side by side with God, lest thou find thyself disgraced and forsaken: for thy Sustainer has ordained that you shall worship none but Him. And do good unto thy parents. Should one of them, or both, attain to old age in thy care, never say "Ugh" to them or scold them, but always speak unto them with reverent speech, and spread over them humbly the wings of thy tenderness, and say: "O my Sustainer! Bestow Thy grace upon them, even as they cherished and reared me when I was a child."*[2]

To obey one's parents, to be good to them, is the best way of being good with God; this is one of the most important teachings of Islam which the Prophet continuously emphasised through strong recommendations such as the well-known *ḥadīth*: "Paradise is under the mothers' feet."[3]

There is only one situation when the son or daughter must not obey their parents, although they have to remain respectful and polite, and that is when their parents ask them to do something which is against God's prescriptions. The most important one is of course not to associate someone with God and if the parents command their children to do so, they must refuse:

> *(Revere thy parents); yet should they endeavour to make thee ascribe Divinity, side by side with Me, to something which thy mind cannot accept (as Divine), obey them not; but (even then) bear them company in this world's life with kindness, and follow the path of those who turn towards Me.*[4]

The refusal to obey such pressure exercised by parents makes clear what the priorities are for authority from an Islamic point of view: a Muslim must satisfy both God and his parents but he cannot disobey the former in order to please the latter. This was confirmed by the Prophet in general terms: "No obedience to a creature in disobedience to the Creator."[5] This means that although blood ties are important, for they are the essential space of identity and belonging for the Muslim, they are not the first and fundamental parameter that determines and directs human relations. If a Muslim has to choose between equity, whose implementation and respect are commanded by God, and himself, his parents or his relatives, he should prefer justice for this is the true testimony of his Faith:

> *O you who have attained to Faith! Be ever steadfast in upholding equity, bearing witness to the Truth for the sake of God, even though it be against your own selves or your parents and kinsfolk. Whether the person concerned be rich or poor, God's claim takes precedence over (the claims of) either of them. Do not follow your own desires, lest you swerve from justice: for if you distort (the Truth), behold, God is indeed aware of all that you do!*[6]

A Muslim first belongs to God and this belonging influences and sheds a particular light on every specific social sphere he deals with and in. To believe in God and to bear witness to His Message before all mankind means that the fundamental values He has revealed, such as honesty, faithfulness, equity and justice, have priority over parental ties. Therefore, a Muslim must respect his family (and by extension tribal, group or national) bonds as long as they do not force him to act against his belief and his conscience.[7] This first space of social relations in Islam associates parents very closely with the concept of family and refers, according to its wide Islamic meaning, to relatives and kinsfolk (*aqrabīn*).

The individual affirmation of the Islamic creed through the *shahāda* and the recognition of the family as the first environment of social life are the prerequisites for entering into the second circle of social relations in Islam. Each of the four practical pillars of Islamic worship has a double dimension, individual and collective. In striving to attain excellence in the practise of their religion, Muslims are immediately called upon to face the community dimension of the Islamic way of life. The majority of Qur'ānic addresses towards Believers are, thus, made in the plural: "*O you who attained to Faith* ..." and when the Muslim recites the opening chapter of the Qur'ān (*Sūra al-Fātiḥa*) in each cycle of Prayer, he presents himself as a member of a community, saying: "*Thee alone do we worship; Thee alone do we turn to for aid. Guide us to the straight way.*"[8] Alone before God, he has to do his utmost to develop a personal and intimate God-consciousness but he should never forget that he belongs to the community of Faith. The Prophet said: "Prayer in congregation is better than that of a man alone at home by 27 degrees."[9] Prayer is the most important pillar of Islam, it is its essence which expresses the link with God as well as the fundamental equality between all Believers, brother beside brother, sister beside sister, all asking for a guidance based on Faith and brotherhood, as they have been taught.

This community feeling is confirmed and reinforced by all other acts of worship and especially *zakāt* which is, essentially, a tax levied for the poor and needy. The stronger our relation with God, the stronger our desire to serve people should be. A good understanding of *zakāt* shows us the strong social Message of Islam: to pray to

God is to give to one's brother or sister; this is the foundation of Islam as understood by Abū Bakr who warned, after the Prophet's death, that he would fight anyone who wanted to distinguish between Prayer and the payment of *zakāt* (and this is what effectively happened with the southern tribes). The same appeal is to be found in the prescription of fasting the month of Ramaḍān. An act of worship in itself, it also draws Muslims to feel the necessity to eat, drink and, by extension, to provide every single human with enough to subsist on. The month of Ramaḍān should be a period within which the Believer strengthens his Faith and spirituality while he develops his sense of social justice. Pilgrimage, obviously, has the same double dimension, for the gathering at Makka is the great testimony of this community of Faith existing among the Muslims. Men and women, together, at the Centre, praying to One God, members of one community sharing the same one hope, that is to please the Creator and to be forgiven and rewarded in the Hereafter.

For Muslims, the day-to-day practise of their Religion gives birth, naturally, to the deeply anchored sentiment of being a member of a community. This dimension is inherent in the Islamic Faith and way of life which, in return, are both strengthened, shaped and directed by this community feeling: "*All Believers are but brethren,*"[10] reads the Qur'ān. Wherever Muslims live we witness the birth of a community first created by and based on common Prayer and the prescribed acts of worship and then growing, as the Muslims start to think of and actually set social activities around the mosque or through the medium of other Islamic institutions. This process is visible everywhere throughout the world in Islamic as well as in Western countries. To say the *shahāda*, which is, as we said, the essence of the Muslim identity, is to uphold this community sentiment with its immediate implication towards social activities. In philosophical terms, one could say that this feeling partakes of the Muslims' identity, namely it is one of its distinctive attributes. The Prophet said: "You must gather, for the wolf does not attack but the stray sheep."[11]

A re-reading of the above analysis regarding the community aspect of the four pillars of Islam shows a progression in the sentiment of belonging. Prayer establishes bonds with our Muslim neighbour, in a specific place, while *zakāt* widens the circle of our social relations for the amount must be spent on needy people within the area it has been levied.[12] The fast develops a still wider feeling of community since we are, through that fast and thought, in spiritual communion with the poor throughout the world. This communion eventually takes on a real and physical effect with the Pilgrimage to Makka, the sacred place of gathering for millions of Muslims, the symbol of the *umma*.

This is in fact the third circle which determines the belonging of the Muslim: the *umma* is a community of Faith, of feeling, of brotherhood, of destiny. As a single Muslim saying the *shahāda*, he should know and understand that his individual act is a part, an essential part, of the *shahāda* borne by the whole community of Believers: every Muslim is individually invested of the common responsibility to bear witness to the Message before all mankind. This is exactly the meaning of the verse we have already quoted which links the notion of *umma* (the body, in the singular) with the duty of Believers (the members, in the plural):

> *And thus We willed you to be a community of the middle way, so that with your lives you might bear witness before all mankind.*[13]

Therefore, every Muslim, man and woman, not only upholds this dimension personally but also understands that it is a duty to spread and to transmit it to his/her children. It is, in fact, an effective belonging which is brought about by an in-depth understanding of *tawḥīd*: the Oneness of God shedding particular light on the *umma* and its responsibility before Him. Therefore, what is happening within the *umma* should interest every Muslim as it is a part of his identity. The Prophet's statement in this respect is plain: "He who is not concerned with the Muslims' affairs is not one of us."[14] To be Muslim, anywhere in the world, means to experience and develop this feeling of belonging to the *umma* as if one were an organ of a great body. the Prophet Said: "The *umma* is one body, if one part is ill the whole body feels it..."[15]

Does this mean that this belonging, based on Faith, affection and brotherhood, has no restrictions and that it is the only parameter of judgement allowing us, for instance, to say: "All that is done in the name of and for the *umma* is good and what is not is to be rejected"? This statement, sometimes uttered by Muslims themselves, by no means conveys Islamic teaching, for just as there are limits in one's obedience to parents, so there are principles by which a Muslim bases his belonging and then his supporting. The greatness of the Islamic *umma* is to be understood in the fact that it is a community of the middle path which must bear witness to the Faith before all mankind. This by defending and spreading justice, solidarity and values pertaining to honesty, generosity, brotherhood and love. The feeling of belonging does not signify that a Muslim is allowed to accept or support an injustice just because its author is his brother in Faith; on the contrary, in the name of his Religion and being a member of the *umma*, he has to stop him and confront him. The Prophet stated with strength: "Help your brother, whether he is doing wrong to others, or is being wronged. A man protested: 'O Messenger of God, I can understand helping one who is being wronged, but how can I help him when he is wrong?' The Prophet replied: 'Stop him from doing wrong: this is your help to him'."[16]

This feeling of belonging has to be directed by the principles revealed by God, otherwise it becomes a kind of blood or tribal attachment which is in complete opposition with the message of Islam. We showed above that even the closest ties, those between parents and children, are subject to the principle of justice and this is the case, obviously, with respect to relations within the *umma* as well as with other peoples or nations. Justice has priority over emotion, be it affection or aversion:

> *O you who have attained to Faith! Be ever steadfast in your devotion to God, bearing witness to the Truth in all equity; and never let hatred of anyone lead you into the sin of deviating from justice. Be just: this is closest to being God-conscious. And remain conscious of God: verily, God is aware of all that you do.*[17]

Therefore, if the feeling of belonging to the *umma* is inherent in the Islamic Faith and part of the essence of *tawḥīd*, we have to stress, however, the fact that this attachment relies on a good understanding of the mission of the Muslim community as a whole, that is to bear witness to their belief in God's presence before all mankind by supporting justice and human dignity in every circumstance, towards Muslims as well as non-Muslims.[18]

The principle of justice is indeed the parameter and, as part of its genuine implementation, there is, in the Qur'ān and the *Sunna*, a very specific situation which is of a nature to direct – and sometimes to restrict – involvement in and for the *umma*, namely when Muslims are bound by a contract or an agreement. When discussing the notion of *shahāda* above, we identifyied the importance of the contract in Islam, and the Revelation is clearly as regards this issue: "*Every contract shall We ask about*"[19] and the Believers are those "*who are faithful to their trusts and to their pledges.*"[20]

This is true to the point that if Muslims are unfairly treated or persecuted in a country with which another Muslim community has signed an agreement, it is impossible for the latter to intervene for respect of the contract comes first. This is clearly stated in the Qur'ān:

> *Behold, as for those who have attained to Faith, and who have forsaken the domain of evil and are striving hard, with their possessions and their lives, in God's cause, as well as those who shelter and succour (them) – these are (truly) the friends and protectors of one another. But as for those who have come to believe without having migrated (to your country) – you are in no way responsible for their protection until such a time as they migrate (to you). Yet, if they ask you for succour against religious persecution, it is your duty to give (them) this succour – except against a people between whom and yourselves there is a covenant: for God sees all that you do.*[21]

Although this verse refers to a situation when there exists an entity – a Muslim state such as that of Madina and a non-Muslim neighbour – it remains possible to infer at least three important teachings from its content:

1. Muslims are not responsible for their fellow Believers who choose to live in another area and who are bound to another state (through an explicit or tacit agreement).

2. It is the duty of Muslims to react when their brothers and sisters are exposed to persecution on account of their religious beliefs.[22]

3. The duty to succour persecuted people cannot be fulfilled if there is a treaty (of alliance or of non-interference), for such intervention would signify unilateral breach of the covenant obligations.

These three observations are of great importance when discussing the notion of *umma* and the characteristics of being attached to it. Part of the Muslim identity is directed by the principle of justice and shaped and restricted by the pacts that can be signed by Muslims – as an individual or as a community – in one circumstance or another.

The *sīra* of the Prophet teaches us that he submitted himself to the clauses of the covenant he signed with the tribes of the Quraysh at Ḥudaybiyya. It was agreed that if someone were to leave Madina for Makka, he would be allowed to stay there, whereas if somebody were to escape from Makka, the Prophet would not accept him and would have to send him back to Makka. When later a Muslim, was freed from Makka and arrived at Madina, the Prophet refused to let him stay for this would have been a betrayal of the pact: to the great astonishment of his Companions, the Prophet sent the man back showing them, by this attitude, that the agreement could not admit any exception. It was only later, when the Quraysh tribes first broke the terms of the Treaty of Ḥudaybiyya, that the Prophet decided to direct his troops towards Makka.

Thus, to summarise our discussion about the notion of *umma*, three observations can be made. First, the notion of belonging based on faith, religion and brotherhood partakes of the essence of Islamic teaching and is one of its distinctive features since it expresses that the link with God (*rabbāniyya*) is completely fulfilled through an active and positive involvement in society, from the small family unit to the encompassing reality of the *umma*. Second, in light of his Faith, the Muslim is subject to the principle of justice which, in any circumstance must be his criterion, rather than an abstract feeling of belonging that relies solely on the fact that "we are all Muslims". Clearly put, a Muslim should feel that he belongs to God first and that the Creator will never accept a lie, a betrayal or injustice by an individual Muslim or a Muslim community for they should be, on the contrary, models of rectitude, honesty, justice and trustworthiness. Third, contracts determine our status, fix our duties and rights and direct the nature and scope of our actions. Once agreed, the terms of a covenant should be respected and if there is a point which seems to work against Muslim rights – or even their conscience as Believers – this has to be discussed and negotiated since Muslims are, unilaterally, not allowed to breach a treaty.

## C. To be a European Citizen

The above analysis should help us tackle the problem of Muslim residents and citizens in a European country. The same questions which were put to the Jews for decades, if not centuries, have arisen among Muslims as to the authenticity of their belonging. Are they members of the *umma* whose orders they are completely bound by or rather true citizens of the state in which they live, bound, as all other citizens, by its constitution and laws. What are they first: Muslim or British, French, German or Spanish? In such a situation, the point is plain: are the so-called European-Muslims trustworthy?

This questioning on such a fundamental issue is legitimate as long as some notions remain approximately defined and vaguely understood by both the Muslims and the indigenous population. This is the case of the concept of *umma* to which the Muslims are attached and feel that they belong to. We have explained above what its horizon is, the way of its actualisation in view of the principle of justice and respect for the treaty. This explanation is of great interest in the question of citizenship insofar as it draws a specific structuring that should permit us to answer its most sensitive point.

Before entering this study, it appears necessary to clarify one essential point which is recurrent when discussing the status of Muslims in Europe: namely, do they consider themselves first as

Muslims or as Europeans? Behind this apparently simple question, one can perceive a set of concerns mixing doubts and suspicions towards these new residents or citizens. Yet even if, at first glance, this questioning seems legitimate, a thorough reflection upon it shows that it is indeed a non-issue insofar as faith and nationality, as understood within the framework of the current national constitutions, are not of the same nature. To be a Muslim signifies to uphold a trust (*amāna*) which gives a meaning to one's life: it is to be inhabited and imbibed by an overall conception of life, death and destiny directed by the belief in a Creator. Philosophically speaking, the "Muslim identity" answers the question of being and as such it is basic and fundamental, since it justifies life itself. The concept of nationality, as understood in industrialised countries, is of a completely different nature: as an element of identity, it structures – within both a given constitution and a given space – the way one is to deal with his fellow citizens or fellow human beings. Muslim identity is an answer to the question "Why?" while national identity answers the question "How?" and it would be senseless and foolish to expect geographical attachment to come first or to solve the question of being. All things considered, it all depends on what we are speaking about. Thus, in the context of a philosophical debate, an individual is *a Muslim of British or French or Belgian nationality* just as it is understood in the case of a humanist or Christian asked to expound his views on life. If the discussion is carried out on the social or political level, then this individual is *British, French or Belgian and of Muslim faith*, just as others are of Jewish or Christian faith. As a matter of fact, the dispute over a terminological choice between "a French Muslim" or "a Muslim Frenchman" is actually pointless.

Therefore the true question is not, from a Muslim point of view, to justify the first attachment of believers – which, naturally, is to God and their faith – but, more specifically, to clarify the nature of the articulation which exists between the prescriptions of the Islamic references and the concrete reality of citizenship in a European country. Do the Islamic sources allow a Muslim to be a genuine European citizen, or is there such a contradiction that would make the union "Muslim-European" impossible to actualise? Some elements towards an answer have already appeared through our discussion about the *umma*, but it is still important to consider them within the framework of this specific issue.

### *1. The current situation*

Before referring to the Islamic legal framework with respect to the Muslim presence in Western countries, we should point out some objective facts so that we can draw an overall picture of the current situation of the Muslims in Europe. It is this reality we have to contemplate for it will be through its prism that we return to the Islamic references in order to formulate appropriate responses. Three overall observations, then, in this respect must be made:

1. Every European country has its own legal framework which refers mostly to a national constitution – the fundamental law – body of laws and a specific jurisprudence. The constitution and the laws work as both a frame of reference and a structure which are the backbone of the nation and the state. This legal framework determines the specific status of citizens, residents, foreigners or tourists.
2. Millions of Muslims – when coming into these countries as workers, students, refugees or after a family reunion – have tacitly or explicitly recognised the binding character of the constitution or the laws of the country they enter into and then live in. By signing a work contract or asking for a visa, they acknowledge the validity and authority of the constitution, the laws and the state all at once.[23] This is clear for residents and passing workers and it is even more obvious in the case of citizens who take a solemn oath to respect their country's fundamental laws.[24] As for young Muslims of second and subsequent generations, they are either citizens, and as such naturally bound by the legislation, or residents, who are bound by the agreement previously made by their parents.
3. As a minority in a non-Islamic environment, the Muslims face problems of diverse types. It is a natural process

known by all minorities throughout the world and over history. It is important, however, to proceed to a meticulous work of classification since the problems are neither of the same nature nor of the same level. We must distinguish the difficulties relating to legislation[25] – which require a specific treatment – from the problems of culture and adaptation that are also greatly influenced by the social and economic situation. Often the latter are confused with the former by the Muslims themselves (for it is often difficult for them to objectively assess their own situation) but also by the indigenous community who sometimes read the laws through their fear of these new and very strange Muslim residents and, in this, make legislation say what it does not say.

These three observations are significant insofar as they allow us to return to the Islamic sources with a clearer perception of the European reality within which Muslims have to live. This is indeed the starting point from which we have to consider Islamic teachings.

## 2. *The Islamic sources*

One of the most frequent questions among Muslims living in the West is to know whether they are allowed to live in Europe or the United States or not, for these areas are part of *dār al-ḥarb* or, at least, of *dār al-kufr*.[26] We have already discussed the issue of an appropriate name – preferring the appellation *dār ash-shahāda* which, in itself, conveys the idea of permission to settle in the West – but we still have to study this question specifically in the light of our references. Such an analysis will open the door to two other important observations relating to the points discussed above regarding the European situation.

1. The question of determining whether a Muslim was or was not permitted to live in a non-Islamic country or area appeared very early on as an issue in Islamic *fiqh*. The *'ulamā'*, from Abū Ḥanīfa up to contemporary *'ulamā'*, were

not unanimous in their answers, which depended on a close study of both the circumstances and the aims. There is an agreement among the *ʿulamāʾ* which stipulates that it is not permitted for a Muslim to stay in a non-Muslim environment in three cases: (a) without a determined need or a clear objective justifying the stay; (b) when the settlement is based only on a selfish will (getting a good job or more money for example) or the desire to follow a Western way of life while neglecting Islamic religious prescriptions; (c) if the Muslim allies himself with non-Muslims for the purpose of fighting Islam or other Muslims.[27] In all other cases – such as working, studying, trading or fleeing persecution – a Muslim is allowed to stay in a non-Muslim environment but only under two major conditions: (a) he should be free to say the *shahāda* and practise his religion; (b) he ought to be useful, by his work, his study and any other activity, to his community as a whole. We should add, according to this analysis, a third condition, which is for Muslims in the West, to bear witness to their Message by reminding people of God and spirituality as well as by being involved in social or economic activities leading to greater justice and dignity.

These rulings have been stipulated on the bases of Islamic references since there are numerous examples of Muslims, in history, who lived in a non-Muslim area. The Prophet Yūsuf (Joseph), for instance, not only stayed in Egypt but also worked for a non-Muslim and himself proposed his services to the polytheist King:

> *And the King said: "Bring him unto me, so that I may attach him to my own person." And when he had spoken with him, (the King) said: "Behold, (from) this day thou shalt be of high standing with us, invested with all trust!" (Joseph) replied: "Place in my charge the store-houses of the land; behold, I shall be a good and knowing keeper."*[28]

Two important observations can be made from these verses and the story they relate: first, Joseph accepted, while he was free and not persecuted, to work under the authority of a king who was not from the People of the Book (*ahl al-kitāb*) and their relations were based on trust, for the King understood that he had nothing to fear from a man who had spoken the Truth and who had shown so much honesty. Joseph, on the other hand, clearly intended to respect the explicit covenant he had made with the King: he knew that the years to come would be of plenty and that they would be able to store sufficient provisions for the foretold years of scarcity. Moreover, he knew that he had a mission to fulfil towards his own brothers first but also within this country as he had already started, when in jail, to talk to his two companions about the presence of God, the Creator, the One as well as his forefathers Abraham, Isaac and Jacob. In Egypt, surrounded by non-Believers, Joseph, the Prophet, understood plainly what it meant to be a witness to the message of *tawḥīd*. Second, Joseph, the Hebrew, whose father and family, as is related in the Qur'ān, settled in Egypt, was, by his decision, responsible for the presence of the Israelite nation in that country. He came as a foreigner, as did his family, and they all decided to stay in a polytheist environment, to remain steadfast in their devotion to the One God and to bear witness to this Truth before the people and Pharaoh. When, after decades, they were persecuted by Pharaoh, the Qur'ān, calls them people (*ahl*) of the country:

> *We convey unto thee some of the story of Moses and Pharaoh, setting forth the Truth for (the benefit of) people who will believe. Behold, Pharaoh exalted himself in the land and divided its people into castes. One group of them he deemed utterly low; he would slaughter their sons and spare (only) their women: for behold, he was one of those who spread corruption (on earth).*[29]

The "group of them" refers plainly to the Israelites, now considered as part of the people of the land subject to discrimination and deprived of almost all human rights.[30] From *foreigners*, the Hebrews, sons of Jacob, became *people of the land* who would flee because of this persecution: this appellation is not meaningless and one must ponder over the transformation of the Jewish status it implies (even if they were persecuted for their belief).

There are other examples in the Prophet's life regarding this issue. He himself, Messenger among his own people, tried to stay as long as possible in Makka. He sought and obtained the support of polytheists, and especially from his uncle Abū Ṭālib who never rejected the old Arab beliefs. When the persecutions became almost unbearable, he received God's permission to send some of the new Muslims away so that they could secure protection. They went to the Christian leader, an-Najāshī, the Negus, in Abyssinia who accepted them even though he was not Muslim himself and nor were his people. The Muslims, thus, lived in a non-Islamic environment under the authority of a leader they respected for he was fair, trustworthy and generous. Umm Salama, who lived in Abyssinia for several years within the small group of Muslim immigrants, explained later how they had appreciated this ruler and how they had hoped that his army, although he and his people were not Muslims, would defeat its enemies.[31]

The Prophet then sent Musʿab ibn ʿUmayr to Madina, which was not a Muslim city. He had to teach Islam to the small group of new converts and also to bear witness to the new Revelation before the people of Madina. The environment was not Islamic, and sometimes even hostile, for the different tribal leaders were afraid of having their authority disputed. When ordered to stop by one of the city's rulers during one of his lessons on the Qur'ān, Ibn ʿUmayr answered: "Could you please listen to what I am saying: if you like it, I shall continue, if not I surely shall stop." Having asked for the freedom to speak, he nevertheless made it clear that he would respect the decision of the ruler since he was under his authority and, as such, bound by the rules governing the city.

Finally, the Prophet himself, subjected to terrible and continuous persecution, was allowed to leave Makka. He had prepared for his departure to Madina for more than a year and eventually left with his close Companion Abū Bakr. In this very crucial situation, for it was a question of life or death, the Prophet chose a very competent and trustworthy polytheist ʿAbdullāh ibn Urayqaṭ to guide them. From this story two important teachings have been inferred: first, that the Prophet himself left a city where the Muslims were in a minority to seek protection. Ten years later, after having conquered his own city of origin and freeing the access to the "Sacred Mosque" (*al-Masjid al-Ḥaram*), he decided to return to Madina which had become his city, the city of the Prophet (*Madinat ar-Rasūl*), the place where he wished to die. The second teaching is also of great significance for this story shows that the Prophet did not hesitate to be in constant contact with non-Muslims and to use their services when he judged them to be competent and honest. The degree of trust was very high for, at that time, he decided to follow a guide who shared the beliefs of his own enemies. The *ʿulamāʾ* of *ḥadīth* have related a great number of situations within which the Prophet used the services of non-Muslims during wars or for running state affairs. Therefore, the Prophet worked together and dealt with non-Muslims on the basis of trust and competence, not only because he and his community were in the minority but as an expression of a fundamental principle directing relations between Muslims and non-Muslims. His respect for the latter was high when they excelled in their work and were true proponents of justice and equity and he conveyed this kind of human recognition even when a non-Muslim died. Once in Madina, while some Jewish communities were plotting against the Muslims, he gave a profound testimony of this respect. A funeral procession passed near the Prophet and he stood up as a mark of respect. Embarrassed, his Companions said, "O Messenger of God, this is the procession of a Jew!" to which the Prophet firmly answered, "Was he not a human being?"[32] This was the teaching of the Prophet and Muslims, especially those living in the West, should remember, and be reminded of the meaning and profoundness of his way of acting.

To sum up the points discussed in this first observation, we must highlight the fact that Islamic sources allow a Muslim to live in a non-Islamic environment depending on the Believer's intention and under three major conditions: to be free to practise, to bear witness to the Message and to be useful to Muslims and society as a whole. Social relations with non-Muslims are based on justice, trustworthiness and honesty and, furthermore, religion is by no means the criterion for the recognition of a specific competence within social, scientific or technological fields. Whether they are in a majority or a minority, Muslims are ordered to be fair and to acknowledge people's skills, whoever they are, in order to work together with and learn from them.

2. The way Muslims should deal with others, Muslim or non-Muslim, is based, as we have seen, on certain important conditions. These have been stipulated over history by the *ʿulamāʾ* according to the situation their respective community was facing: when living, for instance, under the leadership of a Muslim dictator who did not respect the rulings of Islam, when in contact with non-Muslim communities or when in a minority in a non-Islamic environment. Significantly, it was a question of fixing the principles of the Islamic attitude in situations which were considered "extra"-ordinary or "ab"-normal. Normality, in the *ʿulamā*'s mind, being for a Muslim to live in an Islamic society ruled by Islamic references under a Muslim leader respecting the Qur'ān and the *Sunna.*[33] The first principle is that Muslims are expected, in any context, to strive for more justice and to try to change the situation for the better according to the Prophet's saying: "Whosoever of you sees an evil action, let him change it with his hand; and if he is not able to do so, then with his tongue; and if he is not able to do so, then with his heart – and that is the weakest of Faith."[34] Nevertheless, in social, political and even financial fields, human affairs are based on agreements and contracts and,

as identified above, their respect is binding and must have priority in the Muslims' eyes. Fayṣal Mawlawī aptly notes that, according to the great majority of *'ulamā'*, Muslims are also bound by the decisions and acts of a perverted ruler or dictator "as long as he does not commit a sin or something against the Islamic teaching".[35] In such a situation they are no longer bound by his acts since, by doing so, he has betrayed the tacit agreement they had that both, himself and his people, were to respect the authority of Islamic sources. Therefore, they have the right, and the duty, to take over from him, by all legal means.

Following this first observation – which places the emphasis on the importance of agreement – it should be noted that the Muslims of today, even if they do not recognise corrupt leaders or the totalitarian political systems of their country of origin, are bound by the covenants signed by them with other countries as long as they do not impose upon them to accept or do something against their religion. Therefore, these international covenants, as well as the visas they obtain to visit a country, are binding for resident Muslims, and furthermore for the citizens who are under the authority of the national constitution. The overall ruling here is that Muslims are bound by the terms of their contract except for the specific case in which they would be *constrained* to act against their conscience. This precision, regarding the terms used, is necessary for some radical Islamic groups claim that a Muslim cannot be bound by a constitution which allows interest (*ribā*), alcohol (*khamr*) and other behaviour which contradicts Islamic teachings. Yet, if European constitutions effectively allow such transactions or behaviour, they do not *oblige* Muslims to resort to them or to act in such a way. Therefore they must, on the one hand, respect the running legislation – since their presence is based on a tacit or explicit pact – and, on the other, avoid all kinds of activities or involvements which are in opposition to their belief. One can then see that it is clearly in the name of faithfulness to the Islamic teachings of *Sharī'a* and

> *fiqh* that Muslims can live in the West, and that it is their duty to respect the law of the country. In other words, Islamic law and jurisprudence *order* a Muslim individual to submit to the framework of positive law in force in his country of residence in the name of the tacit moral covenant which already underlies his very presence. To put it differently again, *implementing the Sharīʿa*, for a Muslim citizen or resident in Europe, is explicitly to respect the constitutional and legal framework of the country in which he is a citizen. Whereas one might have feared a *conflict of loyalties*, one cannot but note that it is in fact the reverse, since faithfulness to Islamic teachings results in an even more exacting legal *implantation* in the new environment. *Loyalty to one's faith and conscience requires firm and honest loyalty to one's country*: the *Sharīʿa* requires honest citizenship within the frame of reference constituted by the positive law of the European country concerned. How could one be more explicit? Once this is established (the presence of the Muslim in the West and his obligation to respect the law), it is the responsibility of the Muslims, along with their *ʿulamāʾ*, to study every situation where specific difficulties arise, as with mandatory insurance, inheritance, marriage and so forth. Rulings should be formulated – as they already are on numerous issues – by taking into account the legislation of the country, Islamic teachings and the necessities of the original environment which the Muslims are facing.

Three elements, then, are to be kept in mind: first, the Islamic sources make it possible for a Muslim to live in the West; second, he or she is under the authority of an agreement whose terms must be respected as long as they do not constrain him/her to act against his/her conscience. Third, if such an unusual situation should occur, a specific study should be done in order to find a suitable solution for the Muslim, as both a practising Believer and as a resident or citizen. It is clear, from our previous observations, that it is unlawful for a Muslim living in the West, in the light of Islamic references, to act against the laws, to abuse, misuse or cheat.

Once an agreement has been made, to act in accordance with the law is, in itself, an act of worship. Even Abū Ḥanīfa, who went as far as permitting Muslims to use interest (*ribā*) when trading with non-Islamic countries (*dār al-ḥarb*, in his binary terminology), made it clear that trade with non-Muslims was allowed as long as it accorded with the rules, but by no means could Muslims abuse or cheat them. For the citizen, as for the resident, to act with honesty, rectitude and dignity is the best way to protect and affirm one's identity as a Muslim and to bear witness to the Islamic Message of justice before one's fellow citizens and neighbours.

### 3. *The clause of conscience*

We have shown how the idea of belonging to the *umma* is shaped and structured and how, through the notion of contract, the apparent discrepancy between the *umma* and country disappears. Furthermore, the preceding analysis demonstrates that a Muslim is allowed to live in a non-Islamic country as long as he is able to protect his identity and practise his religion[36] and that his residence is based on a tacit or an explicit agreement which, in view of Islamic teaching, he has to respect. As a resident or a citizen, the Muslim is asked to respect the terms of the constitution of the country he or she lives in. This is clearly what the immigrant Muslim has to declare when he decides to naturalise, after having been a resident in a Western country for several years: the oath (*qasam*) he then takes[37] means that he will respect both the country and its constitution. He is not asked to like or to agree with every single law or rule which is in force in that country or to do all that is permissible according to the legislation but, more specifically, he is expected both to recognise (*ya'tarif*) the legislation and to act within the scope of the law (*yaltazim bil-qawānīn*). These are the conditions of the oath and once it is taken the Muslim is bound by it as stipulated in the well-known Islamic rule *al-muslimūn 'inda shurūṭihim*: Muslims are bound by the conditions they have accepted.

Therefore the Muslim, as a citizen, must make allowances and find his way in the Western environment. Within the huge field of what is permissible in these societies he must determine in good faith, as a Muslim, which things he can do and which he must avoid. Some of the latter are very clear, as in the case of what is prohibited by Islam but allowed in Western legislation, like intoxicants (alcohol and what is sometimes called light drugs), interest extramarital sexual intercourse. He has the choice and he should develop the will to keep away from what does not fit his identity and the correct practice of Islam. On numerous other issues, the right way of acting is sometimes less obvious and requires study and clarification, for some questions need specific answers. How should we educate our children in Western society? What health and sexual education should we provide for them? How should we deal with banks? What about insurance or mortgages? and so forth. These are but a few of a considerable number of questions which have arisen within the Muslim communities in Europe during the past 30 years. Yet, these real problems must be distinguished from the upstream question of the legislation in the scope of which Muslims should act. In other words, what the full scope of the national constitution permits is one thing, but what Muslims must choose, among the choices allowed within the said scope, to live according to their faith is another. Muslims are sent back to their responsibility as regards their involvement in education and social and cultural activities in the West, in order to give concrete form to the best behaviour and to provide themselves with answers appropriate to their reality (or possibly with adapted institutions). It is therefore not a strictly *legal* issue since it is, more globally, a matter of thinking out the terms of a specific, participative involvement which will enable us to live our presence in the West, with its requirements and perspectives, in a serene frame of mind.

Once this distinction has been formulated and understood, it appears that the responsibility of Muslim citizens in Europe is great. Not only should they be citizens respectful of their duties, but they must, moreover, determine the foundations and contents of their "Western-Muslim identity" allowing them, in such an environment, to develop a harmonious personality from childhood to adult life. This is indeed a difficult task and a challenge, but it is nonetheless inevitable for it seems the only way (once one acknowledges that it is permitted to settle in the West) for Muslim communities themselves to apprehend and prepare their future in such an apparently disrupting context. This actually means that in every European country Muslims should multiply their efforts to provide their respective communities with all the institutions, organisations and places of worship needed – in partnership with other official bodies – in order to fulfil their task. There is absolutely no contradiction in that matter between their citizenship and their being Muslims: the law allows them to act in this sense, their faith commands it.

Thus, concerning Western legislation, the scope of permission is wider than that of compulsion. Nevertheless, it could happen that citizenship would leads someone to face or to feel a great tension between their faith, their conscience, and the duties related to their nationality. In such situations, they would have to refer to the legal notion of the "clause of conscience" which allows them to make it clear that some actions or types of behaviour are in contradiction with their faith. Such cases are rare – as far as their legal aspect is concerned – but it is still necessary to study them because they perfect the picture we are drawing up of the Muslim European citizen. Three remarks should be brought to the fore: the first two bring in the notion of the "clause of conscience" while the last one is linked to the recognition of "necessity" which implies the idea of the development of Islamic *fiqh* in light of the Western context.

1. We have mentioned above that for a Muslim the "principle of justice" is, after his belief in the Oneness of God, the fundamental parameter of his social, economic and political commitment. This principle comes first, before himself, his parents, the rich, the poor and the *umma* itself. It is exactly the same for his citizenship. If, for instance, he is called upon to participate in a war which is unfair or based on the sole desire for power or control (a territory, interests or something else), a Muslim should not, in good faith, take part in it. He is not allowed to fight or kill for money, land or power, and so he must absolutely avoid being involved in a war of colonisation or oppression. In such a case, in the name of

the "clause of conscience", he must plead "conscientious objection", for as a Muslim his faith and conscience cannot bear a hindrance to the principle of justice before God. This principle has to be respected individually in every situation when it appears clear that the grounds for war have nothing to do with the defence of justice, regardless of the identity and religion of the foe. Numerous personalities have pleaded "conscientious objection" throughout history, and the cases of boxer Muhammad Ali (Cassius Clay) and of so many Christians during the Vietnam war are memorable. They accepted, as objectors, to be sentenced to jail for refusing to obey the State and military order: this is how Muslims should act in such circumstances. Prison is better than committing injustice, as Yūsuf (Joseph) said when prompted to act wrongly: "*O my Sustainer! Prison is more desirable to me* ..."[38]

2. There exists a general Islamic ruling which forbids a Muslim to fight or kill a fellow Muslim and this ruling should be observed at all times.[39] Therefore, a Muslim citizen of a Western country, in order to avoid placing himself in such a situation, should also plead conscientious objection. Nevertheless, it could happen that the attitude of the Muslim leader is unjust and wrong. In that case, a particular decision could be taken after a close study of the whole context and it is then for the *ʿulamāʾ* – in view of both the Islamic teachings and the context – to formulate a legal opinion as to the permissibility of Muslims being involved in such a fight. The ban, however, remains the general rule but still the principle of justice is to be considered and the debates among the *ʿulamāʾ* on this question have been intense throughout history.

3. It happens sometimes that a resident or citizen in the West finds themselves obliged to resort to transactions which are forbidden by their religion. We stated above that the field of the possible is very wide and that Muslims should avoid, when they have the choice, whatever does not fit the Islamic

prescriptions. Yet, some regulations are compulsory (banks, insurance, slaughter, burial, etc.) and need specific considerations. The principles of Islam remain of course the parameter but Muslims, living in a minority in a country whose laws they have decided to accept, should find a way to protect their identity. A close assessment of the situation has to be undertaken by both the average Muslim and the *'ulamā'*, so as to determine the degree of compulsion (and thus the degree of necessity); the existence and the nature of a possible *maṣlaḥa* (if one really exists); the ways which could permit one to act in greater accord with the Islamic rulings. It is only after this that an adapted *fatwā* should be formulated. This has already happened in Western countries over the last 20 years and numerous *fatāwā* have been stipulated regarding Prayers when working, Muslim girls banned from school, dealing with banks, insurance and so forth.[40]

It should be noticed that some of these *fatāwā* are, or must be considered, as temporary, since they provide Muslims with specific answers in a very specific context. Legislation in Western countries has been thought out and elaborated upon for a society from which the Muslims were absent. With respect to some issues, although very rare, Muslim citizens have the right, and the duty from an Islamic point of view, to ask for a genuine recognition of both their presence and their identity and this could mean, in the future, that some laws' content or scope be reconsidered. Western legislation, as well as the current situation of Muslims, is not absolute, timeless or eternal and Muslims, henceforth citizens and at home, must be involved in legal matters and make propositions which permit them to develop and give shape to a balanced Western identity. This by no means signifies that the Muslims are seeking to throw away the foundations of the nation or to appeal to "particular laws for the Muslims" as we have heard here and there. Clearly, and more specifically, Muslims as citizens have the right – within the framework of the national

> legislation – to be recognised as Muslims and it could be that some laws no longer match the current landscape of Western societies. Such laws – very few of them in fact – should be reconsidered or, at least, their foundations discussed. Henceforth, as part of their European societies, Muslims have the duty, according to Islamic teachings, to protect their identity, to respect their commitment towards the laws and, within the wide space of freedom provided, to strive and to act across all the different fields (social, legal, economical and political) to bring about a Muslim personality as well as a Western landscape which, to the largest extent, could match.

Apart from these three overall observations we do not think that is is possible to refer to the clause of conscience. These are the borderline cases which have to be considered and studied closely. Many Muslims claim that it is not possible for them to accept the way marriages are officially established in Europe, the Western school curriculum or other issues of this kind for they do not fit their belief and thus are against their conscience. It is necessary here to be very precise and clear for such claims are of a completely different nature. Some issues which partake of the essence of the Islamic Faith do exist and, as such, they take priority and must be taken into account wherever the Muslim lives. Freedom of worship, respect of the principle of justice, and the prohibition on killing for power or money are of this nature: non-respect for these rulings shakes the foundation of the Muslim identity. They are, as we said, borderline cases and this is why we speak of the "clause of conscience".

Other issues – school, education, marriage, burial – do not fall into the same level of consideration in light of the Islamic teachings. They are certainly of great importance but still it is possible to find solutions within the framework of the legislation, namely in accordance with the terms of the tacit or explicit covenant that exists with the country. Therefore, they have nothing to do with a possible "clause of conscience" but rather require the true involvement of Muslims so that they can find appropriate solutions. We shall discuss some of these issues in subsequent works but still we must acknowledge that some of the absolute and definitive claims made in the name of Islam by Muslims living in the West rely on a partial knowledge of both the European environment and the essentials of Islamic rulings.

## D. Between Assimilation and Alienation

The general and widespread statement that Muslims living in the West must have the right to protect their Faith, their identity and their religious practice seems to rely on evidence which, as such, is not disputed. At least among those Muslims who continuously repeat that this objective has to be achieved. Yet, reflecting on this issue, it appears that the discourse identifying the notion of Muslim identity is very theoretical and imprecise and does not rely on an analysis of the concrete situation of the Muslims in Europe. It is as if the "identity" were a collection of rules sufficient to portray what a Muslim is, and what he is not. Unable to establish distinctions and classify the problems they are facing, Muslims confuse and mix up the different dimensions of the latter. Legal issues are often approached from an emotional angle whereas aspects of one's intimate life and feelings are reduced to a configuration of predetermined rules. We have already discussed some elements of the former but within the notion of identity we are totally engaged in the latter dimension. It is, in fact, a very complex notion since, from an Islamic point of view, the Muslim identity is altogether Faith, rulings, emotions, and feelings which have to be organised, shaped and harmonised within a spiritual and active way of life.

Therefore, we must avoid being deceived and misled by appearances when discussing such a sensitive subject. To be assimilated – that is to lose one's own identity – or to remain alien – that is to live apart from society in order to protect oneself – are not states we can assess simply on the basis of some manifest features. We must be very cautious and tactful when dealing with such notions for they appeal to diverse and sensitive parts of every human personality. What has to be noticed first is that, on the scale of possible postures, when living as a minority, these two extreme attitudes are the more natural and normal ones that a human being seeks to adopt. To try, on the one hand, to appear and act as the majority do, in order to become the least visible possible, is indeed a spontaneous tendency whereas, re-acting to and affirming one's difference through a process based on clear separation, up to the point of sectarian disposition, is also an instinctive posture we witness in all human societies. Therefore, young Muslims who, within European societies, act in one of these two ways cannot be criticised or misjudged for, in fact, there is nothing more natural than to re-act as they do.

The problem, in fact, rests precisely on that point: both attitudes, even if it is not apparent in the first case, are purely a *re-action* to the environment since it is a question of accepting or refusing it. Thus, they are the first natural step in the formation of one's identity in the sense that, at this stage, the identity is defined from outside, through the type of relations the individual has elaborated with his environment. This is the kind of attitude we can witness nowadays in young and not so young Muslims and they can take very subtle forms at the highest level of intellectual development or academic elaboration. Nevertheless, it is clear that such identity is borrowed insofar as "something is missing" which is indeed the assertive reflection and definition *from within* in order to determine what the Muslim identity is *per se*, according to Islamic sources. In other words, what is the identity of the one who says the *shahāda* once we acknowledge that it is not the simple words we pronounce but, above all, a disposition of the heart which we want to keep alive? This was the teaching of the Prophet when he was told by a Companion that a man, who had seemingly said the *shahāda* out of fear, was still had killed. Upset, he been answered: "How were you able to know what was in his heart?"

There is a need today to define the Muslim identity in the West so as to avoid the reacting process. This means considering both the Islamic teaching and the European environment in order to bring about a thorough reflection of very sensitive issues (such as Faith, emotion, psychology, education, study, culture, etc.) and at different stages of human growth (i.e. as individuals and in community) in order to elaborate adapted answers and means of transmission and education in Europe. This seems the only way that will, in the future, permit Muslims in the West to avert the re-active posture and instead direct themselves towards a more assertive and confident self-representation.

This step is of the greatest importance. As long as a consistent number of Muslims do not reach an autonomous perception of their own identity in the West it will be very difficult for them, if not impossible, simply to believe that they have something to give to the society they live in. They will hardly consider that they are able to have a positive impact on this society, let alone have their contribution recognised. Yet, this is the second aspect of *shahāda*, as we discussed above, and Muslims are commanded to testify that their message conveys dignity, justice, generosity and brotherhood. How can this possibly be transmitted through a reactive and nervous attitude which expresses either an attempt to disappear or a strong rejection of others? Between these two extremes, the middle path is the more difficult, the more demanding: to be confident and assertive "in-between" requires acting in the name of both one's Faith and a well understood identity and not re-acting with or against others. This is indeed the less natural tendency.

The new presence of Muslims has created problems in European societies. The sudden awareness, because of their recent social visibility, that there are now millions of Muslims residing in the West and that almost half of them are already citizens, has provoked various and contradictory reactions within the indigenous populations. For some, it is the obvious sign of a perilous invasion whereas for others, still a minority, it is considered as a factor of enrichment. Politicians and academics have attempted to tackle the problem by formulating diverse strategies to integrate this new component of Western society. Sociologists, reconsidering the old concepts relating to minority presence, have tried to classify these strategies and propose a typology of possible approaches. The three patterns – which work nowadays as concepts of reference – are well known: at one extreme we find the assimilationist pattern which supposes a total amalgamation between the Muslim and Western cultural way of living which welcomes him. At the other extreme, there is the isolationist pattern which is based on the preservation of the identity through the creation of an organised religious and cultural community within the global society. In the middle, the integrationist pattern should provide both a protection to the Muslim identity and an individual status of citizenship (like indigenous peoples). This theoretical approach, whilst seeming to clarify the diverse strategies, still reveals several difficulties, not least because the two main concepts, identity and integration, are used outside of their clear and precise definitions. This, in fact, leads to much confusion for a close study shows that neither sociologists nor politicians agree on the exact content of the concepts used and, even less, on the correct appellation fitting such or such society. The French model of integration is considered as assimilationist in the majority of other European countries whereas the British multicultural society is called isolationist in France and, as such, represents the recurrent anti-model. Within the twists and turns of such complicated debates, the reality of the Muslim living in the West seems lost. Yet, it is necessary to draw a more accurate and experimental picture of this reality before trying to propose a definition of the Muslim identity and the modes of a positive integration which signifies, from an Islamic point of view, a genuine "integration of the intimate life of the hearts".

## *1. A European Muslim without Islam*

For the last four hundred years, European societies have gone through a very deep process of secularisation. Faith, Religion, and practise no longer play an important role in social life. It is as if two logics were co-existing without being linked: on the one hand, the social dimension, based on freedom, rights, individualism, work and efficiency and, on the other, the personal dimension within which every single human tries to determine his belief, fix his values and organise his intimate life. The freedom of everyone is guaranteed by the relative neutrality of the public space: Europeans are no longer used to a public manifestation of religious presence in their day-to-day lives and they themselves are, in the great majority, either not practising much or not practising at all. Pope John Paul II, in one of his latest encyclical letters, conveys his fear that secularism, as conceived in industrialised societies, might be a simple appellation, a screen, behind which the reality of atheism and irreligiousness is concealed.[41] Without going to such extremes, we can say that the fact that religion should be a private affair which does not interfere in public affairs leads us to witness, today, contradictory tendencies: on the one hand, an indifference towards religion and, very often, a new and worrying phenomenon called religious illiteracy and, on the other hand, a scattered and sometimes chaotic questioning of values along with an expressed need for spirituality through groups, sects or a very hierarchical community.

The former tendency is of course the stronger today and it is possible to state that our industrialised and modern society is, to a very great extent, *areligious* and that the values associated with its culture, such as freedom, individualism or efficiency, do not echo exactly the religious teachings based on recognition of the Creator, the necessity of Faith and the antithetical notions of good and evil. In the minds of many Europeans, their societies, over the course of history, have positively liberated them of the oppressive yoke of religion. They salute this evolution and perceive it as a process of liberation carried out in the name of the ideal of the individual and his right to freedom. The ascendancy of such a view and its impact on people is considerable, for it is difficult to resist such a strong and vigorous stream, which when backed by the media, films, advertisements, and the way of life itself, sweeps along billions of people not only in the West but in almost all large cities throughout the world. The so-called process of globalisation is, for some scholars such as Latouche or al-Mangiara, nothing but the fulfilment of the thorough Westernisation of the world.

It seems normal and just for some politicians and academics to ask Muslims, in the name of common sense, to join the dominant and, without doubt, positive "train of progress". This means, according to them, that the Muslims have to adopt the same way of dealing with their Faith and the prescriptions of religion. In other words, to become citizens like the indigenous population and to be true proponents of individualism, freedom, efficiency, to be involved in social life as citizens, and only as citizens. As for their Faith and their practices, they are of a secondary nature and pertain to their private life which means hidden, invisible, almost non-existent. No matter what the Muslim identity is or what the Muslims say about it, the fact is that a choice must be made between religion and progress, enslavement and liberation, the old tradition of duties and the modern culture of genuine freedom. Discourses do not convey the terms of these alternatives in such a brutal way and one will hear a great many pleas for recognition of the Muslim identity which are respectful and of incomparable historical value. Yet nothing is said about the content of this theoretical identity which is ceaselessly referred to while, on the other hand, history appears a dimension of little concern.

Whatever concept is used, thereafter, to describe this project of society – *assimilation, integration* or *isolation* – the reality remains the same. In short, the Muslims should be *Muslim without Islam*, for there exists a widespread suspicion that to be too much a Muslim means not to be really and completely integrated into the Western way of life and its values. Once again these statements are general and vague and rely on both the idea of religious people having their own experience and the image of Islam shaped through the spectacular events which take place on the international scene. Therefore, to speak too much about God and His Revelation, to perform daily Prayers, to refer to Faith, spirituality and morality, is to give out signs of non-adaptation and so of suspicious behaviour. If, furthermore, Muslim communities ask for mosques or cemeteries and organise themselves through organisations and specific activities, the picture is perfected: "such Muslims do not wish to live with us ... like us."

This last nuance distinguishing "with" and "like" is less trifling and insignificant than it appears at first glance. If "with us" is to signify "like us", this clearly means that the reference is to "us" and that the pattern of society which is proposed, whatever it is called, rests on the idea *we* have of *ourselves* and *others*. In fact, we would like to integrate the "idea of the other" we have and not his integration as a being who determines his identity by himself in light of both his own references and those of the West. The gap between the integration of a simple representation and one of hearts is great and, in the short as well as long term only the latter provides for a true and positive coexistence. Still its conditions are demanding for it is not a question of simply *adapting* oneself (inwardly or outwardly) to a specific environment but rather of finding the way to feel that the being genuinely *is* and *exists*, that the Muslim has the opportunity to live and develop the essential dimensions of his identity ... his heart, his Faith and his emotions.

For some Muslims, in Europe and even in the Middle East and Asia, to be part of today's world is to adapt oneself to the Western way of life. According to them, Islam most certainly is a universal message, but to be "modern" its prescriptions have to be rethought and actualised following the dominant model of the West which seems to be the universal expression of modernity. By arguing so, they reduce the message of Islam to theoretical values and manifestations of good and moral intent but which, henceforth, are at the periphery of social life. Therefore, the Muslim identity becomes just general prescriptions shared by all people along with some cultural or artistic features exhibited at times of festival or marriage. Such a concept, in fact, is based on the belief – although the apparent discourse conveys the opposite – that Western values and lifestyles are the sole universal ones and, hence, must be followed. The universality of the Islamic message, recognised in theory, is confined to one's intimate life, exiled from public view, invisible, exactly as other religions have become. There is no alternative: to be progressive, open-minded and modern, to be authentically European, means to rethink and even modify the Islamic teachings in such a way that the Muslim identity fits its environment. In such Muslims' eyes it is the latter which is the real norm and at a time of globalisation the intensity of Faith, prescribed values and recommended behaviour must be reconsidered and adapted. They neglect, and even ignore, both the internal dynamic of Islam through its legal instruments and the nature of the Muslim identity; their reference and parameter becomes the dominant model. Their discourses, "open and progressive", please the great majority of Western politicians and scholars for they accord with their own, universal, convictions. No matter if they keep silent about the inner discordances which millions of Muslims in Europe have to face.

The great majority of Muslims living in Europe do not have much concern for these questions and problems. Whether they like it or not they are swept along by the dominant stream and they seemingly live as others do. Nevertheless, the process of acculturation which looks to be irreversible, within second and third generations, is not as efficient as it appears at first glance and the question of identity is arising among young Muslim generations in all Western societies. Although the appearances of integration are safe, the reality is less simple: workers or students, men and women, involved, as is the indigenous population, in the social or political life of their countries, hardly forget their Muslim identity, even though they do not practise their religion. They are, either by the strong influence of the environment or by choice, *Muslims without Islam* but still they are Muslims and the hiatus they feel provokes questioning, doubt and sometimes discomfort and disquiet.

## 2. *Living in Europe out of Europe*

To avoid being absirbed into Western societies, many Muslims, almost instinctively, have found a refuge within community life. When circumstances allowed them, and even pushed them to as in Britain, to gather together in an area they imported or rebuilt the social fabric which had organised and directed their life in their country of origin. The aim is to be "at home", *in Europe but at home.* This process offers an important guarantee for the protection of identity: Muslims coming from India, Pakistan or anywhere else allowed to reproduce a social microcosm within which they live among themselves with few contacts with the indigenous population or society as a whole. From their point of view, this is the most appropriate means of protecting both their ethnic and Islamic identities.

In fact, what is actually protected, for instance in Britain, is strictly speaking neither the Asian ethnic group nor the Muslim identity but rather the *Asian way of living Islam*. Social relations, family bonds and models of education (with the teaching of Urdu or Punjabi languages) are imported and implemented in the micro-society without much attention being paid to the global environment in the West. There is, however, much confusion in the minds of some Muslims who know nothing else except their country of origin and this imported social fabric: Islam, in their eyes, is nothing but the way they used to live it in their cities or villages in India or Pakistan. Thus, to be faithful to the Islamic teachings means to be faithful to the Asian model of actualising them: to question or reconsider the model, for we live in Europe, is understood as a betrayal of Islam that may jeopardise the Muslim identity. Paradoxically here, we contemplate the same shortcoming as above: once again, the Message of Islam is reduced to its traditional or cultural dimension but, this time, for exactly the opposite reasons, because of a fear generated by the environment.

It is not rare, within such communities, to meet young people from second or third generations who cannot even speak English properly or do so with an Asian accent despite their being born in Britain. This phenomenon is very common among young girls who are treated as if they are in India or Pakistan and who are frequently denied the opportunity to accomplish and perfect their studies. The Western environment has, of course, an important influence on the values, fashions and behaviour of our Muslim youth but the way of dealing with these and the method of education are still traditional, adapted to another era in another context. The Muslim identity may be protected in appearance but we observe the same personal, intimate and emotional problems among the majority of young Muslims: seemingly directed by a social fabric and the rules of an Asian environment, they are nonetheless in Europe surrounded by media, fashion, music and a way of life which does not stop at their doorstep. In Europe and out of Europe at the same time, it is difficult for them, if not impossible, to define who they are and what exactly their identity, is between the rules they have been taught and the feelings which impel them.

In the majority of European countries we witness this same tendency among the youth. As already stated it is a natural reaction to an environment perceived as foreign, aggressive and oppressive. Their situation is not as it is in Britain or in the United States, for instance, for the Anglo-Saxon model of integration is based on the recognition of the community space within the idea of multiculturalism. Nevertheless, they try to develop, on a small scale, similar structured groups living according to internal rules as if they were out of Europe. In France, Belgium and Sweden some groups in recent years have tried to protect themselves from society by cutting themselves off from European modes. They do not refer to the specific traditions of their countries of origin but, instead, very often to the way of life of the Prophet and his Companions: they change their dress, wear turbans or *jelabiyya*, assiduously frequent the mosques and avoid contact with the external world and non-Muslims. Confusing Islamic teachings with the way of life and customs of the desert inhabitants of the 7th century, they express the same questioning, the same fragility with regard to their identity: they are Muslims against the European model and the only way out is to live, although in Europe, out of Europe. Their constant and assertive references to the Prophet as well as their inclination to follow the *salaf* of the first great age of Islam seems to give them a kind of confidence but the majority of these youth experience difficulties in remaining constant and they express, by virtue of their behaviour and their indecision, a profound inward questioning.

For some European States such attitudes of confinement are not considered dangerous and indeed the creation of such isolated communities was often encouraged for it appeared to promise social calm and stability. Furthermore, such communities and groups living in a kind of ataraxy were manageable for they were still dependent – socially, politically and even more economically – on the wider society and the State. Finally, the circumscribed presence of Islam and Muslims within certain traditions, cultures or fashions still permitted Western societies to consider their own references and traditions as undisturbed. However, this picture of a strange, alien and still foreign Islam keeps alive an image of what the indigenous peoples *are not*.[42] In this sense, the *very relative* integration of these communities or groups – with only a very vague definition of Muslim identity – was, and still is, of some benefit.

### *3. The middle path*

At a time when the process of globalisation – not only economically but also and above all culturally – is so powerful, it becomes all the more important to determine some milestones in the global landscape. The current is so strong that we cannot be satisfied with some referential concepts which give a very partial idea of the reality of European societies. We can continue to speak about *assimilation*, *integration* and *isolation*, but they are still empty concepts as long as we do not know who the subject, both literally and philosophically, is that we are speaking about. In other words, *who* is this Muslim we want to assimilate, integrate or isolate: without a clear definition of this entity "*who*", these last three concepts could mean exactly the same thing, implicitly conveying different intuitions as to the meaning and content of the Muslim identity.

Furthermore, from an Islamic point of view, the use of the notion of subject is by no means accidental. For Muslims to understand who they are and what they stand for means that they are able to determine their identity *per se*, according to their Islamic references and no longer through the image others develop of them as if they were but objects of some alien elaboration. It is only by acting in this way that European Muslims will feel that they are subjects of their own history, accountable before God, responsible before mankind. To be subjects of their own history also means that they will eventually go beyond this pernicious feeling of being foreigners, of being different, of being an obvious manifestation of an insoluble problem. By having a clear awareness of their identity, a new sentiment will grow, based on a more rooted self-confidence, and this will enable them to realise that their presence can be positive, that they can provide Europe with more spirituality, and a greater sense of justice and brotherhood along with a greater involvement in solidarity.

In light of our earlier discussion about the five essential fields of Islam (*al-maṣāliḥ al-khams*) and *shahāda*, we can identify four elements or dimensions which, altogether, should provide appropriate content for the concept of Muslim identity. It is, in fact, a question of extracting the esence of this identity out of the accident of its actualisation in a specific area or time. In other words, our object and aim is to distinguish Islam from Arab or Asian cultures, traditions or customs so that we can conceive in which manner the image of the European-Muslim is to be portrayed.

1. *Faith, Practice and Spirituality:*

The first and most important element of Muslim identity is *faith*, which is the intimate sign that one believes in the Creator Who has no associates. This is the meaning of the central concept of *tawḥīd*, the belief in the Oneness of God, that is confirmed and testified by the *shahāda*. In this sense, it is the purest expression of the essence of Muslim identity beyond space and time. It naturally takes concrete form in the *practice* of worship (prayer, *zakāt*, fasting, etc.). Closely linked to these two realities as their immediate consequence in the life of the Believer is the fundamental dimension of *spirituality*. Spirituality, from the Islamic point of view, is the way in which the Believer keeps alive, intensifies and strengthens his faith. Spirituality is memory, remembrance and the intimate effort to fight against the natural human tendency to forget God, the meaning of life, and the Hereafter. All the prescribed practices of Islam, and above all, of course, prayer, are in fact a way to remember (*dhikr*):

> *Verily, I – I alone – am God; there is no deity save Me. Hence worship Me alone, and perform the prayer, so as to remember Me.*[43]

Excellence, defined as the ideal behaviour for the Muslim, would be to reach a state where one would no longer forget. Excellence *(iḥsān)*, said the Prophet, is "to worship God as though you were seeing Him, for while you see Him not, yet truly He sees you."[44] That is, to try to be with God in every single circumstance.

In the multiple debates among sociologists and political experts, this dimension is very often neglected as if "faith" or "spirituality" could not be considered as "scientific constitutive elements" of an "objective identity". Yet, the word "Islam" itself means "submission" to God, literally expressing an act of worship along with its spiritual horizon. Therefore, to respect the Muslim identity does mean to recognise this first and fundamental dimension of faith and, by extension, to allow Muslims to perform all the practices which shape their spiritual life. Faith and spirituality underlie those practices which express the presence of an essential *conviction* giving meaning to life: to sever them from that means to sever them from themselves.

Muslim identity therefore is, in its first axis, "a faith, a practice and a spirituality". This is basically the dimension of intimacy and of the heart.

2. *An Understanding of Texts and Context:*

There is no true faith without understanding: for a Muslim, this means to understand both the sources (the Qur'ān and the *Sunna*) and the context within which he or she is living. The responsibility of every Muslim is based on this twofold aspect of "understanding": that is to develop, in concomitance, an "intelligence of the texts" and an "intelligence of the context" in order to find the way to remain faithful to the Islamic teachings. This has been the fundamental teaching of Islamic legal practice since the time of the Prophet, unceasingly kept up by the great scholars over the centuries. As such, *Muslim identity is not closed, confined within rigid and fixed principles*. On the contrary, it is based on a permanent dynamic and dialectic movement between the sources and the environment, in order to find a way to live in harmony. This is why the development of intellectual skills is so important in Islam and, as such, partakes of the foundations of Islamic teachings. The Muslim cannot be satisfied with a hypothetical state of nature: to be a Muslim means to strive in order to increase one's capacity, to seek tirelessly to know more, to such an extent that, in light of Islamic sources, we could state that, once the dimension of worship has been mentioned, "to be a Muslim is to learn". The Prophet said: "Seeking knowledge is compulsory for every Muslim, man and woman."[45]

More globally, this knowledge is the condition to understanding not only the meaning of the Islamic sources themselves, but also the Creation and creatures. According to the Qur'ān, which ceaselessly appeals to human beings to make use of their intelligence, both knowledge and understanding are means of intensifying one's God-consciousness:

> *Of all his servants, only such as are endowed with knowledge stand truly in awe of God.*[46]

This is one of the two aspects of understanding, the other being that the Muslim, having to act according to the Islamic teachings, should use this capacity to make choices between what is right and what is wrong, to find the best way to please God in whatever environment he finds himself. If it is plain that there is no choice without freedom, as we mentioned, we have yet to add that there is no choice either without knowledge and, furthermore, comprehension. Choice and ignorance are antithetical words. Therefore the elements of Muslim identity which come immediately after faith and spirituality are *comprehension based on knowledge* and *choice relying on freedom*. Together they constitute the dimension of *responsibility*.

Muslim identity, in its second axis, can thus be seen as open, since it is based on an intellectual attitude in which the understanding of the texts is allied to that of the context. It is therefore defined through *an active and dynamic intelligence* requiring knowledge, freedom and a sense of responsibility.

3. *To Educate and Transmit:*

Faith (*īmān*) is a trust (*amāna*) and Muslims are asked to pass on this *amāna* to their children and relatives and, as already explained, to bear witness to it before mankind. To be a Muslim is to educate and to transmit and the Prophet himself was so ordered in the early months of the revelation:

> *And warn (whomever thou canst reach, beginning with) thy kinsfolk.*[47]

Once again, the Muslim's identity is not closed and confined within his individual and personal sphere as if it only affected himself and his relation with God. To be a Muslim, on the contrary, is to uphold and to convey a conception of life founded on faith, spirituality and a fundamental comprehension of moral prescriptions. Educating one's children in order to give them the opportunity to receive the *trust* and, afterwards, to choose freely, is part of Muslim identity for a woman, for a mother, for a man, for a father. One of the most important functions of parents, is to offer their children an understanding of *what they are*, and then the children, responsible before God, will choose *what they want to be*, for, the Qur'ān says (6:164), "*No one will bear the burden of another*".

On a larger scale, as we discussed when studying the notion of *shahāda*, Muslims are convinced that the Qur'ān is the last revelation from God and that, as such, it upholds a universal dimension. Their responsibility before God is to make the message of this *trust* known and to explain its contents as much as possible. This responsibility is limited to that, for the idea of converting people has nothing to do with Islam: to spread the message is to call and to invite to a real recognition of God's presence as well as a genuine understanding of His teachings. Conversion is a matter for God only, through His revelation with every single being, and no human being has the right to interfere in this affair of the heart since he would then go beyond both his status and his prerogatives. This is the exact meaning of the expression "to bear witness to the truth before mankind" which conveys the idea that the Muslim should bear the burden of this tremendous trust among his relatives as well as before all mankind. Not only in his speech but also, and even more, through his behaviour.

The third axis of Muslim identity lets it be seen as open and always active since it is based on "being a Muslim" defined through the act of educating and transmitting.

4. *To Act and to Participate:*

The accomplishment of Muslim identity is to express and manifest one's belief through coherent behaviour. Faith, understanding, education and transmission together represent the *substratum* of the Islamic ethic and as such they should direct the Believer's acts. To be a Muslim is to act according to the Islamic teachings whatever the environment, and there is nothing in Islam that would command the Muslim to keep away from society so as to be nearer to God. It is quite the opposite and, "to attain to faith" is often, and almost essentially, linked in the Qur'ān to the fact of behaving in a good way, of "doing good works". The Prophet, as we have seen, was ceaselessly pointing to this dimension of Muslim identity. The authentic flowering of Muslim identity is linked to the possibilities one has to act according to what one *is* and *believes in*.

This action, whatever the country or the environment, is based on four major aspects of human life: to develop and protect spiritual life within society, to spread religious as well as secular education among people, to act for more justice within each sphere of social, economic and political life, and finally, to promote solidarity with all types of needy people. In the North or in the South, in the West or in the East, a Muslim is a Muslim when he clearly understands this fundamental dimension of his presence on earth: to be with God is to be with fellow humans, not only Muslims, but as the Prophet said, with "people", that is mankind as a whole:

> "The best one among you is the best one towards people."[48]

For the individual, attaining to faith must be expressed through coherent action. He can act by himself before God. Yet this is not enough, and it is his duty to strive towards participation, which clearly expresses the idea of acting with others, in a given society with the fellow citizens that make it up. The fourth axis of Muslim identity associates these two dimensions of the active being and the participating being, in other words of the individual and of the social being, which define being a Muslim through the relationship with society and with the world.

These four elements draw the appropriate picture of what the fundamentals of Muslim individual and social identity are, outside its cultural reading in a specific part of the world: the core of *faith, with practice and spirituality*, is the light by which life and the world are perceived; *intelligence of texts and context* makes it possible to structure one's mind as regards oneself and one's environment; in a broader sphere, *education and transmission* allow both to pass on the trust of faith and to transmit the message, and finally, more broadly still, *action and participation* are the fulfilled manifestation of this identity through the way one behaves *for oneself*, towards others and the Creation (*action*) and *with* one's fellow citizens and mankind at large (*participation*). It clearly appears that the definition of Muslim identity can only be seen as open, dynamic, based on principles indeed, but in constant interaction with the environment. The graph below, starting from the core of being, faith, out to the expression of involvement with men, participation, clearly expresses the articulation of the definition of Muslim identity we are suggesting:

Chart VI?: *Muslim Identity*

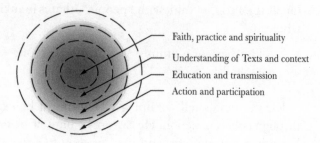

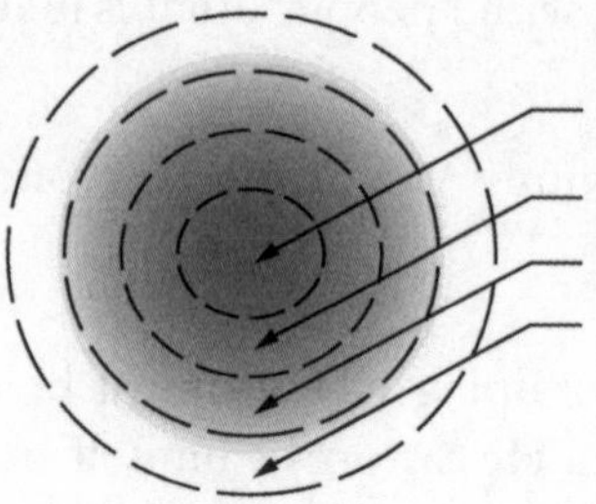


The great responsibility of Muslims in the West is to give an adapted European shape to these four dimensions of their identity in light of their Islamic sources which, as to their conception of life, death and creation, remain the fundamental reference. Keeping in mind both the distinction we presented in the first section between the *uṣūl* (the essential components of religion) and the *furūʿ* (the secondary components), the three levels of the *maṣlaḥa*, namely, *ḍarūriyyāt* (essentials), *ḥājiyyāt* (complementary) and *taḥsīniyyāt* (improvement, perfection) as well as the spheres of implementation regarding *ijtihād*, Muslims, whether scholars or organisation leaders, must provide European Muslims with the appropriate teachings and rulings to enable to protect and fulfil their identity not as Arabs, Pakistanis or Indians, but henceforth as Europeans. This process has been taking place for at least 15 years and is still going on, making it possible to give birth to an original Muslim identity, neither totally diluted within the European environment nor in reaction against it, but rather based on its own foundations according to its Islamic sources. That is the meaning of integration from a Muslim point of view.

On the middle path between being a *Muslim without Islam* and a *Muslim in Europe out of Europe*, there is the reality of a Muslim aware of his four-fold dimension of identity and who is ready, while respecting those requirements, to be involved in his society and play the role which is his, as Muslim and citizen. There is no contradiction, as we see it, between these two belongings as long as the Muslim fulfils his engagement to act according to the law and that he is not asked to sever himself from a part of his identity. This means that his Faith, his concept of life, his spirituality, his need to learn and understand, to speak and educate, to act for justice and solidarity should be respected by the country of which he is a resident or citizen. Nor should the Muslims be discriminated against, legally or administratively, in their freedom to organise themselves and respond adequately and actively to the call of their Faith and conscience. These kinds of hindrances happen every day in European countries because of both the image of Islam conveyed by the media and the widespread feeling that there exists an Islamic threat which in turn is confirmed by the news media relating the dramatic events of Algeria, Afghanistan and the like. Used to living in a secular society, many Europeans, politicians as well as average people, are prone to thinking that the only safe Muslims are those who neither practise their religion nor manifest their Muslim identity. Out of fear, or sometimes bad faith, they interpret the law in a very tendentious and discriminatory way and do not hesitate, at times, to justify their behaviour by resorting to arguments about Muslim fundamentalists and fanatics. One sees such attitudes in the denial of numerous rights to Muslims (the organisation of general activities, the building of mosques, Islamic schools' funding support, etc.) which other religions and institutions, in the name of the law and its implementation, have enjoyed for decades.

Nevertheless, it is the law which should be the reference and the parameter and a close study shows that in a majority of European countries the respective constitutions allow Muslims, to a very great extent, to live in accordance with their identity. On the one hand, they must insist upon a just and equitable application of the law towards all citizens and all religions. On the other, they have to face and assess their own responsibilities in order, within the wide scale of freedom they enjoy in Europe, to provide Muslim communities with courses, study circles, and all kinds of institutions and organisations whose essential objectives are to keep alive the Islamic Faith and spirituality, to diffuse a better understanding of both the Islamic teachings and the environment, to educate as well as transmit the message of Islam and finally, to make Muslims truly involved within society. Nothing prevents them from doing this.

This also means developing a new and confident attitude based on a plain awareness of the essential dimensions of the Islamic identity. This feeling should lead Muslims to objectively and equitably assess their environment. Mindful of the prescriptions of their religion, they should not neglect the important scale of adaptation which is the distinctive feature of Islam. It is this that has permitted Muslims to settle in the Middle East, in Africa as well as in Asia and in the name of the same and unique Islam, to give to its implementation a specific shape and dimension. Once again, as for the form of its implementation, it should be a European-Islam just as there is an African-Islam or an Asian-Islam. To adapt themselves, from an Islamic point of view and as far as new Muslim generations are concerned, does not mean conceding but rather building. They should take advantage of the most efficient methods (education, management, etc.) as well as of scientific and technological discoveries (which in themselves do not contradict Islamic teachings) in order to face their environment armed with appropriate means. These breakthroughs pertain to human heritage and they are part of Western societies and Muslims, especially those who live in the West, cannot neglect or simply reject them for they are not Islamic. The Islamic teaching is plain: as far as social affairs are concerned (*muʿāmalāt*)[49] all the means, traditions, arts, customs that do not, in themselves or by the way they are used, contradict Islamic rulings are not only acceptable but Islamic by definition. Therefore, within the European background and environment, Muslims must make choices in line with their identity. In this way, they can develop and shape the picture of their present and future European identity.

## E. Towards a European Islamic Culture

### 1. *Acquired and selective culture*

We are already witnessing the reality of the settlement of Muslim populations in Europe. This is a fact that no one can contest, particularly with regard to younger generations, and this, in one way or another, is true in all countries; whether the children's parents come from Algeria, Morocco, Turkey, Pakistan or India. This phenomenon is obvious and even if the majority of these youth are still far from a true integration as citizens, we notice that, at the cultural level, they are imbued with the modes, customs and tastes of their country of residence. Their rapport with their environment, their manner of being, of expressing themselves and of apprehending reality, their imagination and even humour have become explicitly European. With this in mind, it is indeed the question of culture that one should consider because this is, in fact, the true parameter of settlement.

Artistic modes of expression, television, the cinema and music (which have become the main language of the youth in the West) all carry, in one way or another, the imprint of the culture that produces them, just as they are the more or less pronounced translation of a concept of life. In a more general sense, there is no free entertainment, or one that is empty of meaning, when it comes to what one makes of being, death or, more simply, passing time. Whoever lives his daily life in Europe or has children knows, feels and understands the urgency of addressing the challenge of entertainment in Europe. For one is faced with two possible choices. Either, in order to protect oneself from all nefarious influences, one forbids oneself any access to popular European culture, because most moral considerations have deserted this domain. This is tantamount to switching off television sets and radios, throwing away newspapers and magazines, and avoiding cinemas, theatres and exhibitions. Such a project is illusary, a crazy, and the young generations, whatever impediments are put in their way, will anyhow be under the influence of this culture in school or through colleagues in class. Alternatively, one acts with a realism suited to such a situation. In this case, it is a question of substituting everything forbidden with a sense of selection and at the same time being creative within Muslim communities in the West. This is clearly the meaning of what we said above with regard to the environment and customs, and this is what Islam taught from its beginning. The savants of *uṣūl al-fiqh* have codified it, and have retained the ways and customs (*ʿurf*) as one of the sources of Islamic law. There is in all the artistic production of European literary, cinematographical and musical works which are not in opposition to Muslim ethics. It is important to facilitate our youth's access to these achievements. The promoters of mass culture and entertainment are more interested in financial gain than in the dignity of the public, and we cannot want our youth to escape from their hold without finding a kind of alternative culture.

The first stage consists in acknowledging that cultural entrenchment has already taken place as regards millions of Muslim-European youth. As a result, one must offer choices within the crushing and, often, stupefying contemporary artistic production. One of the important parts of the Islamic training of the young generations is to arm them with the knowledge of and access to different literatures and to imbue them with art history, so that they can evaluate songs or music and the like for themselves. To forbid everything is tantamount to blinding oneself, whereas to allow everything is tantamount to losing oneself. Nonetheless, it is not a question of imposing censorship, but rather of forming, beginning with the Faith and intelligence of each individual, a critical sense of limitation and a search for dignity, especially in that which relates to entertainment.

Without doubt, however, the most difficult challenge has nothing to do with law, citizenship or social participation. Inevitably, it has to do with the depths of being, and this is in addition to the definition of identity we have given above. Addressing the reality of being European necessitates an awareness of the complexity of the problem of culture and a will to find an acceptable solution to it. We are still far from having attained this stage and very little has been achieved in a well-thought-out and selective approach to literary and artistic production in the West. Undoubtedly, one must first address the simple, controversial question of the lawful or unlawful character of art in Islam. So many things have been said and propagated that, for many, art and entertainment, as such, causes a problem from the point of view of Islam. We are, thus, far removed from the problem we are dealing with. But responding clearly to such questions is tantamount to providing the possibility of at least a framework within which the creativity of young European-Muslims can, in the future, blossom.

## 2. *Islam and art*

It is impossible to expound here all the debates and the diversity of juridical views that have been elaborated in the different treatises regarding the question of art and, more specifically, music and drawing[50] – two modes of expression *vis-à-vis* which controversies have been and remain very vivid. Some have forbidden them, considering them illicit (*ḥarām*); others have considered them licit (*ḥalāl*) under certain conditions. Generally speaking, we can say that the different juridical views concerning music or drawing are divided into the following categories. Some forbid them totally, sometimes basing their views on the literal meaning of a *ḥadīth* and sometimes on an interpretation of a Qur'ānic verse. Others, in disagreement with the interpretation of such sources, refer to other texts in order to permit, within certain limits and under some conditions, both music and drawing. We shall see how, particularly in the case of music, the answers sensibly differ.

◆ *Music and Singing:*

There exist today, in the Muslim world as in Europe, *ʿulamāʾ* who affirm that music and singing are not permitted in Islam. They refer to a number of texts from the Qur'ān and the *Sunna*, and cite some well-known scholars such as Ibn Qayyim al-Jawziyya. It is impossible to remind ourselves here of all the proofs they advance, but it is interesting to note the texts that are most commonly retained. Among the latter we find the Qur'ānic verse: "*Those who purchase idle tales, without knowledge to mislead men from the path of God and throw ridicule on the path.*"[51] According to them, *lahw al-ḥadīth* (idle tales) is, by extension, a reference to singing. The same applies to the following verse: "*And when they hear vain talk, they turn away therefrom.*"[52]

Singing is part of such vain talk (*laghw*) and is therefore considered illicit, since the distinctive trait of Believers is to turn away from it. To these interpretations one may add the *aḥādīth* which, in their view, also confirm this position. Thus they cite the *ḥadīth*: "Any form of distraction is illicit for the Believer except for playing with his family, breaking his horse or training at archery."[53]

Singing and music are not mentioned, which explicitly means that they are not permitted as is confirmed by the following *ḥadīth*: "There will come a day when people from my community will render licit adultery, silk, alcohol and the instrument of music."[54] We may add here the story of Ibn ʿUmar, who when he heard the sound of a musical instrument, put his fingers to his ears and urged his mount to a distance where the sound was no longer audible. He then told his companion Nāfiʿ: "I saw the Prophet acting thus when he used to hear the sound of this instrument."[55] Here again a text seems to back the doctrinal position of those who forbid music.

Those who are opposed to such an interpretation advance argument that the principle, with regard to the things of life and social affairs, is that of permissibility. In order that this be limited, there ought to be a clear and authentic reference. This, in their view, is far from being the case with regard to the texts illustrated above. Ibn Ḥazm[56] points out that nothing in the verse of *Sūra* Luqmān allows one to think that it is singing or music that is referred to. The interpretation of *laghw* as singing is an abuse of interpretation (the word means useless and vain talk and by extension everything that is useless and without importance), and even if one accepts this meaning, one should understand that *al-laghw* is to be avoided but it is not illicit (*ḥarām*). As for the *aḥādīth*, the first one is considered weak (*daʿīf*), whereas the second, even if it is reported by Bukhārī, has in its chain of transmission an uncertain transmitter (Hishām ibn ʿUmar). As for the third *ḥadīth*, it seems that if music was really forbidden, the Prophet would not only have turned his head but he would have also told Ibn ʿUmar not to listen to it and turn away. This, however, he did not do, which renders the text, once more, less explicit as to the reality of its unlawfulness. On the basis of these elements, and relying on other sources, some *ʿulamāʾ*, chief among them Ibn Ḥazm, have considered that music and singing are permitted. Among the most well-known *aḥādīth* in this sense is that[57] where the Prophet was present when two women were singing in ʿĀ'isha's apartment. Abū Bakr, ʿĀ'isha's father entered and wanted to stop them, but the Prophet intervened, allowing them to continue. In another text, it is reported that the Prophet said to ʿĀ'isha, whilst a wedding amongst the *Anṣār* was taking place: "O 'Ā'isha, is there anything there that may entertain them? The *Anṣār* like entertainment."[58] In another situation concerning marriage, Ibn 'Abbās reported that the Prophet asked 'Ā'isha: "Have you sent with her (the young bride) someone to sing? The *Anṣār* are people who have a certain taste."[59] Not only is the mention of singing clear, but the Prophet makes specific mention of the taste of a given people.

On the basis of these facts and numerous other references concerning the practices of the Companions, an important number of scholars have considered that singing and music are licit. However, there are differences with regard to the nature of its permissibility. Some, such as the scholars of Madina following Ibn Ja'far, 'Abdullāh ibn 'Umar or Ibn Ḥazm of the *Ẓāhirī* school, whose opinion is known and respected, have considered singing and music, with instrumental backing, as authorised. Others, following the majority of Companions, the scholars of Makka or Abū Ḥāmid al-Ghazālī, have restrained singing to the voice only, that is without instruments (others have allowed, on the basis of certain *aḥādīth*, singing that is accompanied by percussion instruments).

It is interesting to note that we find, in all the advocates of the licit character of singing and music, conditions attached to authorisation. We can, without being exhaustive, formulate them as follows:

1. The content of singing or the type of music must remain in agreement with Islamic ethics and not bring about an attitude which contradicts them.

2. Interpretation (its mode, moment and place) must also respect these ethics.

3. This kind of entertainment must not lead people to forget their obligation towards God and fellow humans.

4. It is appropriate for the musician and the one who listens to him to measure, in full conscience, the impact and place that this art really takes in their lives. It is a question of establishing a balance of conscience which cannot be but personal and individual.

Those who have considered such things as unlawful and those who follow them have the right to do so, and their view is to be respected, just as they, themselves, must respect those who base themselves on proofs advanced by other well-known scholars. For these, exactness, in the subject of art, remains important since it is a question of offering man a resting space which maintains him as a worthy individual, and which even raises him by means of a "break" which does not entail negligence, excess or exaggeration. Artistic expression in Islam is, in this sense, morally and humanly exacting.

◆ *Drawing and Photography:*

The same rationale may be used *a propos* drawing and photography and the same juridical positions are held by scholars. Some, such as al-Nawawī, have totally disallowed drawing and photography on the basis of Qur'ānic texts or *aḥādīth.* They mention, for example, the Qur'ānic verses wherein it is explained that it is God alone who fashions: "*He it is who shapes you in the wombs as He pleases*";[60] or again: "*He is God, the Evolver, the Bestower of Forms.*"[61]

Moreover, the Qur'ān reports that that which is fashioned by men, such as the idols in the story of Abraham, is the expression of evil and perdition. They also cite the *aḥādīth* reporting the sayings of the Prophet in which he rejects representations and images in places of worship. To this one must add the very clear expression contained in the following two texts: "Amongst those who will receive the worst chastisement from God are those who fashion (or draw) images (*muṣawwirūn*)";[62] and: "Among those who will receive the worst chastisement at the Last Judgement are those who compete with the creation of God (*yuḍāhūn khalqallāh*)."[63] Such texts, and many more besides, which would be too long to quote here, do not allow for, any discussion in their view, and as a result of this drawing, sculpture and, for certain contemporary scholars, photography (in Arabic *taṣwīr*) as well as the cinema are unlawful (*ḥarām*).

There appeared very early on, among the scholars of the first generations (*salaf*), differences concerning the meaning of the word *ṣūra.* In contrast to those whose position we have just indicated above, some scholars, such as al-Qāsim ibn Muḥammad, advanced that this is only a question of "images which have shadows" (sculptured)[64] because the Prophet's saying was addressed to the idol-worshippers who sculptured idols. It is, thus, that they understood the expression "competing with God". They also refer to other *aḥādīth*, and above all that of Zayd in which, speaking of *ṣuwar* (pl. of *ṣūra*), there was mention of the following exception, "except a shape (drawn) on clothes".[65] Following the same line, some scholars have stopped at the literal meaning of the text or words used to designate those who fashion images and widened the field of textual interpretation. According to these, the Qur'ān as in the story of Abraham, and the Prophet, who was living in a polytheist milieu, refer to those who fashion images which are the object of worship or even those who have the pretension of *creating* as if they were gods. The objective (*qaṣd*) of the texts mentioned, beyond the strict literal meaning, is to forbid this specific type of production. This, however, has no bearing on drawings and photographs[66] which do not pertain to the aforementioned categories.

Here again we should not be surprised to find that these scholars who consider drawing and photography permissible have also identified a set of conditions which, are of the same order as those regarding music. We can, thus, suggest the following synthesis:

1. The intention and content of drawing, photography or cinema must not contravene Islamic principles or ethics.[67]
2. On a more personal level, it is up to each person to evaluate his intentions conscientiously and to consider the meaning and place of drawing, photography and cinema in his life in view of his obligations towards God and other human beings.

It has not been possible for us to study all the texts, nor to give an account of all the diverse positions scholars held and hold on the question of art. The account that we have given, however, clearly shows the different stands taken. Broadly speaking, we find here the respective approaches of the advocates of *ahl al-ḥadīth* and those of *ahl al-ra'y*. The former propose a rather literal interpretation, and the latter an interpretative one in accordance with the objective. What is important for our purposes, addressing

Western reality, is the scope available for a cultural Islamic project within the European space. The person who lives under such conditions knows that it is not possible to think of a Muslim presence without nourishing and encouraging an artistic and cultural expression which is an alternative to popular, cinematographical and televisual culture that does not often care about ethics or dignity. Despite all the reticence that some may manifest *vis-à-vis* this reality, at least they should acknowledge that it is irreversible. In the language of the *uṣūliyyūn*, we would say that we must enter, given the state of contemporary popular culture, into the category of *'umūm al-balwā*[68] (generally a negative situation but one which is inevitable) and so find a realistic and satisfactory solution.

Another element seems to us of prime importance in the attitude of those who have considered music, singing, drawing, and photography as licit. This relates to the conditions which they have stipulated in light of Islamic teaching. All of them go along the same line and express both ethical exactness, moderation and individual responsibility. It is indeed this manner of being that seems to us to require a coherent attitude *vis-à-vis* the surrounding culture. Making choices in artistic production, forming a critical awareness, nourishing the sense of a worthy art and aesthetic is, for Muslims, qualified by the aforementioned conditions.

We have cited here only the modes of artistic expression because they have been the most controversial, but it is clear that most of our conclusions are valid with regard to literature, poetry, theatre or cinema.[69] These are part, in one way or another, of the life of Muslims in Europe and so, must be integrated in their Islamic training and, in a broader sense, in the constitution of their social and patriotic personalities.

### 3. *The expression of entrenchment*

There are numerous indications that the question of culture has not yet become a priority in the training of young Muslims. The learning of Islamic principles often remains traditional in an almost complete ignorance of the cultural and artistic environment of the Muslims living in Europe. Here also, all happens as if this environment does not exist or does not have any influence. This shows how far we still are from choosing and selecting an Islamic intellectual and artistic heritage for our youth.

However, one is compelled to note, along with this apparent immobility, that numerous initiatives are being advanced. In fact, in many European countries, young Muslims are initiating the first stutters of a European Islamic culture.[70] The first enterprises are, almost naturally, of a musical nature. Songs are produced according to European taste but in respect of the conditions cited above. It is sometimes a question of the simple use of known genres, like rap, to which added lyrics of an Islamic nature. One may regret such a facile borrowing which remains far from the creativity that should be encouraged in our youth. But one must acknowledge that this is only a necessary, first stage. The lyrics are often little elaborated upon and the process followed is that of imitation. These attempts are either still too Oriental or completely under the influence of popular modes. Rare are the truly original productions containing a new musical elaboration and a real culture of the written. In this sense, the last contribution by Yusuf Islam in Britain is interesting. In collaboration with Bosnian artists and trying to be faithful to the spirit of their traditional culture, he has produced a series of high quality songs.[71] One hopes that more and more Muslims will follow this line and produce lyrics, songs and theatrical pieces[72] which correspond to the expectations and tastes of young European generations. The first signs of this positive entrenchment have already appeared and it is to be hoped that, after a period of transition and adaptation, the Muslim artistic culture will be seen as an original contribution which participates in fashioning the spirit of European culture and aims at directing attention to meaning, values and human dignity. Culture and art should naturally nourish these requirements.

The *ḥadīth* "God is beautiful and He loves beauty"[73] should remind us that the life of Muslims, in trying to be close to God, is linked to aesthetics and the wonder of intelligence and the senses. The Qur'ān is, in itself, a miracle of aesthetics and harmony which renders and transmits all the voices that chant it. The entire universe celebrates the Creator by means of the signs of its beauty, by its colours, perspectives, nature, landscapes and all living beings. To not be sensitive to this dimension is tantamount to plunging into a blindness of heart and being. Art is, and ought to be, the manifestation of this elevation and of this remembrance.

The human being cannot, however, be permanently attentive or receptive to these signs. He must also rest; this is an innate quality of his nature. Artistic expression also plays the role of entertainment, which has its place too, an important one, in the life of each individual. One must give it its due importance, especially in the European space which affords so much free time. The Prophet said to Ḥanẓala, who feared being a hypocrite because he did not always remember God with the same intensity: "O Ḥanẓala, an hour (for this) and an hour (for that)," reminding him that an hour filled with remembrance of God will necessarily be followed by another hour of remoteness without this involving hypocrisy or sin. Even better, the quality of drawing closer is in proportion to the quality and nature of rest or entertainment that follows or precedes this state. This demonstrates the importance that artistic expression assumes, since it is a question of being better in one's environment in order to be better with God. We know how much this relationship is true in our daily lives and it is even more so for people who want to address the challenge of being European-Muslim.

## Notes

1 This means, of course, that he recognises all previous Messengers and Books revealed by God throughout history.
2 Qur'ān 17: 22–4.
3 *Ḥadīth* (Bukhārī and Muslim).
4 Qur'ān 31: 15.
5 *Ḥadīth* (Muslim).
6 Qur'ān 4: 135.
7 We shall return to this important feature of Muslim belonging when discussing the notion of *umma*.
8 Qur'ān 1: 5–6.
9 *Ḥadīth* (Bukhārī and Muslim).
10 Qur'ān 49: 10.

11 *Ḥadīth* (Aḥmad and Abū Dāwūd).
12 They could be spent abroad only if all needs have been fulfilled in the area in question or because of a very strict necessity.
13 Qur'ān 2: 143.
14 *Ḥadīth* (Bukhārī).
15 Ibid.
16 *Ḥadīth* (Bukhārī and Muslim).
17 Qur'ān 5: 8.
18 We have already quoted the Qur'ānic verses of *Sūra* an-Nisā' (The Women) where the Prophet was ordered to acquit a Jew who was innocent and to condemn, instead, the real guilty party, who was a Muslim. See above, Section I.
19 Qur'ān 17: 34.
20 Qur'ān 23: 8.
21 Qur'ān 8: 72.
22 It has to be noted that freedom of worship is a sacred right in Islam which must be protected and defended whatever the religion of the persecuted people. This is not the subject of the present verse, but it is clearly the message of Islam as a whole.
23 If there is no need for a visa, it is because a legal covenant exists between the two states and thus the outcome legally speaking is exactly the same. Muslims, in such a situation, have entered without hindrance thanks to the covenant which is based on the recognition of both the state and the laws of the welcoming country.
24 We shall discuss this oath and the question of citizenship from an Islamic point of view later.
25 European countries, as regards the constitution of their legislation, have a specific history, in which one can witness evolutions, stops, disputes, rivalries between the proponents of one or another political party or ideology. These legislations are of course adapted to the kinds of citizens and religious institutions which have participated in their history and it is quite normal that the presence of Muslims or any new religious community leads to a rethinking of the terms of the law and sometimes its content.
26 Where the Truth of God and His Revelation is denied and rejected by the majority.
27 Ibn Ḥazm and Ibn Taymiyya.
28 Qur'ān 12: 54–5.
29 Qur'ān 28: 4–5.
30 See Muḥammad Asad's comments regarding this verse, *The Message of the Qur'ān* (Dār al-Andalus, Gibraltar, 1980), p. 589.
31 The Qur'ān, in a passage we have already quoted, speaks about the struggle between the Byzantine and Persian Empires. The Byzantines had been beaten and the Qur'ān announced that "*within a few years*" they "*shall be victorious*" and it is added: "*And on that day the Believers (too, have cause) to rejoice in God's succour: (for) He gives succour to whomever He wills, since He alone is Almighty, a Dispenser of Grace*" (30: 30). This means that the Muslims were to rejoice at the victory of non-Muslims and that God supported them as well. For the Muslims it was clear that the Christians of Byzantine were closer to their

beliefs and proponents of rectitude and justice as they had experienced it with the Negus.

32 *Ḥadīth* (Bukhārī).

33 Which became, after the reign of the righteous Caliphs, very rare and even theoretical.

34 *Ḥadīth* (Muslim).

35 Fayṣal Mawlawī, *al-Usus ash-Sharʿīyya lil-ʿIlāqāt' Bayn al-Muslimīn wa Ghayr al-Muslimīn*, p. 101.

36 See the discussion above and especially the conditions we have recalled.

37 Some Muslims claim that it is forbidden to take an oath of this kind for it is like an alliance and the Prophet rejected it in a *ḥadīth* quoted by Muslim, Abū Dāwūd and Tirmidhī: "There is no alliance (*ḥilf*) in Islam; whoever makes an alliance is as in the time of *jāhiliyya* and Islam will but place a difficulty on him." Nevertheless, as noted by Mannāʿ al-Qaṭṭān, the alliance which is referred to in this *ḥadīth* is the one made against Islam and its teachings but not the one which respects the latter or which is taken for doing good deeds (i.e. helping the needy, exchanging experience, protecting oppressed people, etc.). He recalls that the Prophet, who had witnessed when young the *Ḥilf al-Fuḍūl* once said that if he was to be called upon to make a similar alliance he would have answered positively.

38 Qur'ān 12: 33.

39 This could of course happen in the case of manifest injustice by one of two groups as presented in the Qur'ān: "*Hence, if two groups of Believers fall to fighting, make peace between them; but then, if one of the two (groups) goes on acting wrongfully towards the other, fight against the one that acts wrongfully until it reverts to God's commandment; and if they revert, make peace between them with justice, and deal equitably (with them): for verily, God loves those who act equitably!*" (49: 9). Once again, the principle of justice is to be considered as the parameter.

40 We do not want to go into detail here but these matters could be covered in future works.

41 See John Paul II, Encyclique, *L'Evangile de la vie*, ... and *N'ayons pas peur de la vérité* (Bayard-Centurion, Paris, 1995).

42 And, by mirror effect, conveys the idea or feeling of their own identity.

43 Qur'ān, 20: 14.

44 *Ḥadīth* (Bukhārī and Muslim).

45 *Ḥadīth* (Ibn Māja).

46 Qur'ān, 35: 28.

47 Qur'ān, 26: 214.

48 *Ḥadīth* (Bayhaqī).

49 See our discussion in Part One of this study on the difference in treatment between *ʿibādāt* (worship) and *muʿāmalāt* (social affairs).

50 These views have sometimes associated drawing and photography. We shall say a few words below about the necessary distinctions that some scholars have enunciated.

51 Qur'ān, 31: 6.

52 Qur'ān, 28: 55.

53 *Ḥadīth*, reported by the four authors of the *Sunan*.

54 *Ḥadīth* (Bukhārī).
55 *Ḥadīth* (Aḥmad, Abū Dāwūd and Ibn Māja).
56 Ibn Ḥazm, *Muḥallā*, ed. al-Munīriyya, n.d., Vol. 9, p. 60.
57 *Ḥadīth* (Bukhārī and Aḥmad).
58 *Ḥadīth* (Bukhārī).
59 *Ḥadīth* (Ibn Māja).
60 Qur'ān, 3: 6.
61 Qur'ān, 59: 23.
62 *Ḥadīth* (Bukhārī and Muslim). We have indicated two possible translations of the expression *muṣawwirūn*, for there are differences among scholars on the meaning of this word. These differences lead to the elaboration of different juridical views.
63 *Ḥadīth* (Bukhārī and Muslim). Measuring up or competing in the sense whereby they consider themselves creators equal to God.
64 There is unanimity among scholars with regard to the illicit character of sculptured images except those which concern children's toys. In support of this permission, the *ḥadīth* of the Prophet reporting his playing with 'Ā'isha when she was small is quoted.
65 *Ḥadīth* (Tirmidhī).
66 For many contemporary scholars, photography is not even included in what is understood of the word "*ṣūra*" as employed by the Prophet and this even if the Arabic idiom uses the same word, which is not always the case. Photography consists in reproducing whereas it is a question, as we have seen, of fashioning or giving form to something non-existent.
67 The representation for sacralisation, worship or the intent to measure up with creation.
68 This is one of the seven categories for which Islamic law anticipated legal concessions (*rukhsa*, pl. *rukhas*), like forgetfulness, illness, travelling or constraint.
69 The principles enunciated above are of course equally valid for sport. Here again, Islamic teaching orientates and encourages us to engage in an alternative manner in order to never forget the sense of sportive activity, the moderation that we should display and the principle of dignity which must remain the companion of memory and action.
70 The same phenomenon has been apparent in the USA for many years.
71 See his album, *I Have no Cannons that Roar* (1997).
72 Many theatrical groups have been formed in France and the UK such as *al-Khayāl* which has recently produced and played an entire piece.
73 *Ḥadīth* (Muslim).

# III

# A Possible Coexistence

## A. An Observation, and Rifts

### *1. Secularised societies and religious practice*

The Islamic teachings, grafted on faith in the Oneness of God *(tawḥīd)*, are based on the "principle of justice" which, in every circumstance, for or against Muslims, has to be applied first. The life of the heart, emotion or affection, even though they are of great importance in Islam, must be directed and mastered by rules which allow people to live together.

We saw when discussing the notion of belonging in Islam that it is a very important element within Muslim life, but that still it should by no means warrant injustice or betrayal. Muslims are bound by faith, conscience and justice and nothing can justify an exception to this rule, be it towards a Muslim or not. This absolute principle is of great consequence for Muslims living in the West: as residents or citizens they are under the authority of a covenant they have to fulfil. The Qur'ān and the *Sunna* are their references, while they are bound by the terms of the constitution of the country they live in, so long as they are not obliged to act against their conscience. Were they to find themselves in the latter situation, they could, like many other citizens, resort to "moral objection". The law permits it when their conscience requires it of them. In other words, while some scholars wanted, in terms of allegiance, to set the reference to the Islamic way (*Sharīʿa*) against that of a country's constitution, we now realise that it is in the name of the teachings of *Sharīʿa* that Muslims must respect the legal framework of the country they live in. To put it differently, the understanding and implementation of Islamic teaching actually turns out to be a benefitt and a contribution towards securing responsible and self-asserting citizenship.

Beyond the old concepts used by the *'ulamā'*, the Islamic sources, read in light of our contemporary situation, allow Muslims – and have even pushed them – to consider that they are "at home" in the West. The world has gone through considerable geopolitical upheavals and the West is a space where *shahāda* can be pronounced, respected and witnessed. By saying this, it is not only the field of permissibility which is hence open, but above all the exacting horizon of responsibility. As residents and citizens, living in peace and security, Muslims have to provide themselves with all the means that will enable them to protect their identity and, at the same time, to bear witness to the Message of Islam before their native fellow citizens. This two-fold dimension of *shahāda al-Islām* cannot be realised by living in isolation, far from the surrounding society, curled up inside the Muslim community. It is exactly the contrary that turns out to be required: to be a Muslim in Europe means to interact with the whole of society at different levels (from local up to national and even continental involvement).

The youthfulness of Muslim communities in the West naturally led them, for the first two or three decades, to withdraw into themselves and to attempt to solve their problems independently and from within. Those communities had previously perceived the European environment as foreign, alien and often aggressive, and they by no means intended to deal with it nor to be too much involved in it. Although this process can be seen as a perfectly normal stage, at one point in the history of the settlement of Muslims in their new countries, it is no longer the case today. One cannot conceive any future for Muslims in Europe if they are to refuse to deal with their environment and if they do not develop a dialectical relationship which will enable them to be, to give and to receive from others. The laws, as we explained, largely permit a respected presence; the Islamic teachings order Muslims to take advantage of everything, of every opportunity, as long as this does not contradict a principle of their religion. In other words, Muslims must thoroughly assess the current state of affairs in Europe and determine the priorities of their commitment within society.

All the different aspects of the Muslims' presence must be closely studied, for the problems they are facing in the West are not, strictly speaking, of a religious or legal nature only. Pondering over the large range of difficulties affecting young people as well as adults, one will encounter a huge number of questions and considerations. Psychological problems are mixed with educational, social and economic trials. Every field has to be tackled competently and methodically, referring to the Islamic sources, of course, but also by taking advantage of all the studies by Muslim and non-Muslim specialists, who know the environment and are able to provide us with the appropriate means to solve the problems observed and to build our future in the West.

We want to stress here the economic dimension, which is very often neglected as if it did not exist or was of secondary importance. Some *ʿulamā'* and leaders of Muslim organisations in Europe carry on speaking about Islamic rulings and rules, about lawful and unlawful issues, without paying attention to the daily reality of Muslims in the West. They even speak about "integration" in a very theoretical and rigid way: the "Islam" they want to integrate is an ideal Islam which does not exist in reality. In Western "open society", to be a Muslim is to try to find a means to live with a peaceful, tranquil, serene heart, and this is the reality which Muslims must take into account. It is important to recall here what we explained in the first section of the present study: all the Islamic sciences, their formation and development were but means enabling Muslims, in every era and circumstance, to attain a feeling of peace. The Islamic sciences and prescriptions are at the service of Believers' hearts and the latter must not be neglected in the name of the former. The heart is the key:

> *The Day on which neither wealth will be of any use, nor children, (and when) only he will be happy who comes before God with a heart free of evil.*[1]

This consideration has to be kept in mind, especially in the European environment within which true protection is more a healthy and balanced heart giving birth to a peaceful state of mind, than a set of theoretical and ideal rulings. Without playing on words, in an open society such as Europe's, true integration is nothing but an integration of intimate lives. This is our challenge. And Muslims must certainly not mistake their means for ends; in other words, they must not give priority to prescriptions or to Islamic organisations alone over their hearts' needs and spirituality.

This remark basically leads us to tackle the problem of Faith within a secular society. The public space has become non-religious, if not sometimes anti-religious, and growing numbers of Believers find it difficult to face this situation. They are told that they are free to believe privately in Whatever they want, but the power of attraction of the public sphere, with its "sacred values" founded on individualism, money and entertainment, is so powerful and efficient that it seems illusory to imagine that any kind of resistance might be possible. It is as if it were a trapped freedom; the mind cannot but recognise its existence whereas the heart and the senses have no other choice but to submit – out of control. How are we to deal with such a situation? This is what Muslims have to ask themselves and of the society they live in. As they are surrounded by all this high technology, swept along by the current of progress, there nevertheless arises a question, stemming from their hearts, in the name of their identity: What about God? What about spirituality? What is the meaning of all this effervescence, agitation and turmoil we witness in our modern life?

## 2. *Images and suspicions*

These last questions take on particular importance nowadays for they not only lead Muslims to restore things to their correct order, but they also remind everyone that Islam is a Faith, a spirituality and a way of life, and not a problem *per se.* As we explained above, the difficulty of coexistence between Muslims and native populations in Western society is less a problem of law than a problem of warped perception and prejudice.

Too many individuals still link Islam to Arabs or Indians and Pakistanis: they can hardly imagine that one of their fellow citizens might be a Muslim. Were this to happen, it would simply mean to them that as a Muslim that person is not a genuine citizen, for the image of Islam is still associated with some "alien" features. History still inhabits European minds, and the way Muslims are viewed, in the West's passive culture and memory, is related to the Orient, which is seen as exotic, not so remote, but more antagonistic than friendly. Paradoxically, the visible presence of millions of Muslims in Europe by no means modifies this old and deep-seated feeling: quite the opposite can indeed be noticed, and one is always hearing, here and there, hasty judgements stating that there are too many foreigners living within Europe's boundaries. And Islam goes on being treated as if it was still a problem linked to immigration: it seems so difficult to conceive that Islam is now a European reality.

Suspicion is also the rule about the Muslims' true belonging. They have come to the West to take advantage of material progress and to earn money, but their hearts are elsewhere. They are but "profiteers", and we now hear the same reproaches which used to be expressed about Jews. This kind of state of mind still seems to be deeply anchored in many Western countries and especially of course in the regions where Muslims are numerous and where there are unemployment problems.

Yet another dimension must be added to this picture. It is perhaps this dimension, linked to the events which take place on the international scene and which are given spectacular coverage in the media, which has the strongest impact on Western minds. The pressure is so strong that it has become difficult, if not impossible, to assess the various events covered clearly and serenely. Those events, whether in Algeria, Afghanistan or elsewhere in the Muslim world, presented together with images of violence and riots or with quotations from radical and virulent speeches against the West, convey the impression that Islam is inherently and by its nature linked to aggressiveness, violence and war. The confusion is quite absolute and average people today are hardly able to see the difference between a practising Muslim and a "fanatic" or an "extremist". Whenever a European Muslim openly asserts his will to practise his religion, this is mentally associated with widespread television representations. The result is an almost automatic, virtually systematic, rejection. Suspicion is deeply rooted and the idea of an "Islamic threat" gains ground every single day. Thus,

Muslims in Europe are considered as "the wolf in sheep's clothing" or "the Trojan horse", that is to say, the foes' vanguard which has reached the very heart of European countries. Those persistent prejudices are indeed what prevents European societies from achieving harmonious coexistence, at the grassroots, between natives and Muslims. It is urgent nowadays to assess this situation, in order to take the appropriate measures to reverse this pernicious tendency.

It must be clearly stated that Muslims themselves bear a great part of the responsibility for what is going on. They also entertain deep suspicions towards their European fellow citizens whom they trust little, if at all. A new attitude is becoming visible among the new generations but still, events such as those related to "ethnic purification" against Muslims in central Europe are not such as might promote confidence. We can also witness among some Muslims an attitude of rejection of the West, often conveyed without any subtlety, and which is most likely to confirm and reinforce the non-Muslim prejudices. Finally, the lack of clear and coherent discourse coming from Muslims about their religion, their aims and the political events taking place in the world, cannot but give an impression of great confusion, when Muslims continue to avoid answering some fundamental questions about their religion.

Nobody, today, can objectively deny that Muslim leaders in Europe do not convey a plain message about their beliefs and way of life and do not clearly answer the questions they are asked. This is not to say that they should answer every single question put forward by the people around them as if they were in the dock, nor that they should justify themselves and take a specific position whenever a violent action takes place somewhere in the world. They must, of course, avoid being drawn into this logic, which is often very pernicious, for it cannot but nourish a negative and defensive posture. A more assertive presence in Europe relies on a clear and positive self-perception along with a coherent discourse refusing to be reduced to permanent self-justification. Such an attitude makes it possible to tackle problems according to a positive and constructive agenda, on the one hand, and in accordance with Islamic priorities relating to faith, spirituality and justice, on the other.

Still, this does not mean that they are justified in avoiding answering questions asked by sincere people about some Islamic concepts: asking a question is not, *per se*, an expression of enmity – it could, on the contrary, represent the first step on the path of friendship. To understand this reality, this process, means to open and pave the way to dialogue.

## B. Four Priorities

Wanting to succeed in the challenge of a coexistence which would not be *peace in separation* but *living together in participation*, entails that Muslims themselves undertake a number of reforms within Muslim communities in Europe. Each of these undertakings requires considerable work and is, in itself, a challenge to which each Muslim man and woman must contribute. Taking up such challenges seems inevitable, not only for the future of the Muslim presence on this Continent but also with a view to bringing together the prerequisites of a real dialogue with the Muslim world as a whole. Let us mention them here as so many clues to a coherent commitment of European Muslims.

### *1. Intracommunity Dialogue*

It is becoming urgent that Muslims in Europe should rediscover the way to the culture of pluralism which, from the very beginning, was the hallmark of Muslim societies. The apparent unity that binds Muslims together when they feel beleaguered is not sufficient. United *against*, they demonstrate every day how difficult they find it to engage in dialogue or to collaborate *with* others. The fact is obvious, it is easier and more accessible to unite in conflict than in peacetime. But Europe grants us relative social peace and here we are, sinking into division and into endless conflicts for power or allegiance.

Of course we must not be naïve: the intentions of all the actors on the European scene are not always pure and innocent. Some are prompted by love of power and prestige, others are commissioned and controlled by foreign, if not sometimes national, governments to direct and master the processes of organisation and the implantation of different Muslim communities. These are well-known and visible realities, and we should have no illusions about the backstage schemes aimed at controlling the dynamics present at the grassroots. It nevertheless remains that this observation should by no means justify the absence of harmony, the lack of dialogue and the suspicion entertained within Muslim communities today, both at local and national levels.

It is becoming urgent, at least at the local level, to resume dialogue within the Muslim community. The stakes are far too important and the challenges far too serious for us to go on ignoring, criticising and fighting one another. Judgements on institutional or dress appearances, on real or supposed national allegiances, on genuine or contrived Islamic belonging, should no longer prevent those who advocate the idea that it is possible to live in harmony in Europe from holding a dialogue, acting in concert and exchanging views. What matters is not that we should all agree, nor that we should set up one single umbrella association, forgetting our respective pasts and structures, not at all. What matters is that we should respect one another with our differences and diversity and find common orientations and commitments, in specific circumstances or spheres of involvement. Our reference to Islam requires that we reconsider our respective isolation and strive to promote the *culture of dialogue* that each of us individually knows is fundamentally *Islamic*.

Moreover, the distinctions between practising and non-practising Muslims, or between *really Islamic* and *not really Islamic* associations, are quite meaningless. The principle is clear: any person identifying themselves as a Muslim has the right to be considered and to express an opinion, whether they belong to a minority or to the majority: reference to the majority works when decisions must be taken, not as regards consulting and listening to one another or exchanging views. In the latter case, an opinion is an opinion: once expressed, it has the right to be heard, as the Prophet of Islam repeatedly taught us. Restoring intra-community dialogue on as large a scale as possible is imperative and urgent, both between individuals and between associations. Whilst it is obviously impossible to agree with everybody, it is at least our responsibility to hold dialogues with each other.

## 2. *Political and financial independence*

The Muslim presence in Europe, is undergoing an evolution. Whereas it was normal, during the first years, that Muslims should be financially affiliated to their mother countries and to some governments, it is no longer really so today. More and more associations of second, third and fourth-generation Muslims are developing through general self-funding: during cultural activities, conferences, lessons or meetings, participants are asked to pay a subscription or an entrance fee to cover expenses. The time of great projects backed by one government or another seems to be over, although some states still attempt to control European Islamic activities through various mosques, foundations or institutions. The latter are well known, but they are no longer representative of the dynamics running across the Islamic associative fabric in Europe. As Saudi Arabia, Morocco, Algeria or Turkey, among other funding states, are gradually losing the spheres of influence they held for many years, more and more mosques are being funded through locally organised collections. The sums collected are impressive and grant actual independence to the associations themselves, which now really own the mosques.

Foreign and European states are increasingly reacting to these new phenomena in order to try and maintain substantive areas of influence over Muslims' commitment in Europe. It is urgent that associations and their leaders persist in defending their political and financial independence. There are two essential reasons for this: the first is intricately linked to the process of legal and legislative integration we have been speaking about all along in this study. The latter could not be properly achieved under the control and influence of foreign states wishing to impose their own implementation of Islam, as thought out by their own scholars for their own context and society. This reform and adaptation process can only be achieved freely and independently and must not yield to any ideological authority based outside Europe.

The second reason is of a clearly political nature. Controlling Europe's Islamic organisations, for all Muslim countries, means being able to direct and restrict the critical discourse of European Muslims. These Muslims are now the citizens of democratic states which allow them to denounce betrayals carried out in the name of Islam, as well as dictatorships and repression. Relying on their political and financial independence, Europe's Muslims must raise a new, free and honest voice, attached to intellectual probity and exact analysis, explaining and commenting if necessary, and developing a genuine critical discourse on the state of Islam in the world, its achievements as well as its betrayals. This new voice obviously frightens governments, in Europe and elsewhere, but it is beginning to make itself heard, a little more every day, and one of the major challenges of the Muslim presence in Europe is to give it substance, coherence and weight.

### 3. *The Choice of the Rank and File*

Just as we must get rid of foreign take-overs or influences, we must return to Islamic principles as far as Muslims' management of their affairs is concerned. The notion of *shūrā*, the principle of consultation, is often invoked in Muslim circles but unfortunately it is little used in practice. There are still too many struggles "at the top" to decide who will have the privilege of representing the Muslims. In a hurry to unite, one runs the risk of dividing. This is indeed, unfortunately, what we can observe today.

As we have repeatedly said, the Muslim presence is a recent one and we cannot expect Muslims to get organised in two or three generations – unless we resort to dictatorship and sham pluralism, speaking in the name of everybody but deciding alone. "The one who stands in front" (*Imām*), in Islam, is chosen by "those who stand behind". They must all be competent, some to be chosen, and others to choose. It is out of the question to argue that Muslims are "still unable to choose well" and to take decisions about their affairs without consulting them. Islamic principles require that we take the time to train people in pluralism, in consultation and discussion. The choice of the rank and file cannot be done without, and the issue that must preoccupy us is to determine the middle and long term stages in the implementation of this basic principle of community organisation in Islam.

It seems necessary that we begin to organise things at the regional level. Setting up pluralistic coordination platforms at town and regional level, determining the priorities of concerted action, fixing agendas as to local and regional action and finally associating the broadest possible range of social and political partners, are initiatives which should be given priority everywhere in Europe. Concrete initiatives of this kind are being undertaken in Germany, Britain, Sweden, France and Spain, and they should become more numerous and be carried out with the coherence appropriate to such commitments. If it becomes for imperative, that a national platform be created, nothing prevents us from organising a temporary and plural council accompanying the birth of a really pluralistic organisation stemming from the grassroots.

### 4. *Citizenship*

Once we have admitted that we are at home in Europe, we must examine the modalities which must lead to a genuine presence and a substantial participation by Muslims in the life of the city and of society. Muslims, like all the nation's citizens, must become involved in the elaboration of a clearly-defined programme of civic training. The abdication of civic responsibility we witness today in industrialised societies is serious and a legitimate source of worry. The risk of negative contagion is great among citizens of the Muslim faith, even before citizenship has been really promoted within the Muslim communities present in Europe. This will be a major challenge to take up: prompting Muslim men and women to become interested in the history of the country they live in and the way its institutions work, and to participate as citizens at all levels of the social scale, from local and town level to national and governmental level. The stake is actually to fashion a citizen's consciousness constituted of a deep-seated sense of responsibility and a self-asserting knowledge of one's rights.

Such civic training and citizen involvement necessarily means facing some risks which are, in themselves, quite serious and which could, if we do not pay sufficient attention to them, lead to future deficiencies in the pluralistic scheme. Participating citizenship should be based on the awareness of one's responsibilities and not on a vague feeling of belonging. This is a major difference in the making of choices, especially during election time. For a Muslim European, political choice must be based on the principles to which his conscience and intelligence are attached, rather than on identity considerations alone. It is not enough for a man or a woman to have an Indian, Pakistani, North African, or more generally Muslim sounding name, to justify choosing him or her. The reference to Islam demands of our conscience, just as democratic reason requires it of our intelligence, that the true criteria of a genuine citizen's choice, concerning elections for instance, be founded on the candidate's *honesty* and *competence*, whether he or she be a Muslim or not. We must absolutely avoid the self-centred attitudes in which the political sphere is considered as a space of expression for community aspirations, either between ourselves, or against others.

This risk must also be pointed out to a number of politicians in Britain, France and Belgium (the most advanced countries today as far as participation is concerned) who, in order to attract the mainly Muslim voters of immigrant descent, place a few "exotic names" on their respective lists. The race for votes makes them forget their own purported principles of opposition to community-centred isolation. This situation is serious and quite unacceptable for the pluralistic future of European countries: to have a few individuals elected today, they run the risk of developing rifts between communities and encouraging the already too widespread system of lobbying and pressure groups. This is not the way to build a peaceful future, and little respect is shown for citizen involvement when it is systematically reduced to this unhealthy seduction game. Besides, were the whole of society to fall into such practices, Islamic references forbid Muslims to accept this kind of management which is close to bribery and partiality.

## C. Common Challenges

What matters today is no longer that we know what the *place* of Muslims in Europe is, or will be. The question that now matters to us is rather that we know how they will *contribute* to their respective societies. In Part One, we recalled some of the central principles constituting the Islamic concept of the world and of man. When discussing Muslim identity, we then presented the essential axes of spirituality, education and participation. These three themes are strong elements which nourish and accompany Muslim men and women wherever they live. Together, they constitute the question of meaning and preoccupation with values. Muslims are certainly not the only people asking themselves such fundamental questions; women and men of faith or conscience, humanists in the broad sense of the word, are all preoccupied with the future of our societies, increasingly oriented towards productivity, performance and greater spending. The challenges are numerous, heavy and complex, and we must learn to take them up together.

1. *Learning subtlety and complexity again:* listening to a woman or a man, being attentive to their expectations, to their problems, to their doubts, is acceding to complexity. Our concept of the world may be simple, our principles may be crystal clear, but life is complicated – as are the hearts and intelligences of everyone of us. Anyone who is attentive and to his own needs others knows this. It is strange indeed that what we know almost instinctively in our daily and emotional relationships should vanish into thin air as soon as we consider others, belonging to another religion, another culture, another history. Here, our relations are built on concise, quick, clear-cut, almost definitive information: as if we wanted to understand our friends deeply, but found it sufficient to gather superficial information about other people's realities. We give some people, out of friendship and love, what we refuse others out of indifference and prejudice. Yet all the time we advocate dialogue. What we know about others seems obvious, not because we have taken the time to listen to them and to understand, but because we have heard it repeated again and again. With speed and the era of satellite communications, the obvious, what is obvious *to us*, has changed in nature.

It is vital that we relearn the meaning of study, of in-depth understanding, and accede together to a deeper perception of the complexity on which other people's lives are organised. Listening, learning to understand again, admitting at times that we do not understand, are all paths leading to deep, subtle thought, often silent and without judgement. Our enemies, today, are *caricature* and *prejudice*: lack of information used to keep us ignorant of some cultures, some realities or some events; now sketchy, superficial information, if not misinformation, gives us the illusion of knowledge. But today's illusion is far more dangerous than yesterday's ignorance: it breeds complacency, definitive judgements and intellectual dictatorships. The movement goes both ways: one should, on the one hand, be careful to avoid simplification, and on the other hand, grant others access to the complexity of one's being and perceptions. This seems to be the challenge of dialogue in a culturally plural society.

2. *Spirituality:* we insisted at length, in Part One, that the essence of the Qur'ān's Message is that of spirituality and love, directed to the heart. According to the teachings of Islam, the goal of human spirituality is to live one's relationship with God constantly inspired by the experience of rememberance and nearness. This is the enlightening path of spirituality along which moral norms are but milestones and landmarks. All the world's religions are concerned with protecting this intimate spirituality which encourages balance, harmony and contemlation of our humaneness. In short, that which gives us our humanity and dignity. Even agnostics are always speaking of their desire to live and give meaning to a spirituality, a vital inspiration, the consciousness of a meaning that must be preserved. We all speak about this, and we all realise how terribly difficult it is to live a coherent spirituality at the heart of the ways of life which engulf us. How, then, must we live our spirituality? How can we protect it? How can we transmit it? When living it for oneself is so difficult, how can we transmit its taste and strength to others, to our daughters or sons? When we wish to live with them in conscience, how can we educate them in the light of inspiration, of meaning, how can we accompany their hearts, how can we nourish their conscience?

Living and protecting one's spirituality in an over-modernised society is difficult, it is a real challenge that we must take up together. Spirituality, meaning, values, are all areas which must preoccupy us: or else tomorrow, because we neglected or avoided debates on fundamental issues, we may have to admit that we have left an open field for all sorts of sectarian and exclusion-fostering deviations. We are faced with real questions that must occupy the sphere of reflection of human beings living in affluent, industrialised societies. To be concerned with spirituality and the heart is to ask oneself what role faith plays in one's daily life, how one's conscience influences one's choices, what value and meanings things have beyond their financial quantification. How can we be with God today? How can we live with men? These may be deeply unsettling questionsfor someone who starts to reflect on the course of their life and the lives of their children.

3. *Education:* educational systems in the modern world are always being questioned and criticised as if they alone were responsible for all the failings of society. Teachers become scapegoats for every frustration: school is no longer what it used to be and "everything is wrong". Muslims, like all other citizens, are interested in this issue: the school system as a whole, teaching curricula, life at school, are social issues and must involve all the actors in society. Whether in Muslim families or in any other family, the old clear-cut divisions (the family providing education whereas school provides learning) are dead and gone: such spaces of ideal complementarity have now given way to a sort of haze in which respective vocations are hard to define and discussions often lead to placing responsibility on others: parents have abdicated their responsipility, teachers say; teachers are over-permissive, the parents reply. As each side thus judges the other, generations of children pass through and are offered very little hope, unless they are handed down a strange and very precocious weariness.

Education is one of the most weighty concerns of modern times. Discussing it requires that all the actors in our European societies, whatever their faith, their spirituality, their humanist beliefs, work in concert to determine the vocation of school education and its place in our society in light of our common project. A community, a nation of responsible beings, can be assessed through their readiness to invest in the education and training of tomorrow's adults. Our aim cannot be only to transmit abstract learning and skills leading to an almost total mastery of the environment and enabling individuals to obtain social recognition with a good salary. What exactly do we want? It is high time we asked ourselves this question together. What is it we want? To train worthy and responsible beings? To live together in respect for others and in plurality? To defend right and justice? Does our global educational scheme lead to such objectives? The least we can say is that the heavy pressure schools are under to produce the most efficient academics and executives through selection and out-and-out competition is very far indeed from these idealistic expectations.

Pupils, students and academics more or less guess where they are being led, but they no longer really know *who* they are as they acquire such training. An often curtailed memory of their history and particularly blurred horizons of their cultural identity blend with the most widespread religious illiteracy. All these elements contribute to multiplying fears and misgivings: how can one serenely and respectfully recognise others without having a clear notion of one's own identity? A pluricultural society demands exacting and adequate education, or else it may produce the worst possible racist and xenophobic deviations. The role of school education, today even more than in the past, is to express and train, to enable students to question meanings, to discuss values without remaining confined to a mere selective management of abilities and performances. This issue concerns all responsible citizens, whatever their faith.

4. *Social rifts:* European societies are going through deep social and economic crises. The question of unemployment is haunting and more and more pockets of marginalisation, exclusion and delinquency are developing. Violence and insecurity are the daily lot of many towns, cities and suburbs throughout Europe. We know only too well that all those factors are liable to increase racism and xenophobia because the populations who are the most deeply struck by such scourges are often those of immigrant descent. It is urgent that we develop partnerships at local level in order to fight

all types of social deviations. Short range work is an indispensable first step but it must be accompanied with strategies for upstream intervention, at the level of the choice of social and urban policies. All citizens, whatever their beliefs, must take part in this effort towards social reform and justice which must be distinguished from purely voluntary and cooperative action. The latter is indeed necessary but it should be considered as an additional contribution rather than as the only commitment in the political sphere.[2]

Fighting unemployment, opposing employment discrimination (when names, colours or clothes seem to come from elsewhere), promoting social welfare, intervening against suburban violence or looking after marginalised persons (the poor and the elderly) are so many challenges that we must take up together, as partners and fellow citizens.

A fundamental need today, therefore, is to promote better mutual knowledge between Muslims and the society they live in. Fighting historical liabilities as well as the huge weight of prejudices is not possible through mere speeches or sincere testimonies of "good will". The conflict seems so deep and so tense that the process leading to establishing mutual trust between Muslims and natives will take a very long time; it will, above all, have to rely on better understanding which stems from genuine dialogue, joint activities and necessarily dynamic coexistence. From the Muslims' point of view, this means they should acquire the confidence that they are *at home* and that they must become more involved within European societies, which are henceforth their own, at all levels, from strictly religious affairs to social concerns in the broad sense we have just mentioned. The reactive posture we discussed above, expressed either through total dilution in the environment or through violent opposition to it, cannot go along with the idea of building a future out of trust, respect and collaboration.

Islam is primarily the fundamental expression of the essential links of the heart's life to God. The widespread negative image of Islam today has completely concealed this aspect of its teachings and Muslims, by their often purely emotional reaction, are themselves far from living and expressing this dimension of their religion. Islam is a concept of life which directs Believers towards spirituality and meditation over life's meaning. It is both a simple and a very demanding way of life which requires from the Muslim that he does his utmost to be better tomorrow than today and to choose, at any price, the way of generosity, honesty and justice. Muslims in Europe, drawing the principles of their religion from their traditional Asian or North African implementation, should come back to these fundamentals and play their part within industrialised societies. Together with the members of other religious communities and all men and women of good-will, they must participate in the necessary debate about faith, spirituality and values in the modern and post-modern era. Their new presence could be a positive mirror considered as revelatory rather than aggressive: for Muslims will henceforth have to ask questions, not alone, not *against* the whole society, but now *with* their fellow citizens through a sincere and genuine shared preoccupation. This means that a wide involvement in favour of dialogue on ethical as well as religious issues should be promoted from the grassroots up to leading and specialised institutions in all Western countries.

The Qur'ān encourages people to mutual knowledge:

> *O men! Behold, We have created you all out of a male and a female, and have made you into nations and tribes, so that you might come to know one another.*[3]

The explicit meaning of this verse calls upon the members of specific nations and tribes to do their utmost to know their fellow humans from other groups. However, the implicit meaning is that people of the same nation already know each other, for it appears obvious and should be taken for granted. Yet this is far from being the case today, and the members of Western pluralistic nations, both Muslims and non-Muslims, should attempt to reach this apparently obvious and at any rate essential state.

As we have seen, insufficient civic knowledge is clearly evident among the young in almost every European country. They are no longer interested in politics and they hardly know how national institutions and the various executive and legislative bodies work.

This, downstream, brings about a serious malfunctioning of the democratic process in modern societies. For instance, the low rate of participation in elections or decisions of public or national interest, often not exceeding 30 or 40%, is a matter of great concern for the future of Western democratic societies. It is as if a chasm were to be dug between the political and economic classes, always deciding the nation's fate, and a majority of the population more interested in their immediate and daily problems.

This attitude is, ultimately, the same among a great number of Muslims: they all too often consider political institutions as foreign to their life in Europe. There is substantial ignorance among Muslims concerning the laws and political institutions and the different spheres of decision-making of the nation they live in. Some of them are already citizens – or have been residents for more than 20 years – but they know nothing of the overall constitutional framework of their country and it has never occurred to them to take advantage of their rights. We explained above how the Islamic references, through the examples of Yūsuf (Joseph) and of the Prophet and his Companions, allow Muslims to be involved in a society whose people are majority non-Muslim, and this attitude must be encouraged in the West. In other words, we should promote all forms of civic instruction among Muslims; this instruction would refer to the legal and political landscape, the way institutions work, the stakes of the different votes as well as the citizen's role at a local and national level. In light of their Islamic sources, the leaders of Muslim organisations should first of all promote social and political involvement at the local level in order to familiarise young Muslims with the neighbouring political sphere. Working with other local organisations, organising civic instruction sessions for Muslims and non-Muslims together, and meeting local authorities, appear to be some of the means which could bring about a real encounter, based on a shared feeling of mutual responsibility.

The natural consequence of this process is, of course, more effective involvement in the social field. Faith in Islam is linked to the *principle of justice* which, as we have said, must be defended in all circumstances. If being a Muslim is to act, then it is a duty and a responsibility to be active in Western societies. This Muslim participation is undoubtedly the most appropriate means of developing a better relationship between Muslims and the social workers or institutions around them. Up to now, Muslims have been used to working alone and believing that, since it was impossible to rely on society in religious matters, the situation would be the same for solving their broader social problems. This confusion, mixing up religious education in the West and social involvement, has led to an isolation of Muslim organisations at all levels, from the grassroots to academia. More serious still, this isolation has deprived Muslim associations of social recognition, which is so important to keep alive the energy and commitment of human beings, whatever the intensity of their faith in God. Women and men, whether young, adolescent or adult, need to be acknowledged by their peers, and a society only gives credit to those it knows and recognises.

The outlook which may have contributed such isolation must be reformed immediately and Muslims must share common concerns with their fellow residents or citizens on the crucial issues we have presented above. The Muslims' religion commands them to strive for more justice, but this certainly does not mean that they should be concerned only with themselves and not collaborate with all those who try to reform society for the better, in the name of human dignity and respect.

## Notes

1 Qur'ān 26: 88–9.
2 This is often the type of involvement which predominates within Muslim associations, showing that the incorporation of a citizen's identity is not yet fully achieved. In his own country, at the heart of the place he lives in, a citizen defines his involvement in the name of law and its fair implementation. Although resorting systematically to "voluntary" and "cooperative" action is commendable, it nevertheless often reveals fear and overcautiousness in facing one's reponsibilities and making explicit a specific involvement asserted in the name of mature and clearly avowed citizenship.
3 Qur'ān 49: 13.

# Conclusion

The approach that we have proposed in this work has two objectives. First, to consider the question of the Muslim presence in Europe with different yardsticks than those which seek to evaluate this same presence through the problems that it poses to Muslims themselves and to the welcoming societies. Inevitably, these yardsticks are not neutral and, in addressing the problem, they may prevent an objective and serene look at the tenets of the Muslim religion and the different margins for manoeuvre offered to Muslims in order to take charge of their own destiny in Europe. Far from the incriminating or xenophobic statements of the one or the other, it is for Muslims to consider their sources and to put their conviction, to the test so as to find solutions that allow their identity to blossom in Europe. They will certainly not act alone, and on the way to their becoming established they must count on the laws of the countries of which they are citizens or where they reside, just as they must associate with their social and political partners at all levels. To do so, it is necessary to go beyond a reactive attitude, to go back to the Muslims frame of reference. This is what we have tried to present in Part One of this work.

Both for Muslims – who because they are or feel misunderstood, end up reacting and confusing ends and means – and for non-Muslim Europeans, it seemed necessary to make a circumstantial study of the fundamentals of the Islamic religion and, at the same time, present the available juridical tools so as to facilitate a positive Muslim presence in the West. The general rules of *uṣūl al-fiqh* that we have studied, even though insufficient, are of vital importance in helping Muslims to adopt and participate in the future of European societies, without being cut off from their own faith and traditions. This theoretical framework is irreversible and the modalities of *ijtihād* elaboration, with its conditions, stages and priorities, in accordance with the environment and *maṣlaḥa,* must be kept in mind.

The second objective of the present work is to clarify and answer some questions of jurisprudence (*fiqh*) relating to the presence of Muslims in Europe; these sensitive questions have been tackled in Part Two. Starting from the definition of space (*dār*) as it was defined, in a binary mode, by scholars of the 9th and 10th centuries, we have tried to move forward the treatment of themes by making constant reference both to the theoretical level and to the reality on the ground. This is in order to better comprehend the current situation in Europe.

The questions of identity, citizenship and culture seemed to us to be essential. We have established that a coexistence which rejects both assimilation and isolation is possible. The Islamic points of reference allow and encourage Muslims to engage in their society fully in respect of its legal framework. The definition of Islamic identity that we have given brings to the fore the fact that it is not closed and shaped once and for all, far from the evolution of societies and their dynamics. On the contrary, this identity, whilst always remaining faithful to its principles, is characterised by a constant necessity to interact with its context, to question and to understand it so as to find the most satisfactory and harmonious solution. It remains for Muslims to accede to a perception of themselves which is affirmative, responsible and constructive. This is not an easy task as it is, undoubtedly, the major challenge of the coming decades: to reform the image that Muslims have of themselves.

The presentations which were construed by a number of Europeans go equally along this line. The question of Islam is above all a problem of presentation and mentality. The future will also depend on the effort that one makes to better know and inform oneself. The degree of mutual misunderstanding remains alarming after decades of coexistence and centuries of dialogue. The Muslims and social players, at all levels, whether local, regional or national, must assume their responsibilities in order to go beyond this state of suspicion and rejection.

At this end of century, we can see signs of very tangible progress. The questions which we have tackled, the answers that we have provided by referring to the works of the *'ulamā'* are, on the whole, new. An awareness that the Muslim presence in Europe has become a fact is recent and one must acknowledge that matters of law and jurisprudence are increasingly treated and considered. Younger Muslim generations have forced their elders to provide clearer Islamic answers. We are still far from a thoughtful and systematic study but the process has been irreversibly set in motion.

One is obliged to note that on the level of citizenship, social participation and artistic production, a profound movement is taking shape amongst different Muslim communities in Europe. With varying rhythms, according to the modalities proper to each country, the outline of a European Muslim identity is in the course of being drawn, far from the statements of catastrophe presented by the media. European social players and intellectuals are increasingly feeling this and are already engaged in constructive dialogue and engagement in the field with their Muslim partners. This is, in our view, the way that should from now on be taken in order to link the theoretical framework of jurisprudence that we have presented with its real application on the ground. This challenge is of great importance, and it is the responsibility of the people of Faith and conscience to try to defend and live upto their principles regardless of the results obtained, even if it seems that the whole world is against them. This because they know the price of faithfulness to God and to their own conscience.

# Appendix I

## Introduction to "Islamic Tendencies" in Europe and the World

The landscape of Islamic groups in Europe does not immediately show – to say the least – any very clear or particularly precise contours. Beyond the multiplicity of groupings, one discovers tendencies and currents that can be identified only with difficulty: Who are they in this group? What are they after in that group? What are the modes of thought of this third group? Some people do not bother with nuanced distinctions and divide Muslims without reserve into two camps: on the one hand, "fundamentalists" or "radicals" (who are therefore to be mistrusted), and on the other hand, "moderates" (who alone are to be supported). A binary scheme of things, straightforward and easy to handle, but one that in no way corresponds to the reality of a terrain far more complicated and complex. In this appendix we wish to bring a somewhat more precise and nuanced light to bear upon the reality of these tendencies as they present themselves in Europe and which, in a more generalised way, correspond to the dynamics of the Islamic world as a whole.

### Principles of Classification

It seems necessary to recall, in respect of the Islamic currents as a whole, that their sources are the same and that the fundamental principles on which the Muslim religion is based (save particular and rare exceptions) are unanimously accepted. In this sense therefore, *Islam is one*, and presents a framework whose fundamental axes are identifiable and which are, in spite of the great diversity of the different currents or schools of thought, accepted by all of them. What explains that diversity cannot be rendered by the simple device of a plurality, as one may read in certain recent studies. Faced with the apparent impossibility of suggesting a juridical, political or ideological classification, they end up simplifying the matter by using the expression "Islams". Such use of the plural, intended as a clarification to begin with, is more problematic than truly effective for that purpose: pointing to the diversity, it confuses any reading of the explicitly convergent viewpoints and, more particularly, it says nothing about the clear and often precise boundaries of the divergent viewpoints. An expression applied after realising the one fact of diversity and divisions can neither justify nor explain their causes or their articulations, may indeed mislead the observer as to the very nature of the different positions adopted. The method is thus anything but productive of sound knowledge.

It seems to us necessary to state here a clear principle on the basis of which a study of the various tendencies can truly find some direction. If it is unanimously admitted that the scriptural sources of Islam are indeed the Qur'ān and the *Sunna* (the two fundamental sources not disputed by any of the schools of thought), it seems legitimate to investigate the various currents according to the manner in which they relate themselves in fact to the Texts. This approach, as we shall see, has more explanatory efficacy because it investigates the attitudes that give rise to the religious, social or political language and action. This approach in no way casts doubt on the fundamental belonging to Islam of this or that group, but it does seek to disclose their respective postures *vis-à-vis* their manner of reading the sources – the status of the Text, the margin of interpretation, the degree of literality, the role of reason, etc., are significant measures that explain the differing and differentiated commitments of the various groups. Clearly, Islam is one but its textual sources permit a plurality of readings (albeit such readings must, in order to be accepted, respect certain normative criteria).

It is not possible for us to study here all the currents of thought one by one. They are numerous and their names differ from one country to the next, even the same title may represent diametrically opposed tendencies according to which continent one is referring to. Every country thus demands a distinct treatment and the subject-matter would then become extremely confused and forbidding. We shall therefore confine ourselves here to delineating the distinctive characteristics of certain major tendencies. These are represented, from one country to another, by groups calling themselves by different names. Nevertheless, they stick, in large measure, to an identical reading of the Texts and, flowing therefrom, to doctrinal and social attitudes consequent upon that reading.

## Six Major Tendencies

1. *Scholastic traditionalism.* This is a tendency that has some adepts in Europe and is also present in different regions of the Islamic world. Reference to the scriptural texts, the Qur'ān and *Sunna*, is fundamental for the partisans of this current of thought, with this peculiar characteristic that they refer rigorously, at times in an overtly exclusive way, to one or other of the schools of law (Ḥanafī, Mālikī, Shāfiʿī, Ḥanbalī, Zaydī, Jaʿfarī or others); moreover, they do not allow themselves any right to differ from the juristic opinions established within the framework of the school in question. The Qur'ān and *Sunna* are the sources as mediated through the understanding and application thereof laid down by the accepted *ʿulamā'* of the given school. The margin of interpretation of the Texts is very narrow and does not permit any development. Numerous currents enter, in one manner or another, into this type of reading of the source texts: whether these be the *Deobandīs*, the *Barelwīs*, the *Ahl as-Sunna*, or the Afghan *Ṭālibān* or the *Tablīghī Jamāʿat,*[1] we come across the same traditionalism, insisting on fundamental elements of worship, on dress code, on the rules for the application of Islam, and, in doing so, depending on the opinion of the *ʿulamā'* as codified, most often, between the 8th and 11th centuries. There is nothing here of *ijtihād* or renewal in the reading of the sources, any such being regarded as baseless and an unacceptable liberty or "modernisation".

The movements of scholastic traditionalism are present in Europe, notably in England among Indo-Pakistani Muslims or in Germany among the Turks. One finds small communities of this type spread over other countries also. Their concern is primarily with worship and they do not envisage, within Europe, any social commitment, civil or political. Their reading of the Texts, and the priority given to strictly traditional practice makes them disregard, even refuse, any involvement in European society, a domain in which, quite simply, they do not see themselves as able to participate. The discourse they elaborate and the teaching they provide are based on the sacred as reflected through the prism of a traditional reading of the juridical principles of a given or accepted school.[2]

2. *"Salafī" traditionalism.* This current is often confused with the preceding one although the differences between the two are of some consequence. In contrast to the first type, the "Salafī" traditionalists in their approach to, and reading of, the Texts, refuse the mediation of the schools of law and of the *ʿulamā'* to whom they refer. They call themselves "Salafī" because they are concerned to follow the "Salaf", the title given to the Companions of the Prophet and to the pious Muslims of the first three generations of Islam. The interpretation of the Qur'ān and *Sunna* is thus done in a manner that is immediate and goes beyond the confines marked out by the schools. What distinguishes the traditionalism of this current is the *literalist* character of their approach which, while insisting on reference to the Texts, forbids itself any interpretative reading. This school of thought is in direct line of descent from those who, very early on, were called *ahl al-ḥadīth*[3] and who opposed interpretations based on the search for the aim or object (*qaṣd*) of an injunction or prescription, the attitude which characterised the *ahl al-ra'y*.

The "Salafīs" insist in all circumstances on the necessity of reference to and authenticity of the Texts called upon in order to justify this or that posture or action, in matters of worship as in matters of dress or of community life. The Text alone, in its form and its literal meanings, must be followed and may not be subjected to interpretations which, in being interpretations, lead to error and innovation (heresy, *bidaʿa*).[4]

Permanently linked to certain *ʿulamāʾ* based mostly in Saudi Arabia, in Jordan, in Egypt or in Syria (and linked, most of the time, through former students of their respective educational institutions), the doctrinal stance of the *"Salafī" traditionalists* and of their groups in Europe is the refusal of any type of involvement in any space regarded as non-Islamic. The concepts of *dār al-kufr* or of *dār al-ḥarb*[5] remain operative and explain the relationship of the *Salafīs* to their social environment, which is primarily defined by separation and by a practise of the religion that is literalist and protected from European cultural influences.

3. *"Salafī" reformism.* The reformist "Salafīs" share with the traditionalist "Salafīs" the concern to depart from the confines marked out by the schools of law in order to rediscover the pristine energy of an unmediated reading of the Qur'ān and *Sunna.* They too, therefore, relate themselves to the "Salaf", the Muslims of the first generations, with the aim of avoiding the commentaries that accord a unique authority to the interpretations dating from the 8th or 10th centuries. However, what distinguishes them from the traditionalists – in spite of the fact that they likewise insist upon the necessity of reference to the Texts – is that they tend towards a reading based upon the aims and objectives of the law and of its jurisprudence (*fiqh*). Nearer in this respect to the *ahl al-ra'y* school, they hold that the practice of *ijtihād* is an objective, constant and necessary assumption for the application of *fiqh* to every epoch and every place.

Most of the reformist "Salafī" currents present in Europe were born out of the influence of the reformist thinkers of the end of the 19th and first half of the 20th centuries who enjoyed a wide hearing in the Islamic world. The well-known names are al-Afghānī, ʿAbduh, Riḍā, al-Nursī, Iqbāl, Ibn Bādis, al-Bannā, al-Fāsi, Bennabi, al-Mawdūdī, Quṭb and Sharīʿatī. To that list it is necessary to add the names of others whose influence was restricted to the national level. These reformists are far from having all shared the same ideas. It is impossible here to demonstrate their differences but what unites them is, clearly, a very dynamic relationship with the scriptural sources and a consistent will to use reason in handling the Texts so as to take account of the new challenges of their epoch and of the social, economic and political development of societies.

The arrival in Europe of reformist "Salafī" intellectuals followed the repressions which took place after independence, as in Egypt or in Syria with the Muslim Brotherhood (in the sixties and seventies) or, later, following other local political events as in Tunisia with *al-Nahḍa* movement, in Morocco with *al-'Adl wal-Iḥsān*, or in Algeria with, among others, the partisans of *al-Jaz'ara* or the Muslim Brotherhood. What lies behind these influences, as with others in the Islamic world as a whole, is set to give rise to two different currents. The first, in the legalist tradition of the most famous "Salafī" reformists, is to follow and adapt the application of reformism in the European context. The original school of thought continues to be a point of reference in that the methodological approach to the Texts remains open to the possibility of interpretation and requires the necessary application of *ijtihād* in response to the new contexts of life. However, fidelity to reformist thought and methodology, henceforth very loose, does not necessarily mean any sort of structured adherence – the thinking being done having gone beyond, the authority of this or that group or organisation. The thinking being done has evolved a good deal in Europe and, indeed, precisely in that respect it remains loyal to the original reformist spirit. It is concerned to protect its Muslim identity and the practice of worship, to recognise the constitutional framework in Europe, to be involved at the social level as citizens and to live in sincere allegiance to the country to which they belong. Reformist "Salafī" thought is widely diffused in the West and a great many groups are influenced by its manner of reading the Texts which they borrow and adapt as needed and with initiative.[6]

4. *The political and literalist Salafiyya.* This is the second current of which we spoke above and the child of the repression that has been rampant in the Islamic world: at first attached to the reformist

legalist school, some of the *ʿulamāʾ* and intellectuals drifted into strict and exclusively political commitment (while they were yet based in the Islamic world). They retained nothing of the reformism except the concept of social and political action which they married to a literalist reading of the Texts with a political entail concerning the management of power, the Caliphate, authority, the law, etc. The whole yields a complex mixture tending towards radical revolutionary action – it has to do with opposition to governments, even in Europe, of fighting for the establishment of the "Islamic state" and ultimately of the Caliphate. Their discourse is sharp, politicised, radical, and opposed to any and every notion of collaborative involvement in European societies, something that would appear more as treachery. The movements of *Ḥizb at-Taḥrīr* or *al-Muwwahidūn* are the best known in Europe. They call to *jihad* and opposition by every means to the West (always regarded as *dār al-ḥarb*, the realm of war). These currents, which secure a lot of public attention, nevertheless represent less than 0.5% of the Muslim population resident in Europe.[7]

5. *"Liberal" (or rationalist) reformism.*[8] Born out of the influence of Western thought during the colonial period, the reformist school, called "liberal" or "reformist", supported the application in the Islamic world of the social and political system of organisation which emerged from the process of secularisation which took place in Europe. The liberals defended, for example, Mustapha Kemal Ataturk's programme of secularisation in Turkey, and the definitive separation of the sphere of religious authority from the management of public and political life. In Europe, the supporters of liberal reformism favour the assimilation-integration of Muslims, expecting thereby a thorough adaptation to the European way of life. They do not insist on the daily practise of the religion and retain essentially only its spiritual dimension lived individually and inwardly, or, instead, an attachment to the culture of birth. Most of them are opposed to any manifestation of distinctive dress, synonymous with seclusion or even "fundamentalism". Bearing in mind the evolution of societies, the Qur'ān and *Sunna* can no longer be in their view the authoritative frame of reference for norms of behaviour, and it

is applied reason which must henceforth determine the criteria for social conduct. The term "liberal" thus refers back to the sense the word has acquired in the Western world which privileges rationality and rests upon the primacy of the individual.[9]

6. *Sufism.* We must not omit, from the European landscape, reference to the Sufi currents. They are indeed many and very diverse. Whether they belong to the *Naqshbandī*, *Qādirī*, *Shādhilī*, or to any number of the many other, *ṭuruq* (pl. of *ṭarīqa*), the Sufi circles are essentially oriented to spiritual life and mystic initiation. That does not mean that the initiates (*murīd*) do not have any communal or social involvement whatever; indeed, the opposite is very often what happens. At the end of the day, the issue is above all one of priorities differently distributed: the scriptural texts have a profound meaning which requires, according to Sufi teachings, time for meditative reflection and understanding. It is a call to the inward life, far from agitations and discords. The Text here is the ultimate source because it is the way to remembrance (*dhikr*) and to nearness (*taqarrub*): it is the only route to the experience of nearness. The *ṭuruq* are circles of initiation more or less internally organised with a particular hierarchy that reaches from the initiate to the guide (*shaykh*). Each order has its particular mode of operation.

We must also note that there also exist in Europe some brotherhoods that are very organised and directly linked to brotherhood systems in Asia and North and West Africa. One knows, for example, of the organisational capacity of the *Murids* or the *Tijanes* who operate most of the time in a closed circle, but who nevertheless sustain a very effective network, within that circle, of support and solidarity in Europe and in the United States.[10]

This account of the major tendencies in contemporary Islam is far from exhaustive but it has, we hope, the merit of elucidating the scene by demonstrating some nuances, in contrast to the over-simplifying reading with its binary opposition of "liberals" against all the others – "fundamentalists", "radicals", etc. The situation is much more complicated than that, and the boundaries more subtle: they have their roots in history, to be sure, but above all in their particular ways of understanding the textual sources. For the scholastic traditionalists, the traditionalist "Salafīs", and the politicised and radical "Salafīs", the Texts, be it the Qur'ān, or the *Sunna*, or the opinions of the great *'ulamā'*, do not admit of either interpretations or distortions. Reason is useful for the purpose of understanding the Text, but not, by extension, for the purpose of determining its objective. For the reformist "Salafīs", the Text certainly remains the point of reference, but reason, depending on rules of deduction and inference (*istinbāṭ*),[11] is allowed, through the exercise of *ijtihād*, a considerable latitude for interpretation and elaboration. At the other extreme from the doctrinally fixed positions, "liberal" reformism gives priority to rational elaboration where the primary role of the scriptural texts is to provide some spiritual orientation and broad ethical injunctions, but always of a personal-individual kind (reflecting the role of religious texts *vis-à-vis* social and political life that developed in the West).

The distinctions we have described above, hinging on the mode of reference to "Texts/reason", can be represented diagrammatically as follows:

Chart VII: *The principal Islamic Tendencies and their relationships to Texts and Reason*

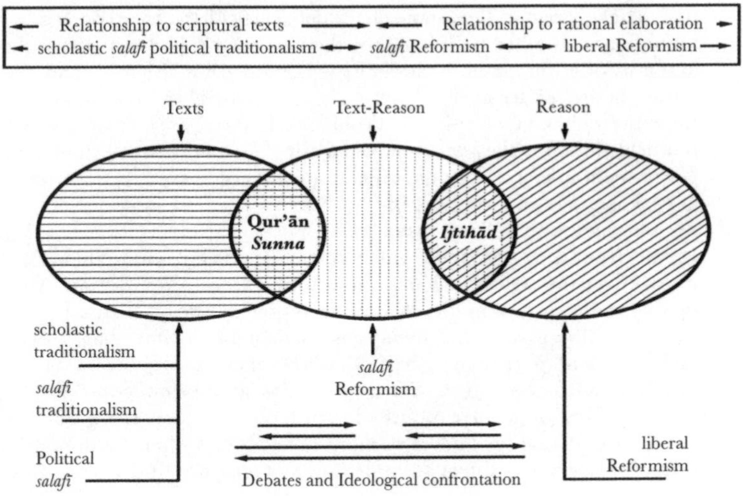

## Notes

1 Being a part of this broad tendency does not mean that the different groups are of one mind. On the contrary, their reference to a particular school of juristic thought sometimes exacerbates attitudes of exclusivism and rejection *vis-à-vis* other schools within the same tendency. Contentions, whether historical or doctrinal, can provoke fierce opposition – as between the *Deobandīs* and the *Barelwīs*. The latter are also opposed, from a doctrinal viewpoint, to the partisans of the *Tablīghī Jamā'at* whose school of thought is founded on the acceptance of different scholastic allegiances, their principle of action being to avoid matters of controversy and to concentrate on the essentials of worship.

2 In the Islamic world, these movements do not in general take part in politics. In a majority Muslim country they recognise the authority of the powers that be and do not offer themselves as an "opposition". They are to be regarded, if one may use a political term, as "conservatives". It remains the fact that certain currents of the scholastic traditionalist type have demonstrated, in certain situations of social unrest, a determined political involvement. This has most often been limited to particular occasions and circumstances (in Pakistan, in India, in Turkey and in certain regions of Africa). The case of the Afghani *Ṭālibān* is significant in that, in the opinion of all specialists, nothing predetermined these students to get involved as they did in the political domain: they were encouraged and invited to do so by Pakistan (with the agreement and support of the United States and Saudi Arabia).

3 See Part One, Chapter 1.

4 In the Islamic world, this current numbers among its *'ulamā'* those who enjoy the highest esteem in the Islamic sciences (notably in the sciences of *ḥadīth*), authoritative scholars such as al-Albānī, Ibn 'Uthaymin and Ibn Bāz, recognised and respected worldwide for their breadth of learning and their scholarly rigour. They show, on the political field, the same conservative attitude as the other traditionalists: they accept without opposition the authority of government, whatever it may be, since it is "Islamic", and they refuse the use of terms like "election", "parliament" or "democracy" as these are neither Qur'ānic nor Prophetic. Refusing involvement in the political domain, they often serve, wittingly or not, to legitimise the government in place, since their literalism and arguments, do not contain any competitive political content.

5 See our discussion in Part One of this work.

6 In the Islamic world, the legalist reformist "Salafī" movements are engaged in the political domain and most often in opposition. Most defend the idea of a model Islamic society which respects the Islamic sources – notably, on the social, political plane, a State based upon law, political pluralism, parliamentarianism, elections based on universal suffrage – without this meaning any submission to the Western model. They make it a point of principle to "play the game" of institutional legality. They are, more or less everywhere, although in different degrees, subject to imprisonment, torture and persecution.

The position of the different groups varies in line with the history of the societies in which their actions take place.

7 Radical political movements exist in the Islamic world and are, almost everywhere, petty groups. They hold the foreground of media attention by means of their violent and sensational actions. In Algeria, a faction of the FIS drifted into this type of posture after the halting of the electoral process and the repression that followed.

8 We have chosen here the name which the partisans themselves of this movement use to define themselves in the West. In the Islamic world, the terms most often used are *ʿalmāniyyūn* (whose root points to the idea of being essentially attached to the management of worldly matters, thereby separating them from any inspiration from the Texts or from the religion), or again *ʿilmaniyyūn* (whose root refers to the scientific dimension of the movement, meaning a sort of *scientism* dependent upon an exclusively rationalist approach to the handling of collective affairs). These two concepts are used in Arabic to translate the idea of secularism. Opponents of this tendency name it using a series of terms that express, in various degrees, the idea that this type of "rationalist reformism" is in fact the product of a Westernisation of thought.

9 The liberal reformists are a minority in the Islamic world, sometimes in government and sometimes in the leftist opposition. They have many "outlets" in Europe where they are often presented as the only true democrats in Islamic countries. The reason for that is largely the fact that the articulation of their discourse is immediately intelligible and agreeable to Western ears since they espouse points and lines of reference familiar in the West. The reality in their democratic posture remains to be proven since certain reformists, labelled as "liberal", have not hesitated to support dictatorial regimes as in Syria, in Tunisia, or the "eradicators" (a wing of the ruling military junta) in Algeria. However, the pretext of battling the "fundamentalists" (which to their way of thinking covers all other tendencies than their own) cannot justify their alliances with despotism.

10 The Sufi circles are practically apolitical in Europe and this is likewise their distinctive feature in the Islamic world. However, this last observation needs to be greatly modified in view of the fact that the Sufi *ṭuruq* were often, in the former Soviet Union and in Turkey, bastions of fierce political resistance to colonial occupation and oppression. The Sufis were often partisans of a so-called "parallel" Islam, refusing allegiance to governmental authority in order to defend a true faith removed from the compromises accepted by those religious dignitaries in the pay of government and representing "official Islam".

11 See Part One.

# Appendix II

## Immigration, Integration and Cooperation Policies – Europe's Muslims Find a Place for Themselves[1]

**Abstract**

*Immigrants are welcome when their labour is needed but they find themselves rejected as soon as the effects of an economic crisis are felt. Whether in Europe (as shown by the growth of the National Front in France) or in Southeast Asia (see the article by Solomon Kane and Laurent Passicousset), they fast become scapegoats. However, there are signs that we are on the way to a real integration of the Muslims living in Europe. To be sure of success, we need a conscious decision by governments to reject the slogans of the extreme right, and for people to abandon simplistic views of Islam.*

In the Europe of the Middle Ages, Islam made major contributions to the rationalism, secularism and modernity of Western thought. However, the current Islamic presence in Europe is a more recent phenomenon, dating back only 60 or 70 years. In historical terms, it is therefore very recent. It took other national and religious minorities (like the Jews or the Orthodox Christians, to mention just two groups) centuries of debate and conflict before they found a place for themselves and won rights in their new-found countries. Is it reasonable to expect the problem to be solved for Muslims within the space of only one or two generations? Furthermore, the first waves of Muslim migrants were workers from North Africa, Turkey, India and Pakistan, and they were generally poor, driven to migration by economic necessity. Their level of education and the precariousness of their status made it unlikely that they would think in terms of a European Islam. It took the arrival of the second and third generations to modify the ways in which these migrants saw their presence in their host countries. This has been clear in France, although in Britain migrants have tended to stay within their own communities, reproducing some of the social structures of their countries and regions of origin. A third factor has been the impact of international events. Beginning with the Iranian revolution of 1979, these have had a tremendous effect on people's view of Islam in Europe and given rise to the negative perceptions which are so widespread. From the Rushdie affair to the excesses of the *Ṭālibān*, from the violence and killings in the Middle East to the daily horrors in Algeria, all this has engendered a climate of fear. This has become more pronounced in the context of the social crisis sweeping Europe as a result of unemployment, exclusion and urban violence. It is what makes the debate on the Islamic presence so difficult - some would say impossible. Particularly when, under the pressure of crisis, it becomes confused with the problem of immigration. One can actually speak of a kind of "Islamophobia", as in the title of a valuable study commissioned by the Runnymede Trust in Britain in 1997.[2] The image of Muslims has become demonised, and this prevents serious evaluation of the dynamics affecting their communities in Europe. However, the second and third generations have played a determining role in the evolution of people's thinking within the various Muslim communities in Europe, for reasons which at first sight appear mutually contradictory.

## The Impact of the Second Generation

The rate of religious observance among young Muslims is relatively low, which means that for many of them integration into their host countries has actually meant assimilation.[3] This fall-off in observance has forced first-generation mosque leaders and leaders of Islamic associations to rethink their ways of working.

Religious leaders, who have tended to be either appointees of governments or Islamic militants in exile, have found themselves obliged to adapt to the situation of their young people, speak their language, reshape the format of religious education and redefine their structures of social and cultural activity. On the other hand, the renewed fashion for religious observance among a minority of young people has led to the creation of a large number of Islamic associations. In the space of 15 years, their numbers have doubled, perhaps even trebled. The forces behind this have been Muslim youths, who are becoming increasingly active, and those in their thirties, born in Europe and often students or graduates from European universities. Their commitment has led to major changes in many people's ways of thinking because they see themselves as having a right to be in Europe and they expect recognition of their civil rights. This has led to a rift between generations, because, unlike the first-generation immigrants, these young people are out to create roles for themselves at the intellectual and social level. Their dynamism and their European culture have pushed their elders (often former members of Islamic movements in North Africa, the Middle East and Asia) to a thorough re-appraisal of their ways of working and their intellectual stance in relation to Europe. At the top, this has led to important debates within Islamic communities, particularly among Islamic elders (the *'ulamā'*). When consulted on questions of Islamic jurisprudence (*fiqh*), the *'ulamā'* have also been obliged to re-evaluate their positions, pronouncing new judicial opinions (*fatwā*) more in line with the realities of life in the West. The growing presence of associations such as the Young Muslims (YM) and the Islamic Society of Britain (ISB) in the UK, along with the Jeunes Musulmans de France (JMF) and Association des Etudiants Islamiques en France (AEIF), and many others elsewhere in Europe, has raised major issues, including the need for the *'ulamā'* to arrive at theological and judicial frames of reference which are clearer and better adapted to the European context. Thus the 1980s and 1990s have seen a growing awareness of the need for a renewal of Islamic thinking in Europe. Young Muslims are now Europeans, and, directly or indirectly, they are asking questions which demand explicit answers. Should Europe still be considered, in the term used by the *'ulamā'* of the nineteenth century, as a *dār al-ḥarb* (the space of war), as opposed to the *dār al-Islām* (the space in which Muslims live as a majority, in security and under their own legislation)? In other words, is it possible for Muslims to live in Europe? If yes, then how should Muslims relate to the national legal systems of the countries in which they live? Is it permitted for a young Muslim to acquire European nationality and play a full role as a citizen of his country? Thus far, Islamic legal experts have not given any of these questions a detailed, global, substantiated answer.

During the 1990s, growing numbers of meetings were held to discuss theological and judicial issues – *'ulamā'* from the Islamic world joined in debate with *imāms* and intellectuals living in Europe, and fundamental issues were addressed.[4] As far as Islamic jurisprudence was concerned, major results were achieved. Five basic principles were arrived at, and these now provide the basis of a virtual consensus among both Islamic experts and the Muslim communities of Europe:[5]

1. A Muslim, whether resident or citizen, should see himself as involved in a contract, both moral and social, with the country in which he lives, and should respect that country's laws.

2. European legislation (which is secular in nature) allows Muslims to practise at least the basics of their religion.

3. The old concept of *dār al-ḥarb* – which does not derive from the Qur'ān, and is not part of the Prophetic tradition – is seen as outdated; other concepts have been suggested as ways of reading the Muslim presence in Europe in more positive terms.

4. Muslims should see themselves as citizens in the full sense of the term, and should participate (while at the same time seeking respect for their own values) in the social, organisational, economic and political life of the countries in which they live.

5. In European legislation as a whole, there is nothing to prevent Muslims, or any other citizens, from making choices that accord with their religion.[6]

## Breaking the Mould

Alongside the development of this theoretical framework, a renewal of Muslim identity has also been much in evidence. Despite the pressures to which they are subject, young people are doing a lot to ensure that national legal systems guarantee respect for their identities. Very often discrimination comes from reductive or biased interpretations of laws that may be xenophobic in nature, as was demonstrated in the report by the Runnymede Trust. Suddenly, there is a growing energy and commitment among Muslim associations. They are also placing greater value on civic education and citizen participation, which are seen as necessary stages in the acquisition of legitimate rights. At the local level, sensitivity sessions are being organised, often in partnership with specialist organisations. Another sign of a determination to break out of isolation is that the language of the host country is increasingly being used at conferences and at Friday Prayers. In Britain, faced with influential traditionalist movements (e.g. the *Barelwī* and *Deobandī*), youth associations such as The Federation of Students' Islamic Societies (FOSIS) and the Young Muslim (YM) are combating the ghetto tendency. While they recognise that the multicultural Anglo-Saxon system has made it largely possible to protect the cultural identity of Britain's Indo-Pakistani populations, they are intent on fighting against discrimination deriving from the ghetto factor. European Islam also seems to be finding ways of remaining politically and financially independent. Some major mosques and institutions are still tied to governments, but more and more Islamic associations are becoming totally independent, so that many places of worship are now built with funds collected within their communities. The activities of Muslim youth are either self-financing or enjoy subsidies offered by governments,[7] and this means a degree of independence. In Europe, Islamic communities are moving away from a situation in which leading notables battle it out over who is to have the right to speak as official representatives of the various national communities. This is a positive development, opening the possibility of real representation emerging from the groups' broader membership, chosen by that membership, and politically and financially independent, particularly since there is now a stronger commitment to pluralism within those communities. While the resistance to this should not be underestimated, there have been important signs of progress in the make-up of the Islamic Council of Spain, the Higher Council in Belgium and the recently formed Muslim Council of Britain, set up in November 1997. The final indicator of the profound changes under way is the number of artistic and cultural projects involving Muslims in Europe. In Britain, Spain and France, a variety of groups are working at creating a real European Islamic culture. While some of them limit themselves to imitating familiar forms and genres (rap, variety shows, popular theatre and so on), others are creating striking syntheses. These artistic expressions are slowly disengaging from their specifically Arab, Turkish or Indo-Pakistani antecedents, and are attempting to recreate Islamic values within national mores and cultural tastes. We can soon expect to see the emergence of even more original syntheses, the creation of a European Muslim identity capable of becoming accepted at the mass level. However, the realities of daily discrimination, suspicion and rejection have not gone away, and many Muslims are having a hard time of it in Europe. The road to coexistence is something of a minefield, not so much because of discriminatory legal systems, but because of an increasingly widespread prejudice that Islam and Muslims are by definition "incapable of integration".

This indicates an urgent need for education and information. People's simplistic perceptions of Islam prevent the public at large from being aware of the major progress that has been made in the area of integration. There are many initiatives that have already opened doors: the organising of open dialogues, the efforts made by Muslims themselves to make themselves known (inter-denominational religious gatherings, open days, university debates etc.) and the rejection of stereotypes by some intellectuals and members of the media. The doors may be narrow, but they open the way to a future of mutual respect. Instead of thinking in cold, formal terms of a passive integration of Muslims, we should be looking enthusiastically to Muslims to make a positive contribution in building a new Europe. Their presence is a source of enrichment: it contributes to reflection on the place of spirituality in secularised societies, and on the egalitarian promotion of religious and cultural pluralism. In broader terms, Muslims are the natural allies of all those who challenge society on questions of meaning, ethics and social justice.

## Notes

1 This is an article written originally in French by the author and published in the monthly newspaper *Le Monde Diplomatique*, April 1998.
2 Commission on British Muslims, chaired by Professor Gordon Conway, *Islamophobia: A Challenge for us All*, Runnymede Trust, October 1997.
3 Between 60% and 70% say that they fast Ramaḍān, but only 12% to 18% pray every day; 75% to 80% either do not speak their language of origin, or speak it very badly.
4 Ten *ʿulamāʾ* from the Islamic world met in July 1992, and again in July 1994, at the European Institute for Human Sciences in Château-Chinon, in order to draw up an Islamic judicial framework for the Muslim presence in Europe. In Britain, the Islamic Foundation has organised a number of initiatives in this direction since 1990. London also saw, in March 1997, the creation of a European Council for Judicial Opinions and Research. See the bulletin *Ṣawt Uruba* (The Voice of Europe) published in Arabic by the Federation of Islamic Associations of Europe, Milan, May 1997.
5 Groups such as *Ḥizb at-Taḥrīr, Al-Muwaḥḥidūn and Al-Muhājirūn* are calling aggressively for a reductive application of *Sharīʿa* law in Europe. Despite the exaggerated publicity accorded to them by the media, these groups are in fact very isolated.
6 As regards the possibility of obligations laid down by law being in contradiction with Islamic principles (a situation which is currently fairly rare), there is a need for research in order to identify priority principles and/or prospects of adaptability.
7 In 1997, Islamic associations in Britain and France successfully put in applications to the European Commission's "A Soul for Europe" programme. See the Commission's annual accounts, Annual Report 1997, General Secretariat of the European Commission, Brussels.

# Glossary

## 1. Some Concepts Used in Islamic Sciences

***ʿAqīda:*** faith and all the matters related to the six pillars of *Īmān* (God – His names, His attributes, the angels, the books, the prophets, the Day of Judgement and predestination). In general, it studies what is beyond sensory perception. It does not exactly cover the sphere of theology nor that of Christian dogmatics, as some Orientalists have tried to suggest, neither does it correspond to the sphere of philosophy, understood in the sense of Western philosophy.

***Fiqh:*** Islamic law and jurisprudence. It comprises two general sections which are based on different and opposed methodological approaches: *ʿibādāt,* worship, where only what is prescribed is permitted; and *muʿāmalāt,* social affairs, where everything is permitted except what is explicitly forbidden.

***Shahāda:*** the profession of faith and its testimony through the formulation with the heart and intelligence of "I bear witness that there is no god but God and that Muḥammad is His Messanger". It is the foundation, the axis and the determination of "*being a Muslim*".

***Sharīʿa:*** There is no single definition of the concept of *Sharīʿa.* Scholars have generally circumscribed its meaning from the standpoint of their own sphere of specialisation. Starting from the broadest to the most restricted usage, we may present the definitions as follows:

1. *Sharīʿa,* on the basis of the root of the word, means "the way", "the path leading to the source" and outlines a

comprehensive conception of creation, existence and death and the way of life it entails, stemming from a normative reading and an understanding of scriptural sources. It determines *"how to be a Muslim"*.

2. *Sharī'a*, for the *uṣūliyyūn* and jurists, is the corpus of general principles of Islamic law extracted from its two fundamental sources, the Qur'ān and the *Sunna*, while also using the other main sources (*ijmā'* and *qiyās*) and secondary ones (*istiḥsān, istiṣlāḥ, istiṣḥāb, 'urf* ).

***Taṣawwuf:*** Sufism. It is the science of mysticism, which has a specific framework, norms, and a technical and specialised vocabulary. It requires an initiation. It involves the study of the stages and states which lead towards intimacy and nearness to God. It is the dimension of *ḥaqīqa*, of truth, of ultimate spiritual Reality, that only the nearest can know.

***Uṣūl al-fiqh:*** The fundamental principles of Islamic law: it sets out the principles and methodology by means of which the rules of law and jurisprudence are inferred and extracted from their sources. It involves the study and formulation of rules of interpretation, obligation and prohibition, universal principles, *ijtihād* (*ijmā'*, *qiyās*), etc.

## 2. Some Technical Terms

***Aṣl,*** pl. ***uṣūl:*** root, origin, source, foundation.

***Āya,*** pl. ***āyāt:*** sign, indication but also verse.

***Dalāla,*** pl. ***dalālāt:*** meaning, implication.

***Dalīl,*** pl. ***adilla:*** proof, indication, evidence, scriptural support and source.

***Far',*** pl. ***furū':*** branch, subdivision, secondary element as opposed to roots, foundations (*uṣūl*). It also means a new case in the practice of *qiyās*.

***Farḍ 'ayn:*** personal, individual duty or obligation.

***Farḍ kafā'ī (kifāya):*** collective obligation. If part of the community takes care of it and fulfils it, the rest is relieved of it.

***Fatwā,*** pl. ***fatāwā:*** specific legal ruling: it can be a mere reminder of a prescription explicitly stated by the sources, or a scholar's elaboration on the basis of a non-explicit text or in the case of a specific situation for which there is no scriptural source.

***Ḥadīth,*** pl. ***aḥādīth:*** reported and authenticated traditions about what the Prophet said, did or approved.

***Ḥukm,*** pl. ***aḥkām:*** rulings, values, prescriptions, commandments, judgements, laws stemming from Islamic law.

***Ḥukm taklīfī:*** restrictive law defining rights and obligations. It is based on human responsibility.

***Ijmā':*** consensus of opinion, in the sense of unanimous or majority opinion.

***Ijtihād:*** literally "effort", it has become a technical term meaning the effort exercised by a jurist to extract a law or a ruling from non-explicit scriptural sources or to formulate a specific legal opinion in the absence of texts of reference.

***'Illa,*** pl. ***'ilal:*** the reason for a specific ruling. It makes it possible to understand a ruling through its cause and thus opens the way to elaborating other rulings through analogy or extension.

***Istiḥsān:*** judging something good, it is in fact the application of "legal preference".

***Istiṣḥāb:*** presumption of continuity of what was previously prescribed.

***Istiṣlāḥ:*** consideration linked to general interest.

***Istinbāṭ:*** both inductive and deductive extraction of the implicit or hidden meaning of a given text. More broadly, it means extracting and pointing out the laws and rulings specified by a scriptural source.

***Jumhūr:*** majority trend, when referring to the majority opinion among the conflicting views of scholars; this does not affect the validity of a minority opinion if it is justified.

***Kalām:*** literally "speech". In *ʿilm al-kalām,* it is linked to Islamic philosophy but also concerns fields which, according to the Western repartition of domains, partake of theology or dogmatics. This science is, in several aspects, situated at the intersection of the three above-mentioned spheres.

***Madhhab,*** pl. ***madhāhib:*** juridical school.

***Makrūh:*** abhorred.

***Mandūb*** (or ***mustaḥab***)***:*** recommended.

***Maqāṣid, sing. maqsūd:*** objectives, aims.

***Maṣlaḥa,*** pl. ***maṣāliḥ:*** consideration of public interest.

***Mubāḥ:*** permitted.

***Mukallaf:*** someone having reached the age of puberty and in full possession of their mental faculties.

***Muqayyad:*** limited, restricted, defined, determined, circumscribed. This also qualifies a *mujtahid* who formulates legal rulings within a specific juridical school.

***Muṭlaq:*** absolute, unrestricted. Also qualifies a *mujtahid* who is competent to formulate legal rulings beyond juridical schools, directly from the sources.

***Qatʿī:*** clear-cut, explicit, definite, leaving no scope for speculation as to its interpretation.

***Rukhṣa,*** pl. ***rukhaṣ:*** alleviation of or concession in the practice or implementation of prescriptions due for instance to age, illness, travel, poverty, social conditions, etc.

***Rukn,*** pl. ***arkān:*** pillar, fundamental principle.

**Ṣaḥīḥ:** authentic, meeting specific authentication criteria.

***Sharṭ,*** pl. ***shurūṭ:*** condition, sometimes criterion.

***Shūrā:*** consultation.

***Takhṣīṣ:*** restriction from a general to a specific meaning.

***Taklīf:*** responsibility, obligation.

***Taqlīd:*** imitation. In legal matters, it means the blind imitation of one's predecessors without questioning, assessing, checking or criticising their legal opinions.

***Ta'wīl:*** interpretation, more specifically in the sciences of faith: allegorical or metaphorical interpretation.

***Tazkiya*** (*an-nafs*): effort of spiritual purification, initiation to spiritual elevation.

***Umma:*** community of faith, spiritual community, uniting all Muslim men and women throughout the world in their attachment to Islam.

***Wājib:*** obligation, often used as a synonym of *farḍ* except by Ḥanafī jurists.

***Ẓāhir:*** manifest, apparent. The literal meaning of the text.

***Ẓannī:*** unexplicit, leaving room for conjecture as to its origin and/or allowing scope for interpretation as to its meaning.

## 3. Terms used to Qualify the Status of Scholars

***'Ālim,*** pl. ***'ulamā':*** literally, "the one who knows". A scholar in a broad sense, who may be specialised in one particular branch of Islamic sciences. It can today qualify those who graduated from university with a degree in a field related to Islamic sciences (the term ***mawlāna*** is also used to express the idea of "scholar" or *shaykh*).

***Faqīh,*** pl. ***fuqahā':*** literally, "who understands deeply". Generally defines the jurist who masters the sciences of law and jurisprudence, but this title is sometimes used for scholars of very diverse abilities. By referring to etymology, one may apply this term to an individual possessing great religious knowledge, without thinking of a particular field of specialisation. In the language of specialists, the term rather refers to someone who is conversant with legal matters without necessarily being competent to develop and formulate specific or new legal rulings. His knowledge may relate to one particular school or to several, he may know the views expressed about a given legal issue. He may for instance know the points on which scholars disagree, he may also express one or several already formulated legal rulings, but this is generally where his competence ends. The *mujtahid* or *muftī* are generally acknowledged *fuqahā'* but a respected *faqīh* is not necessarily a *mujtahid* or a *muftī*.

***Imām,*** pl. ***a'imma:*** literally, "the one who is placed at the front". Applies to any person, specifically trained or not, who directs Prayer or officiates during Friday sermons. More particularly, this term is used to qualify a scholar who has historically left his mark on the development of Islamic sciences and knowledge, especially in the field of law and jurisprudence. One thus speaks of the "great *imāms* (*a'imma*)" when thinking of Abū Ḥanīfa, Mālik, ash-Shāfiʿī, Ibn Ḥanbal and Jaʿfar as-Ṣādiq, for instance. This may express the recognition of the community as a whole or sometimes, more specifically, of the circle, the school of thought or organisation in which the said scholar may have been involved.

***Muftī:*** some scholars have made undifferentiated use of the terms "*mujtahid*" and "*muftī*", as for instance ash-Shāṭibī (whom we mentioned in the second section of the first part). The link indeed seems natural since the practice of *ijtihād* is necessary to the formulation of a *fatwā* (same root as *muftī*). A *muftī* is therefore someone who formulates specific legal opinions on the basis of unexplicit texts or in the absence of specific texts. Three slight differences have been pointed out by scholars to clarify the differences in denominations and functions. The *muftī* is clearly at the disposal of the community or of individuals, his function is to *answer* questions and the latter direct his reflection; this is not the case for the *mujtahid* who is not necessarily asked questions and who can work upstream. More than the *mujtahid*, since he works downstream and interacts more directly with his environment, the *muftī* must know the people and society he lives among; this is also required of the *mujtahid* but less expressly. Lastly, some have noted a mere institutional difference: the *muftī* is a *mujtahid* who has been employed by the state or who serves a specific institution to formulate legal rulings and direct the administration of affairs.

The *muftī* would thus simply be a *mujtahid* who has become a civil servant. The same distinctions exist among scholars as regards the *muftī muṭlaq* and the *muftī muqayyad*.

***Mujtahid,*** pl. ***mujtahiḍūn:*** a scholar working on scriptural sources in order to infer or extract judgements and legal rulings. He is recognised as competent to practise *ijtihād* (same Arabic root, *ja-ha-da*) on unexplicit texts or in the absence of specific texts. Numerous qualities are required to reach this level of competence: 1. Knowledge of the Arabic language; 2. Knowledge of Qur'ān and *ḥadīth* sciences; 3. Deep knowledge of the objectives (*maqāṣid*) of the *Sharī'a*; 4. Knowledge of the questions on which there was a consensus: that makes it necessary to know the substance of the works on secondary questions (*furū'*); 5. Knowledge of the principle of analogical reasoning (*qiyās*) and its methodology; 6. Knowledge of the historical, social and political context; that is, the situation of people living around him (*ahwāl an-nās*). 7. Recognition of his competence, honesty, reliability and uprightness (see the detailed analysis in the second section of Part One).
Scholars have distinguished two types of *mujtahid* for whom the required competence criteria are different:

1. *al-mujtahid al-muṭlaq* (absolute): extracts legal rulings and opinions directly from the sources and beyond all specific school criteria. His recognised knowledge of texts and methodological principles enables him to formulate views which do not necessarily refer to juridical schools and their rules.
2. *al-mujtahid al-muqayyad* (limited): simply extracts prescriptions within the framework of a specific juridical school. The conditions required for the latter are of course less demanding; they also include the knowledge of the deduction rules linked to the juridical school to which he belongs or refers.

***Shaykh,*** pl. ***shuyūkh:*** literally "old": generally qualifies persons who have a degree in one branch or another of Islamic sciences. It is also very broadly used to express students' respect or recognition of a teacher's abilities even if the latter does not have an official degree. One can note some obvious instances of excess in this respect. In mystical paths and circles, the *shaykh* is the initiating master who guides and accompanies the *murīd* (the initiate in search of knowledge) on the path to knowledge and elevation.

***Uṣūlī,*** pl. ***uṣūliyyūn:*** a scholar conversant with the knowledge of the fundamental principles of Islamic law. He works on the Qur'ān and the *Sunna;* he must master the juridical instruments and know the principles and methodology by means of which the rules of law and jurisprudence are inferred and extracted from their sources. He studies rules of interpretation, the fields related to obligation and prohibition, as well as general orientation rules. The principles of implementation of *ijtihād*, *ijmā'* or *qiyās* also fall within his province although this does not mean he is competent to implement them himself. His knowledge is first of all essentially theoretical. A *mujtahid* or a *muftī* necessarily masters the field of knowledge and competence of an *uṣūl* scholar but the latter is not immediately nor necessarily a *mujtahid* or a *muftī*, since his knowledge may be only theoretical, merely enabling him to identify the instruments of extraction and deduction without being competent to make use of them.

# Index